Praise for *The Good Lif*

"At once revolutionary and conservative . . . revolutionary in its insistence that the results of philosophical reflection be put into practice . . . Positively warm, oddly free of moralizing, welcoming of disagreement and engagement. By the end, you are ready to have a beer with the authors—and you feel they would welcome the opportunity. . . . Boldness in embracing controversy—enabled by the calm confidence of the authors, which supports their willingness to transparently and undogmatically engage—continues throughout, to excellent effect. . . . 'Find[ing] a goal proportionate to life' (to life, not to our essential nature) is the animating project of *The Good Life Method*. Inviting and guiding the reader through a set of reflections—even spiritual exercises—aimed at that discovery is a very Good Thing." —Pamela Hieronymi, *Los Angeles Review of Books*

"For those looking for a self-help guide at the start of the new year, philosophy professors Sullivan and Blaschko recommend skipping diet books and pop psychology for Aristotle and Thomas Aquinas. Their book is based on a class they teach at the University of Notre Dame called God and the Good Life. The time-tested principles they set forth include living generously, working with integrity, and accepting responsibility. Looking around, it's clear that those are all easier said than done, but the payoff promised in the book's title—the good life—is worth it."

—Jim Kiest, *The San Antonio Express-News*

"[A] wise and accessible guide . . . entertaining and insightful . . . Those pondering the perennial question of how to live a good life should start here."

—*Publishers Weekly* (starred review)

"A warm, empathetic guide for examining the quality and meaning of one's own life . . . Thoughtful contemplations about thorny moral questions."

—*Kirkus Reviews*

"*The Good Life Method* is a compulsively readable book. I found myself squirming in places but pushing forward, reflecting on how much all of us stand to gain from trying to ask and answer the questions that Sullivan and Blaschko pose. They offer a method more than a manual, one that lends itself not only to conversations among families, friends, colleagues, leaders, and voters, but also invites thoughts of a grand national experiment."

—Anne-Marie Slaughter, CEO of New America

"I know of no question more worthy of our time and attention than, 'What is a good human life, and how do I live it?' Meghan Sullivan and Paul Blaschko have crafted a fascinating class, God and the Good Life, which has engaged and inspired our students at Notre Dame about that question. They now offer observations and insights from that course to readers of this book."

—Rev. John I. Jenkins, C.S.C, President of University of Notre Dame

"'Make religion attractive,' Pascal remarked, cryptically, in *Pensées*. That remark came to mind again and again as I read *The Good Life Method*; individually, collaboratively, energetically, enthusiastically, Meghan Sullivan and Paul Blaschko make philosophy attractive."

—Paul Elie, author of *The Life You Save May Be Your Own*

"In writing about *The Good Life Method*, Sullivan and Blaschko have provided a flexible yet focused approach to help us all ask—and answer—life's most important questions. They weave together timeless truths from great thinkers with contemporary research on college student well-being and their own lived experience as scholars, teachers, and mentors to provide a practical approach to making meaning in a world of choices and challenges."

—Penny Rue, PhD, former vice president for Campus Life at Wake Forest University

"John Henry Newman remarked that 'a habit of mind is formed' through humanities-based thinking, 'of which the attributes are freedom, equitableness, calmness, moderation, and wisdom.' For Newman, this shapes the 'idea of a university.' As a professor at West Point, I'm particularly struck by how close those personal intellectual attributes are to the ideal of shared public discourse in the republic my students choose to defend. As a poet, though, I can't help but suspect that moral inquiry begins with a little of what Keats called 'negative capability'—the habit of 'being in uncertainties, mysteries, doubts.' We all are. How do I live in my own home with my family and neighbors as the person I want to be? How do I be or become the person my children believe that I am? *The Good Life Method* isn't a script or prescription. It's a book about strong questions and how to face them, how to live with and through them. It's about setting conditions—both personally and in our communities—for our most enduring habits of mind in our everyday lives."

—Matthew Salyer, associate professor of English at the United States Military Academy at West Point

ABOUT THE AUTHORS

Meghan Sullivan is the Wilsey Family College Professor of Philosophy at the University of Notre Dame and director of the Notre Dame Institute for Advanced Study. She has published works in many leading philosophy journals. Her first book, *Time Biases*, was published by Oxford University Press. Her work has been supported by grants from the National Endowment for the Humanities, the Andrew W. Mellon Foundation, and the John Templeton Foundation. She teaches God and the Good Life and in 2021 received Notre Dame's Joyce Award for Teaching. Sullivan has degrees from the University of Virginia, Oxford University, and Rutgers University, where she earned a PhD in philosophy. She studied at Balliol College, Oxford University, as a Rhodes Scholar.

Paul Blaschko is an assistant teaching professor at the University of Notre Dame, where he teaches God and the Good Life and courses on the philosophy of work. He's the director of the Sheedy Family Program in Economy, Enterprise, and Society in Notre Dame's College of Arts and Letters, which helps students connect interests in business and the liberal arts in pursuit of meaningful work. He regularly consults with professors across the country about how to create better, more innovative philosophy courses. He received his PhD at Notre Dame in 2018.

The Good Life Method

REASONING THROUGH THE BIG QUESTIONS OF HAPPINESS, FAITH, AND MEANING

Meghan Sullivan
and Paul Blaschko

PENGUIN BOOKS

PENGUIN BOOKS
An imprint of Penguin Random House LLC
penguinrandomhouse.com

First published in the United States of America by Penguin Press,
an imprint of Penguin Random House LLC, 2022
Published in Penguin Books 2023

ISBN 9781984880321 (paperback)

THE LIBRARY OF CONGRESS HAS CATALOGED THE HARDCOVER EDITION AS FOLLOWS:

Names: Sullivan, Meghan, 1982– author. | Blaschko, Paul Leonard, author.
Title: The good life method : reasoning through the big questions of happiness, faith, and meaning / Meghan Sullivan and Paul Blaschko.
Description: New York : Penguin Press, 2022. | Includes bibliographical references and index.
Identifiers: LCCN 2020054704 (print) | LCCN 2020054705 (ebook) | ISBN 9781984880307 (hardcover) | ISBN 9781984880314 (ebook)
Subjects: LCSH: Virtue. | Ethics. | Conduct of life.
Classification: LCC BJ1531 .S85 2022 (print) | LCC BJ1531 (ebook) | DDC 170—dc23
LC record available at https://lccn.loc.gov/2020054704
LC ebook record available at https://lccn.loc.gov/2020054705

Printed in the United States of America
1st Printing

Designed by Meighan Cavanaugh

FROM MEGHAN:

To all the students who've come with us on this journey and to all the ones I can't wait to meet.

FROM PAUL:

To Shayla, Solomon, Maria, and Lydia.

My goodness.

Contents

Introduction

> Are you not ashamed of your eagerness to possess as much wealth, reputation and honours as possible, while you do not care for nor give thought to wisdom or truth or the best possible state of your soul?
>
> —Socrates, in Plato's *Apology*

We all have goals. This trait is something that sets us apart from other animals: we are self-reflective creatures. We keep score with grade point averages, bank accounts, hours slept, or calories burned. And we're constantly trying to improve. Our particular methods vary. Some of us keep journals or make pacts with friends to get better. Maybe you are the kind of person who writes down an annual plan in a leather-bound journal every January first. Maybe you just casually check in now and then with your partner to look at whether you've spread yourself too thin between family, work, and the long list of everything else. Some of us wait for a big turning point to redraw our life maps—a graduation, the birth of a child, a reorganization at work. Maybe a big crisis trips your planning switch.

We often take up these goal-setting missions as a way of responding to what we perceive to be our shortcomings. We try to build back better. Yet as we make progress on one part of our lives, inevitably something else changes. We think we are on track to assembling that better life, but then we find the pieces aren't fitting together. We have to begin again. But where? In these moments we start to see the problem: setting and accomplishing goals is one thing, but where should our goals come from? What should we ultimately be aiming at?

We believe that there is a more sustainable way to approach this deeply human work—a method for thinking about our goals that is among the oldest, the most holistic, and the most battle-tested: philosophy. You may not think of philosophy as being so practical. But many philosophers, from the ancients right up until the modern day, have seen the discipline as indispensable to the good life.

In the fourth century BC, Aristotle opened his course on happiness by telling students, "We are conducting an examination . . . so that we may *become good*, since otherwise there would be no benefit from it." You might associate philosophy with studying very abstract theories of logic, human nature, the universe. But Aristotle thought he was teaching his students the most practical subject on earth—how they could become better at being human by learning to direct their lives toward worthy goals.

Following in Aristotle's path, we've dedicated our careers to helping our twenty-first-century students view their "good life" problems through the philosophical framework he inspired, and it resonates with them deeply. If you read around in the roughly two-thousand-year history of philosophy, you discover a persistent theme of people trying to find a solid foundation for their goals, a vision that they can then use to direct their everyday lives.

In ancient Greek, a *telos* is an aim that gives meaning and direction to an activity. For teleological creatures like us, finding the right life goals, and figuring out how to accomplish them, is *the* essential human task. Aristotle thinks we are like archers, always trying to fix a far-off target in our sights. He called the goal *eudaimonia* (yoo-die-mo-nee-ahh). The Good Life.

Other ancient philosophers describe this fundamentally human task as "joining up your circles"—joining your short-term plans with more essential goods; your present moment with your past and future; your own life with the lives of others around you; your current desires with a vision for how your life will all fit together into a coherent and meaningful whole. The Greeks and Romans thought that this urge to "join up" is what makes us different from all of the other animals: we have a capacity to see these connections in our lives and make adjustments to strengthen the links. And they thought that to undertake this work seriously, we need a lot of philosophical coaching. Socrates, Plato, Aristotle, the Stoics, Saint Thomas Aquinas—and the philosophers who have continued their work in subsequent centuries—have all worked out proven methods for bringing direction to tumultuous lives. It is shocking how vibrant and relevant these time-tested guides still are today. Many of these philosophers lived their own lives during deeply volatile periods. They developed their theories precisely because the circles were getting hard to join up.

Philosophy has long been in the business of practical, timeless self-care. But in the modern world, when we are of a mind to work on our goals, we often turn to the *newest* research we can find. We buy popular business and positive psychology books, and search out diet and fitness plans to experiment with. If what we're looking for is life-directing wisdom—if we really want to make deep and lasting changes for the better—some brief reflection is enough for us to realize that these aren't the sources we should be seeking out. They often just add to our disorientation. Advice from a 1970s diet book ("Avoid fat at all costs!") is completely different from what doctors recommend today ("Skip the sugar if you want to lose weight!"). Happiness advice from psychology similarly shifts directions every few years. In the 1980s, the trend was to promote self-affirmation—accept and love whoever it is that you happen to be. In the last decade, the advice was to develop grit instead—buckle down and toughen up. And in our own time, all of this guidance seems . . . insufficient to the moment.

Sometimes we're not even sure what sources are worth consulting; we feel stuck. Do you really need an ambitious career to be fulfilled? How involved should you be in your children's lives? How do you in particular contribute to something bigger? You might be at sea on how you could even settle such questions. Or maybe you recognize that your life is wonderful, but you simply aren't able to say why. This need for clarity is itself a problem when you try to talk to your friends, your parents, your spouse, or your kids about who you are and why you make the choices you do.

We're all looking for direction: an inner voice, a trusted mentor, or a book of wisdom to illuminate the path ahead and to shape our answers to the "Why" questions for each of our goals. You've probably encountered people who have this kind of plan. There's an enviable contentment about them. The big questions of life don't seem to derail them. In fact, they seem to become deeper, even better versions of themselves in the face of the biggest challenges.

Now imagine you had a plan like this.

You could go to it whenever you hit a rough patch or whenever you wanted to reflect on this life you are living. When you feel at sea, it could serve as your compass. Its sections would contain the insights you need for connecting up your current goals with their deeper reasons.

You might ease into your plan by tackling some common good life challenges:

> How should I allocate my money and time?
>
> How should I love the people in my life?
>
> How do I balance learning, working, family, friendship?

Maybe starting to work out the plan for these aspects of your life would make you a bit more daring. You'd tackle some trickier questions:

Where do I stand on religion?

Where do I stand on politics and community life?

Whom will I follow, and why?

As your skills and knowledge grow, you may even start to consider some of life's most challenging questions:

What will I worship, and why?

What will I do when the people I love suffer and die?

Why am I confident that all of this will be meaningful in the end?

Some religious traditions seem to come with such a plan ready-made: the Bible, the Talmud, the Qur'an. But even wisdom literature doesn't function like a personal user manual: you have to do the work to think rationally about how it applies to your life.

Many of us choose instead to follow our winding paths through education, career, and relationships and build as we go. We cobble together our plans for health and longevity; we run experiments with money and mindfulness and collect bits of advice along the way. That internal dashboard tracks salaries, friends, and achievements. We rely on these metrics to drive our lives.

But here's the important truth—one that both ancient and modern philosophers know all too well: your good life plan is one that *you* need to be constantly and actively writing. Philosophy can supply the methods, but the material has to be generated by the experiences of *your* life brought up against the fundamentally human problems faced in every era.

Not only is this work possible, but with a bit of curiosity you can start doing it now and reaping the benefits. Giving you this philosophical footing is the goal of this book.

For the ancients, the question was, Can people *learn* what it takes to have a good life? And if so, is it more like learning how to cook, or learning how to solve a math problem, or learning how to play in a band? The Greeks debated this relentlessly and concluded that happiness is a form of knowledge that combines the intellectual with everyday practices.

Their approach to philosophy is often called virtue ethics. The core idea is that there are goals for a good life and achieving them requires developing certain habits and traits, which the ancients called virtues. Virtues appear in each domain of day-to-day life (our finances, our child rearing, our approach to education). The "ethics" in virtue ethics is less a fixed system of rules and more like a "work ethic"—internal principles that drive you toward something.

Virtue ethics offers a set of tools that aim to sometimes complement and to sometimes challenge the happiness advice we seek in other spheres. In this book, we'll teach you the main skills and the philosophical story behind them:

1. Strong Questioning: posing the kinds of questions that uncover our deeper reasons for believing and doing what we do
2. Agency: developing your intentions and telling the true stories about what you are doing and why
3. Loving Attention: paying the right kind of attention to others' true stories, discovering common goods, and joining your lives
4. Making Meaning: beholding how the episodes of your life fit together, reasoning through major course corrections when you must confront them, and joining up all the circles

Each skill builds on the others, and at the foundation is the skill of desiring philosophical reasons for the way you live your life.

STRONG QUESTIONS

The philosopher's central job has always been to teach others the art of loving the truth. In Greek, *philo* means "love" and *sophia* means "wisdom." Often we aim to uncover the truth about the problems that human beings just keep crashing into. Sometimes this requires heavy machinery, like a whole system of arguments or a grand account of human nature, love, or the meaning of life. More often, though, the work is done with smaller, more delicate instruments.

Questions are like brushes that can be used to carefully separate the dirt from whatever underlying truth you are trying to see. The philosopher suggests the questions, knows a bit about answers that others have revealed, and can help you see how these questions and answers are showing up in your own circumstances. That is the work we are trained to do. Some of our questions might seem madcap at first, but in answering them, you uncover another layer of insight about what drives you.

Here's a thought experiment: Suppose there were a pill that causes an immediate and *permanent* sense of pleasure and well-being. Would you take it? In wrestling with the question, you might realize that some of your goals don't have much to do with feeling pleasure. Would taking the pill make you a bad friend? You think about someone you love who is going through a nasty divorce; if you were on the pill, you wouldn't be able to empathetically care for them. Would taking the pill reduce the uneasiness that spurs you to push and develop yourself? It might make you boring, or shallow, or insensitive.

How you answer the question in this thought experiment gives you a clearer picture of the kind of life you find really valuable. It can help shed light on your views about the relative value of pain and pleasure. It reveals another layer of your good life goals. Indeed, sometimes taking a goal and imagining a pill or some other method just magically "zapping" it into reality can be a good prompt for reflecting on what role *you want to play* in achieving and controlling the goal, which is itself a very important philosophical insight.

Getting in the habit of asking philosophers' questions can also shape our moral lives. Do news stories or conversations about current events with relatives frequently irritate you? Try asking questions as part of your approach to the news. Read the headline, feel the twinge, but then make yourself pause to ask, What would it take to change my mind on this topic? Philosophers know that with the proper kind of skepticism, interactions that can feel like blood sport are reframed as opportunities to grasp something you have been missing.

Skepticism is itself one of the delicate instruments; some of our fragmentary good life views are still coming together, and they need to be carefully cultivated. Arriving at stable views is work we need to do with other people. A great philosophical question is one that you'll want to discuss with your parents, your kids, and your friends. Here are a few starters:

1. What were the moments in your life when you felt most in control?
2. What's the difference between loving someone for their own good and loving them for what they can do for you?
3. How have you figured out what risks in life were worth taking?

The ancients thought that really good conversations have the power to open our lives up to one another. By learning more about the reasons we each have for doing what we do, we can better appreciate how our friends are striving to make their own lives good. These philosophers sometimes even describe this process as coming to live "second lives" through the experiences of those we love.

Most important, asking philosophical questions (and wanting their answers) starts to give us a power that philosophers call personal agency—the capacity to understand and then direct parts of our lives.

Of course, it is one thing to have the capacity to better direct your life, and another thing entirely to know what you are directing it toward.

We often establish our goals indirectly, by observing the actions of those around us. We notice that our fellow grade-schoolers tend to value athletic prowess, so we beg our parents to sign us up for basketball and then spend hours practicing our dribble in the driveway. We wonder what promotions we should go for at work, so we look at what job titles our colleagues seem to prize. We often quickly move from noticing somebody else has a goal to assuming it is ours as well.

Such goal exploration is a necessary part of healthy self-discovery. But it can also go disastrously wrong, partly because the model allows us to adopt goals in a way that bypasses our own reasons, emotions, and consciences. As a result, we can end up striving for things that we don't value for the long haul. This is one reason why the big new house can feel as metaphorically empty as it is literally, or why the corner office can become more of a trap than a trophy.

THE SURVEYED LIFE

You might acknowledge all this but still not realize how many of your goals are coming from the outside. In the era of big data, we tend to think tackling the question of happiness is something we should do more "scientifically," by conducting studies.

For example, our local supermarket in South Bend, Indiana, asks customers to tap a smiley or frowny face at the checkout station. They are collecting data about what kinds of in-store experiences correlate with customers' reporting at the end that they had a good shopping trip. This data is then used to generate better in-store experiences. This is an externalized feedback loop: ask a question → collect happiness reports → make adjustments to improve the experience.

This survey approach to happiness is everywhere in our lives right now. And in the right doses, it can be healthy. Although the constant data collection and behavioral management can get a bit intrusive, there's a reason we let our phones count our steps, monitor our heart rates, remind us to meditate, and organize reports in easy-to-digest diagrams. Wishful thinking and laziness often conspire to make us think we're more active than we actually are. The breathing exercises and meditation effectively help us to chill out. The diagrams keep us honest.

Still, the survey approach is radically insufficient to address the bigger questions. A well-lived life is integrated and thoughtful; it doesn't consist in robotically conforming our lives to whatever the data suggests at the moment. A device can't tell you how to feel, what goals are ultimately worth measuring, or what your genuine reasons are. That hasn't stopped some from trying to extend the survey approach to the bigger existential questions.

Positive psychologists like Martin Seligman, for instance, spend their days surveying which personality traits and opportunities seem correlated with overall life happiness. The psychological approach looks for cross-cultural agreement about traits that are thought to be important to happiness. If attention to detail is prized in some cultures but not others, but courage is prized across cultures, then courage is determined to be more likely a part of the good life. Seligman notes that people with some form of religious attachment tend to report higher life satisfaction. Though he doesn't think "scientifically minded Westerners" could reasonably believe in the claims of particular theistic religions, he recommends from the data that you add some kind religiousness to your good life.

The logic of the survey approach goes like this:

> *Premise:* Some activity _____ (fill in the blank with one of the many options studied by this approach: eating beans, cleaning your closet, writing thank-you notes, having children, having access to parental leave, being religious) corresponds with higher reports of well-being and life satisfaction.

Conclusion: Therefore, this activity should likely be part of your good life.

This is a widespread and tempting form of argument, but it is not a good one. The conclusion does not follow from the premise—just because a majority of people think something is good doesn't mean it *is* good. And the surveys are only relevant so long as the people and situations they study are relatively stable. If the day-to-day conditions surveyed are upended, the data is useless. Moreover, from a philosophical perspective, we doubt that these studies will help any of us identify the missing ingredient in our good life. They don't go remotely deep enough.

In Silicon Valley, there's been a recent push to expand the survey approach to happiness with technological precision and design thinking. The guiding assumption is that engineering can make progress on our goal setting where non-technological solutions have seemingly failed us.

Stanford teaches a very popular happiness course out of their design school called "Design Your Life." The lead faculty—Bill Burnett and Dave Evans—are industrial designers and, like many college professors, they want to teach courses that will help students be productive and happy adults. Their formula is to use the same prototype-and-evaluate process that works for product design. The hidden premise is that you are relevantly similar to a product—your function is the kind of thing that can be the subject of market research and your goal is to have a great consumer experience with life.

There is a saying among software engineers: "Nobody touches running code." The idea being, if a system is working toward a goal, don't try to mess with it from the inside; instead add to it from the outside to solve problems as they arise. Subbu Vincent, an engineer and ethicist at Santa Clara University, suggests this is the predominant approach to ethics in the culture of Silicon Valley. Let the engineers, managers, and consultants do their jobs; offer philosophy and ethical advice as enhancements on the *existing code.* There is even a euphemism for this add-on approach to ethics: tethics. Tethics only has the bandwidth to deal with ethical questions that can be solved before a product is shipped; questions like why or whether the product should even exist are typically avoided.

Burnett and Evans have a noble mission, but the design-based approach to the good life inherits all of the "tethical" baggage. One key takeaway from their program is that the secret to happiness is a bias to action—don't overthink your choices, but instead experiment and then modify any ideas that don't seem to be working. They urge risk taking, since—according to their design-process approach—failure simply isn't a possibility.

As *good life* advice, this is deeply misleading. There are many roads to living a meaningful life, but there are also serious ways someone might fail.

Suppose Paul is in his midthirties with three young children at home, and he decides to abandon his wife and family to run an experiment with a new career as a painter in Tahiti.* Paul might learn something from the experiment, but—we'd argue—he would not be living the good life. And that's because good people don't abandon their loved ones to try new painting adventures. Some of our goals must be shaped and limited by other, much more important ones. We learn this by reflection, not by experimentation.

Equally questionable, this design-based approach also seems to put the "good life" within reach of only the privileged. It plays into the false narrative that the most pressing problems we face concern decisions like whether to be management consultants or engineers, whether to marry young or marry late, whether to live in London or San Francisco, whether to retire early or stay in the workforce as long as possible. It requires being lucky enough to have choices over careers and how you'll be treated by

* This is exactly what the French Impressionist painter Paul Gauguin did, except Gauguin had five young children.

others, not to mention plenty of time and discretionary funds. You might think there is something pretty hollow about defining the goal of a life as something that only the rich or the educated or the powerful can achieve.

This design advice (like all products) also comes with an expiration date. The jobs and relationships and other daily options we are experimenting with will change, often faster than we can imagine.

We don't just want hacks to make us *feel* happy—we want to know why certain goals are continually worth wanting. And we want to do the work to discover these truths about ourselves and the world.

So what kinds of questions and life experiments should we be performing? And how deep can we go?

The alternative to the survey approach is a life lived deeply from the inside, a life in which the goal itself is something that you have seen, loved, and defended. A goal big enough to encompass a whole life rather than just to optimize the day-to-day. A goal you share with others—that joins up your circles. This is where philosophy becomes indispensable. We have to learn how to integrate the answers to our questions into a theory of who we are. We need an alternative to the surveyed life.

THE EXAMINED LIFE

A remarkable feature of human history is that we all started wondering philosophically about how to live better lives at roughly the same time—between 600 and 300 BC. In China during the Zhou dynasty, Confucius was helping people try to find harmony with their families and authority figures. In India, Siddhārtha Gautama taught theories and practices aimed at stopping the relentless cycle of suffering. In the Middle East, the authors of the Book of Job and Ecclesiastes were raising questions about the nature of God, faith, and the challenges of leading a meaningful life. The resulting insights would inform the philosophical basis for Judaism, Christianity, and Islam. And over in Greece, Socrates, Plato, and Aristotle were devising methods and theories that would come to be the cornerstone of Western approaches to thinking about happiness. It's as though around the third century BC, the lights abruptly came on for humanity. We realized we wanted *reasons* to guide our lives—and that with intellectual effort, we might be able to find them.

All of these virtue ethics philosophies (and others that have appeared since) have three key ingredients. First, they offer a hypothesis about our starting point: who we are, what we need, and why we struggle. Second, they offer a hypothesis about our goal: What would the good life be for someone with our starting point, and why should we go after this goal? Third, they offer practical guidance for how to get from here to there. What should you do first thing if this is your goal? How should you change your relationships? What kind of work is worth doing, and why? Sometimes, especially for the oldest traditions, the practical advice needs a bit of translation. Philosophy helps there as well.

Consider Aristotle, who taught his "good life" course at the Lyceum in Greece during the fourth century BC. We know about his ideas because we have his lecture notes collected in a book called the *Nicomachean Ethics*. (Nicomachus was Aristotle's son, presumably one of his intended audiences.) Aristotle hypothesized that every type of thing has a particular function, and he thought that knowing that function helps us grasp the appropriate goals for that thing. For example, the function of a knife is to cut things efficiently. So a good knife is supersharp, a bad knife is dull, and if your knife gets so dull that it can't cut anything . . . then it isn't a knife at all. It is just a metal stick. The features that allow a thing to fulfill its function well are its virtues: sharpness is a virtue of knives. Things that inhibit the functioning of an object are its vices: dullness is a knife's biggest vice.

Living things also have functions, and these, too, can be studied. The function of a gray wolf (*Canis lupus*) is to live and hunt in packs, reproduce with a mate, live with their offspring, and prey on animals in its geographic range. You can tell that a wolf is sick if it's unable to do these things. Functions also help us distinguish between kinds of things. You can tell a knife from a fork by how well it cuts, a wolf from a Chihuahua by whether it would appreciate a nice pat on the head.

For Aristotle, answering the happiness question requires us to first answer a corollary one: What is our function as humans? This is not something you can simply decide for yourself, or determine by making observations about how people happen to live, or by conducting market research. To answer the function question, Aristotle asks a related question: What do we think is special or distinctive about our lives as humans? He reasons it out in one of the most famous (and most complicated) passages in virtue ethics:

> We posit the work of a human being as a certain life, and this is an activity of soul and actions accompanied by reason, the work [function] of a serious man being to do these things well and nobly. . . . Human good becomes an activity of soul in accord with virtue, and if there are several virtues, then in accord with the best and most complete one.

So what's special about us compared with, say, knives, wolves, or iPhones? Aristotle insists in other parts of the *Ethics* (and in his political writings) that we are a kind of *social animal.* We need animal goods like food, shelter, and health to be doing well. We need companionship and to be coordinated with others in our species. But we are also *rational*—we can think about ourselves rather than just being ruled by instinct. Would I be a good parent if I have offspring? Why am I in this community rather than some other one? These are planning questions other animals simply do not face.

In fact, the main thing that distinguishes us from other animals is this capacity to understand our lives as good or bad. A wolf can't really know whether it is good or bad at doing what wolves are meant to do. A human can worry about this every single day.

Aristotle thinks we can use this understanding to direct our lives in powerful ways. He's not averse to using feedback and feelings as a tool, but crucially he doesn't stop there. If we are fearful, we can take up projects to become more courageous. If we are unhealthy, we can adopt new diets and fitness plans. Other animals are stuck with their preprogrammed habits and instincts, but we have some control over how we program our vices and virtues; we have a hand in shaping our characters.

Socrates, the grandfather of Greek virtue ethics, thought that this "care for the soul" is the most important work any of us can do. He famously challenged his contemporaries to want more from life. "You are an Athenian, a citizen of the greatest city and with the greatest reputation for wisdom and power; are you not ashamed of your eagerness to possess as much wealth, reputation and honors as possible, while you do not care for nor give thought to wisdom or truth, or the best possible state of your soul?"

This isn't a platitude. So many goals—prestigious college, big paycheck, charming family—insistently recommend themselves to us as the "good life." And then they leave us short. The Greek philosophers saw their role as provoking their friends to reason through better answers to the question of what's worth organizing your life around.

The "ultimate good" for human beings will involve satisfying our animal needs while also building up virtuous traits of character, over time and in a rational way. That is the kind of happiness Aristotle called eudaimonia. Contemporary philosophers often translate it as "flourishing"—the complete state of being a well-developed, accomplished, and happy (in the good-feeling sense) person. Those who achieve this goal will feel and act in ways that represent the best parts of our nature. They will acquire all the virtues—like courage, generosity, and wisdom—and will integrate them seamlessly in an intentional and purposefully lived life. The hard part is figuring out how to nurture these virtues over the course of living our lives.

GOD AND THE GOOD LIFE

Which brings us back to the question—how do you learn this? Design thinking and survey methods can be taught (and they are!). The philosophical approach to happiness can be taught as well.

Our university, Notre Dame, like many Catholic schools, has every student study philosophy. Until a few years ago, if you asked students why, they'd respond with a standard Catholic answer for everything: we do it because, uh, tradition.

Back in 2015, Meghan was a newly tenured professor and Paul was a teaching-minded PhD student. For a while, we'd both been growing restless with the usual approach to teaching the Philosophy 101 requirement. We followed the typical intro script: A few weeks spent on logic, followed by a crash-course historical overview of Plato, Aristotle, Descartes, and Kant. Some mind-bending logic puzzles mixed in for fun. Midterm and final exams asked students to reproduce the logical maneuvers from the lectures. Our students gave the class high evaluations, but if you saw those students in the coffee-cart line the next semester and asked what they remembered from Philo 101, you'd get a blank stare with a sheepish smile. Many of them admitted on anonymous end-of-term surveys that they never did the readings.

Meanwhile, our students were slammed with philosophical problems: we knew this well from our discussions with them outside of class. Students may not get much out of writing an essay about Camus, but they think a lot about nihilism. They just call it burnout. Ask students if they worry that all of their projects lack meaning, and you'll get candid, sometimes terribly sad responses.

These college students are extremely intelligent. They are community-minded high achievers. Most of them are fortunate enough to come from emotionally stable and economically secure family backgrounds. Many have had some exposure to philosophy and spirituality, and if they don't know much about religious traditions before they arrive, they pick it up quickly on our very overtly religious campus. More than anything, they want to be successful adults, and they are hyperresponsive to advice they get from parents, teachers, and role models in their orbits. On paper, these students seem like they're well on their way to living happy, fulfilling lives. This is why their nihilistic tendencies seem so puzzling.

They have access to an endless stream of tools, resources, time management systems, and goals that promise to deliver a good life, but they often wind up paralyzed with anxiety. If we're honest, many of us feel the same way long after graduation.

Imagine that you had to "win" everything you needed for a good life in a series of tournaments. Each round has a set of judges who set the criteria, and other people are sometimes on your team and occasionally your competition. Throughout each day, these judges observe you from a distance, sometimes letting you advance a level, sometimes holding you back. Sometimes smiling with admiration, and even clapping. Sometimes gasping and shaking their heads in disgust. You're not exactly sure what the prize is, or what criteria are being used. Here's what you do know: whatever these judges decide will ultimately determine your fate.

This thought experiment is closer to real life for many of us than we may want to admit. We're caught up in systems of evaluation, which we never fully opt in to, that determine nearly every aspect of our lives. These systems have the power to set your career trajectory and to determine your future earnings and income level; they even have some influence over the likelihood of your getting married and having a family, where you'll live, and how you will or won't enjoy aging. When we are young, well-meaning parents, teachers, and mentors tell us that we have to earn high grades, volunteer two hundred hours by senior year, and get a certain score on the ACT or risk spending the rest of our lives jobless, in debt, and unhappy.

These systems are crushing us, and it starts with our teenagers. According to survey data gathered by the American College Health Association in 2019, 57.5 percent of college students reported feeling that "things were hopeless" in the last year, 67.4 percent reported feeling very lonely, 66.4 percent reported feeling "overwhelming anxiety," and 14.5 percent reported having "seriously considered suicide." Suicides have increased in the United States in the last decade, especially among young people.

Three trends coincide with crises of meaning in young adults. First, what they view as the goal of a good life has shifted. More than 80 percent of college freshmen in the 1970s said that one of their important goals in life was to find meaning and purpose. By 2018, that number was down to 42 percent. What are they aiming at now? More than 80 percent of them said that one of their primary goals was to become rich. Second, young Americans now report historically low levels of feelings of personal accomplishment—they have changed their goals but feel no closer to achieving them. Third, psychologists observe plummeting levels of social trust among young people—they have less satisfying goals, less capacity to accomplish them, and believe nobody is going to help them.

The trends look equally bleak among the broader adult population. According to the economists Anne Case and Angus Deaton, after 1998, the mortality rate was predicted to continue falling at 2 percent. But unlike in other wealthy countries, it instead began rising for many demographics in the United States (especially for those in the fragile middle class). U.S. deaths caused by suicide, drug overdose, or alcoholic liver disease are persistently on the rise. The surprising thesis to come out of this work is that these deaths are better explained by a loss of meaning and community connection than by what we typically think of as risk factors, such as job loss or declines in access to material resources. This raises the issue of how we measure meaning and practically how we help each other to meet these profound needs.

In our own lives, philosophy has been a deeply personal resource. It is how we pay the bills, but it is even more so a "way of life." Philosophy is the way we read the news, what we talk about with our friends, where we go in quiet moments when we are struggling to make big decisions. We are both Catholics (though with pretty different experiences in the religion) and philosophy has given each of us the tools we needed to talk with others about the weird and gripping faith we have embraced.

In 2015, our understanding of our students' struggles with meaning and value came from the frustrations we observed when talking with them; we didn't know all the wellness and economic data then. We certainly had no way of predicting that tumultuous elections in Europe and the United States were about to make it feel harder than ever to have authentic and productive discussions with other people about moral issues, or that a global pandemic would make all of our lives far more tenuous and expose our interdependence.

We saw that the good life was in retreat on our own campus. We knew we had to act locally. We thought philosophy could offer our students hope and the benefit of ancient wisdom during a turbulent period of their lives.

The God and the Good Life course was built on the idea that philosophy is care for our souls. We decided we would ask our students four crucial questions facing all of us in this pursuit:

1. How do you decide what (and whom) to believe?
2. What are your moral obligations?
3. Should you practice a religion?
4. What (if anything) can you do to make sure your life is meaningful?

These are the questions that still keep us up at night. Seeking answers to them goes a long way to giving our lives direction. In our course, we teach students to reason out their answers to these questions in the context of real-world problems, especially the problems appearing in their lives.

We designed the God and the Good Life course with the optimism that in the right environment and with a bit of training, twenty-first-century seekers can develop sincere, well-reasoned, and persistently useful goals to guide them through the world.

The results have been inspiring. While admittedly it is a core requirement, the class is the most popular undergraduate course on the Notre Dame campus. We can't keep up with student demand, which is gratifying but also indicative of the need for this work with young people. As the course gained a national reputation, we started fielding more and more requests to share lesson plans with adults looking to add philosophical depth to their goals. We realized this is work we need to do throughout our lives. In fact, the Greeks warn us that work like this cannot be contained in a course for young people.

In ancient virtue ethics, physical fitness is a surprisingly common metaphor for living well. There are obvious, literal connections between health and happiness—if you don't take care of your body, you'll be miserable, or you may not even have a life to make excellent—but the Greeks took interest in the connection at a deeper level.

First, they recognized that virtue requires training, and that we need to start learning and practicing the right habits at an early age. As those of us who have only realized the importance of regular exercise later in life know, there's only so much strength and mobility you can recover. Likewise, if we wait too long to work on our souls, we might miss a crucial window of opportunity. We might become hardened in our ways of thinking, and we might not know which direction to turn when life hands us the really difficult problems. As we age, of course, our needs change again, and we find ourselves wanting to go deeper into the answers that ring true in our experience. We reach out to friends, or we become more involved in meaningful communities, and use the resources we find there to build on, and better appreciate, what's true, good, and beautiful in our lives.

Second, the Greeks recognized that even though we have different needs at different stages in our lives, and that what it takes for us to be happy in these stages might look radically different, there's a kind of underlying unity in our pursuit of the good life. There's nothing relativistic in the doctor's order to exercise vigorously in your youth but then tone down the running as you age. Likewise, Aristotle and Plato recommend seeking out moral mentors, or making sure to educate and cultivate yourself when you're young. And this is perfectly compatible with their advice to lean more on your own experience and wisdom to think through moral problems later in life.

If the virtue ethicists are right, then our souls change as we acquire the education, experience, and ultimately wisdom characteristic of a well-lived life.

If we're going to take this metaphor to its natural conclusion, we should note that we think *our* role in all of this, and the role that this book can play, will be different depending on which season of life you find yourself in right now. If, like our students, you're just starting out, and you want to make sure to put your life on the right track, we'll provide the questions—and some of the answers—that philosophers have found to resonate down through the ages. Their sheer resilience throughout history proves that they're not going to go out of style anytime soon.

If you're going through the transitions characteristic of midlife, you'll find concrete stories to illustrate *our* answers to some of these questions. Compare these stories against your own experience, as you would with a friend over a long and leisurely afternoon walk.

And if you find yourself nearer to the finish line, you might use the ancient wisdom in these pages to give color and detail to the way you appreciate or understand the life you've lived. The pursuit of happiness, like the pursuit of health, is an activity undertaken from the moment you realize it's possible until you take leave of life itself.

THE GOOD LIFE METHOD

There are many traditions within good life philosophy that can guide you as you try to live more intentionally. Any of these traditions is worth considering in its own right and might very well resonate with the particular philosophical problems you are facing. So why do we choose to start with the ancient Greeks' tools? Unlike Confucianism, the Greek philosophy "travels well"—many of the Greek hypotheses about the good life are meant to be universal, not limited to families in the Zhou dynasty. The Buddhist views of the good life have a higher entry cost in understanding very specific metaphysical claims about selves and the universe. And Jewish, Christian, and Muslim philosophies have all inevitably been shaped by exposure to the Greek methods, though, as we'll see, their relationship is complicated.

Finally, for Western audiences at least, the views of Socrates, Plato, and Aristotle are likely to be relevant to philosophical questions already occupying your mind. They are cultural operating systems for our moral lives the way that Shakespeare always seems to be running in the background of our literary lives.

From Socrates, we get a role model for how to ask hard questions about the good life and care about the answers.

From Socrates's student Plato, we inherit the idea that society needs dedicated wisdom lovers if we're to have any hope of living together in justice and harmony. And he gives us the idea that a crucial part of any individual's good life is the dogged pursuit of the truth, even if it means disrupting comfortable routines.

From Plato's student Aristotle, we inherit the idea that living a happy life is something that will crucially depend on whether we are able and willing to devote our lives to the cultivation of our personalities by developing the virtues. Aristotle also gives us the method: "It is necessary to examine what has been said [by philosophers] by bringing it to bear on facts and life, and if it harmonizes, we should accept it; but if it is dissonant, we should suppose it to be mere words." In short: Philosophy should matter to you, it should be relevant to questions you face in your own life, and, if applied correctly, it should help you be happier. Moreover, the thoughtful study of our own good life problems can advance our understanding of the philosophical nature of happiness.

This is a bold sales pitch! We believe this "facts and life method" is just as possible for us as it was for the Greeks.

Many ancient philosophers held that thinking seriously about how to live a good life is something that can only happen in a community where knowledge is shared and wisdom is passed down. Aristotle was even more adamant: having these deep philosophical conversations about our goals is the material on which true friendship is built.

If our experience is representative, these ancient hopes ring as true today as they did at the onset. For the two of us, the God and the Good Life project has been personally life-changing. While teaching thousands of freshmen to wrestle with these questions, we've also been trying to answer them in our own lives. We've been writing our own philosophical apologies. And we've been rediscovering the surprising, enlivening ways that our academic training in philosophy can redirect our goals. Along the way we've formed incredible friendships with our colleagues, students, and each other.

In the coming chapters, we'll talk you through variants of the questions, providing you with arguments—some ancient wisdom and some more cutting-edge arguments—that will help you live more intentionally. Each chapter takes up an area of life where we often have goals, then fills out the layers with philosophical depth. Aristotle teaches us how to be better parents. Plato and W. E. B. Du Bois advise us on living through politically turbulent times. Our questions will inevitably push us to key virtue ethicists in other periods. Søren Kierkegaard and William James and Saint Thomas Aquinas are here to help us wrestle with faith and risk and God. Elizabeth Anscombe helps us grapple with what is (and isn't) our responsibility. Seneca and Marcus Aurelius coach us through thinking about fear, disruption, and death. All are fellow travelers and advisers as we try to get eudaimonia in our sights.

The book follows the structure of our course, which really ought to be called "The Good Life and God." In the first half, we think seriously about the day-to-day philosophical challenges that life deals us—questions about money, work, family life, and political friction. Developing answers to these questions inevitably pushes you to consider more difficult philosophical puzzles: your attitudes toward risk and death, your views about fostering an interior life, your assumptions about why your life is good. In the second half of the book, we'll turn to the existential matters—faith, suffering, the kinds of questions that religious belief might make easier to answer, and the ones that religious belief can make even harder.

For us, this method of pursuing the good life has been as much an intellectual journey as it has been spiritual. Questions about the rationality of trusting a religious tradition or alleged sources of divine revelation—or even whether it's possible for a self-respecting philosopher to believe God exists without demonstrable proof—have shaped the story of our religious lives. These are stories that we'll share with you, along with the answers we think we've found and our own outstanding questions, as we encourage you to examine your own ideas anew. But you certainly don't have to share our conclusions to benefit from the Good Life Method. We welcome skeptics and believers alike on the journey.

AT THE CONCLUSION of each chapter, we leave you with some concrete practices related to the four key philosophical skills—asking strong questions, writing your "inner story," paying attention, and making meaning. The final assignment of our course is a written reflection that is part rigorous philosophical argument, part personal narrative, and part map to the good life that offers students' own answers to the four big questions of our course. We call this assignment the "Philosophical Apology." It's a goal-planning document on steroids.

The word "apology" comes from the Greek *apologia*, which means "speaking in one's defense." Over time, it has come to define a genre of writing in which authors lay out their philosophical approach about some big good life questions and then defend the approach in two ways—by illustrating their reasons in support of the position and by showing how this view is being enacted in events in their own lives.

Socrates delivered the most famous *Apology* in 399 BC. It was a literal defense: he'd been put on trial for embarrassing the rich and powerful in his pursuit of the good life, and he used his final speech in the Athenian Assembly to urge his fellow citizens to care about the truth. Augustine apologized in *The Confessions*, one of the first memoirs in history and a philosophical defense of his sudden religious conversion. The Roman emperor Marcus Aurelius wrote his apology—*Meditations*—while in the battlefields of northern Europe, never once mentioning the war but instead reflecting on his contemplative life. W. E. B. Du Bois wrote his apology *Dusk of Dawn* on the eve of World War II, wrestling with a lifetime of encounters with racism. Friedrich Nietzsche wrote his apology to explain why he was rejecting conventional morality and striving to become the superman.

In our class, we use the conventions of the apology to help students think clearly and philosophically about their beliefs, and to incorporate that thinking into the broader story of their lives. Along the way it inevitably turns out to be a very effective vehicle for thinking through our good life goals and learning how to share them more deeply with others.

Life makes philosophers of us all eventually—the ethical and existential challenges come at us whether we are ready or not. Now we want to invite you into our class and this experiment in modern virtue ethics.

Soulcraft: You Owe Yourself an Apology

Our project in the next ten chapters is to teach you to see your life in its many dimensions as a philosopher would. If you're looking for a way to organize your philosophical journey, and make it more concrete, you might start by giving some thought to the overarching assignment we give students on their first day of God and the Good Life.

THE APOLOGY ASSIGNMENT

> ***Purpose:*** Develop the ability to tell a persuasive philosophical story about your beliefs and how they fit into the ongoing story of your life; explain and defend your core philosophical beliefs with reference to major philosophers and traditions, while anticipating and responding to likely objections to your views.

Each "section" of an apology should deal with a different big question about the good life, like whether close familial relationships are essential to your happiness or whether you should be donating money to charitable causes and how to figure out which ones to pick. You can organize your thoughts using the Big Four from our class: Belief, Morality, Faith, and Meaning.

Each building block of your apology will contain the following major elements:

(1) **THE STORY OR "STARTING POINT."** Tell a story from your life so far that conveys how you glimpsed an answer to this particular good life question.

(2) **THE ARGUMENT FOR A "GOAL."** For virtue ethicists, the answer to these good life questions is typically to become a certain kind of person. What do you think people like

you should do in response to this question? The goal should be partly inspired by the insight from your story, partly argued for using philosophical reasons and insights.

(3) **PLANNING FOR THE "MEANS."** What habits, practices, and relationships are going to get you from your current life to the good life (eudaimonia)? How much help will you need and what kind of help? How will you know if you are on the right or wrong track? The final ingredient in a great apology section is a reflection on how you plan now to direct your life toward the goal and how you anticipate inevitable setbacks and complications.

It may seem daunting, but we'll be giving you small and very doable philosophical exercises to help you along throughout this book. We call these breakouts "soulcraft," after Aristotle's poetic way of describing what happens to you when you live in a good community. We will suggest practical experiments you might try if you want to infuse your life with a bit more of the virtues these philosophers recommend. And we'll give you some examples from our own apologies and those of our students and colleagues, showing you how we struggle through philosophical puzzles raised by our own finances, families, tragedies, ambitions, and turning points.

Aristotle warns us about falling into the gap between theory and action, "like patients who listen attentively to their doctors, but do none of the things they are ordered to do. As the latter will not be made well in body by such a course of treatment, the former will not be made well in soul by such a course of philosophy." So if you want this to work, we're going to encourage you to start brainstorming about the stories, people, and experiences in your life that these theories might connect to. And prepare to enlist others in your soulcrafting experiments to come.

I.

The Good Life

1.

Desire the Truth

> Don't you realize what a great evil comes from dialectic as it is currently practiced? . . . When young people get their first taste of arguments, they misuse it. . . . They imitate those who've refuted them by refuting others themselves, and, like puppies, they enjoy dragging and tearing those around them with their arguments.
>
> —PLATO, *Republic*

DECISION 2016

We launched the God and the Good Life course in the fall of 2016. Two months into the inaugural semester, we thought that we were crushing it. Our in-class lectures were lively. Students wrote halfway decent essays. Our course website was crashing less often. GGL was a campus hit. But it wasn't until that November—the week of the presidential election—that we really started to understand the risks and potential rewards of what we were attempting.

The day before the general election, we invited Pete Buttigieg, then the mayor of South Bend, to help us lead a class debate about the role democracy plays in the good life. While Meghan and Pete have somewhat different political and religious outlooks, they've enjoyed the big debates since their early twenties. Pete and Meghan were in the same cohort of Rhodes scholars at Oxford in the early 2000s. Both started new jobs in South Bend in 2011. When Pete deployed to Afghanistan in 2014, Meghan lived in his house. (Paul partied there.) Pete's been dragged in as a "celebrity guest" for many of Meghan's seminars, talking about modern moral dilemmas and local government, Enlightenment philosophy and local government, Greek philosophy and local government. As they discovered, there is pretty much no subject of a philosophy course that cannot be interestingly related to problems of local government.

Paul has a more complicated relationship with Mayor Pete. From the time Paul arrived in South Bend, he has been involved in community organizing. In 2016, the mayor's office announced plans to sell its largest public park, which was the site of both the most biodiverse lake in the county and an underused municipal golf course. Paul helped spearhead an effort with activists from South Bend's Catholic Worker house to oppose the sale. He became a thorn in the side of the city government, publishing op-eds in the local paper and passionately arguing at city council meetings that maintaining the park was vital for the local community. To Pete's credit, he was willing to engage with the group, though he disagreed. Ultimately, the sale never went through.

On November 7, 2016, we brought Pete in to debate with us about Book 8 of Plato's *Republic*. In the chapter, Plato goes to great lengths to argue that democracy is a tragic form of government and that living in democracies will gradually destroy our souls. We thought this would be a funny class session, foregrounding the big U.S. vote. Meghan represented some of Plato's more extreme views: you can't trust the electorate; the other side is likely corrupt; people don't know what they should want; political rhetoric has absolutely no connection with the truth. Pete represented the pro-democracy side: we are more alike than we are different; we have to learn to live together; we are "political animals" who need to be civically engaged. We figured we would all have a good laugh about Plato's misguided cynicism.

Philosophy (and the professoriat more generally) skews pretty blue, and this can lead professors to off-base assumptions about our students' views. In the past few years we've heard a lot about "bubbles" and "echo chambers," but back in 2016 we were unknowingly living in one. Walking into the lecture room on November 7, we just assumed that we knew the political views of these particular students. *Of course* people in their demographic support Clinton over Trump. *Of course* they think the current American political process is unequivocally good for our souls. Mind you, we'd never asked the students directly about how their political views figure into their conceptions of the good life.

Plato versus Pete seemed to go off as planned. At the end of class we did our own Decision 2016 poll of the two hundred students in the audience, using an anonymized polling app. "Who would you vote for tomorrow?" The results were . . . surprising.

- Gary Johnson 7%
- Jill Stein 2%
- **Donald Trump 44%**
- Hillary Clinton 37%
- Other 6%
- Would Not Vote 4%

Trump won the God and the Good Life election? It seemingly defied reason. Of course, in the next twenty-four hours we'd learn that the political diversity in our class was a microcosm of our nation.

On November 9, a few hours after President-elect Trump's victory speech, we were back in the auditorium and, according to the syllabus, about to switch units and begin discussing the life of contemplation. That felt wrong. For one thing, we realized we had completely screwed up the class on the seventh. The Platonic questions—Can we trust rhetoric? Each other? Do democracies work?—were suddenly very live, very divisive issues. Protests spread across Notre Dame's normally placid campus that morning; some students were demanding the university make statements on immigration policy. Some wore MAGA hats to class; others showed up crying. It was like we went to bed Tuesday night thinking we were one unified utopian campus and woke up Wednesday realizing that we were two different cities secretly living on top of each other.

The fundamental question Plato poses is whether we can be the kind of people who both love the truth and love life together. Is there any way to reconcile the two desires in a single life? That morning after the election, we realized how much we needed Plato.

LET NO ONE UNAWARE OF GEOMETRY ENTER HERE

Some philosophers are charismatic; you read their vision of the good life and you're immediately drawn to them. Plato is not such a philosopher. He can be judgmental and paranoid. He takes long digressions on topics like how to tame horses. It's not even always clear whether he believes what he is writing or is just being ironic. Still, if you go through Plato's training, so much else in philosophy falls into place.

In the *Republic*, Plato asks a great question: If we wanted to set up a city to help everyone achieve the good life, in a unified way, how would we do it? And he has a weird starting point to answer the question: geometric puzzles.

Legend has it that above the entrance to Plato's school, the Academy, there was an inscription: *Let no one unaware of geometry enter here.* For Plato, there is a direct connection between geometry and happiness, one with surprisingly profound implications for our current political conundrums. Caring about geometry is a warm-up for the much harder work of caring for the truth and convincing others to as well.

At some level, many of us find puzzles strangely fun. Area mazes are a very popular puzzle system in Japan; you'll find them in newspapers and books at train stations. Japanese schoolchildren work through them the way American kids do word searches. The goal in an area maze is to use just a bit of arithmetic and some logical maneuvers to figure out a mystery fact about a rectangle. The only geometry you need to remember is that the area of a rectangle is the width times the length. Here is an example of an area maze puzzle. Give it a shot.

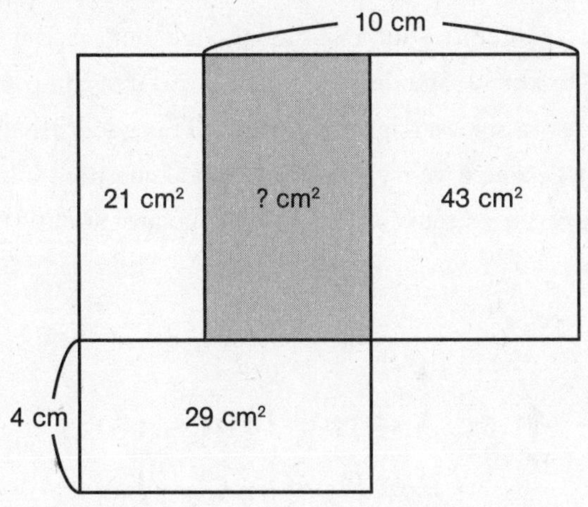

Maybe you found the answer (if not, check the endnotes for this chapter). Now ask yourself, How does it feel to *not* know? And how does it feel to figure it out? And how do you feel about another person if they patiently work through it with you?

Most of us love that feeling of putting the pieces together and solving a puzzle, either by ourselves or, even better, with our friends. If you aren't a math person, think about how you feel guessing the culprit of a murder mystery or remembering that celebrity name after hours of racking your brain. There is a distinctive kind of pleasure that comes along with intellectual curiosity, achievement, and integrity. This is our rational capacity, the same part of our personality that gets frustrated when we know we need a good reason for some decision, but we can't find one good enough. This is one of those goal-seeking traits that separates us most profoundly from other animals, which, as far as we know, do not spend time devising area mazes for themselves.

Plato thought geometry puzzles have the capacity to activate the parts of our personalities that love the truth. He wanted beginners at the Academy to at least recognize they want the truth, so they might be willing to undertake the hard work of finding it. Without this recognition, Plato thought, our communities and institutions could not survive.

But as Plato knew, sometimes it can be a real struggle to be someone who perseveres in the search for the truth. This good life puzzle turns up on campuses, where we try to ask hard moral questions but sometimes fumble the necessary discussion. It also turns up profoundly in family life.

Just Asking Questions
(Paul's Apology)

A few years after the Sandy Hook Elementary School shooting, I got an email from my mom. The subject line read something like "What's going on here?!" The body of the email was just a link to a video on YouTube. It was a thirty-five-minute, extremely low production value "documentary film" that laid out the most popular arguments for the conclusion that the shooting never happened; that it was all an elaborate government hoax to promote stricter gun control laws. The arguments were frustratingly specific, and took the form of questions that are difficult to disprove without special knowledge of the events:

Why doesn't the police timeline match that of first responders? Why is there helicopter footage of armed men without uniforms in the nearby woods at the time of the event? Why do the shadows in two photos taken at the school—allegedly on the day of the shooting—seem to indicate radically different times of day?

I felt a flash of anger, then disbelief that someone would care so little for the victims of an unfathomable tragedy that they could create something so vile.

Then I felt fear that my own mother was being sucked into a void of misinformation. I both wanted to engage with her and feared that if I did I was walking into a trap. Perhaps ignoring it, while it wouldn't make it go away, wouldn't actively push her further out into space. Perhaps the best thing to do in such situations is to refuse to engage.

But there was also a tiny voice in the back of my head that said, "Well. If it's so obvious that this is false, if this conspiracy theory is so stupid and ridiculous, then what are the answers? Why don't the timelines add up? How hot does jet fuel burn? How could a pathetic defector have made three perfect shots from the sixth floor of the book depository?"

And this, perhaps, was the most terrifying moment of all.

I'm embarrassed to say that I didn't respond very charitably to my mom's email. I let the fear turn into outrage. I fired something off that included a lot of CAPITALIZED WORDS. I accused her of harming the victims of the families by spreading this kind of bullshit and said that I wouldn't even stoop to the level of discussing such internet garbage. I overreacted.

And what good did that do? Well, for a while my mom stopped sending me links to any videos. But we also talked less about the world, current events, and big questions we thought were important.

Then, one day, she sent another link—this one having something vaguely to do with vaccines for newborns. I felt the rage welling up again.

But this time, instead of firing up the engines of righteous indignation, I took a breath and emailed back a question: "Why did you send that to me?" She responded that she couldn't help herself. My wife and I were expecting our first child at the time, and she was worried about the baby. What if some newborn vaccines were unsafe? What if they had irreversible and devastating effects? I took another breath. "I appreciate your concern," I said. Because I did. "It would be tragic if we unintentionally harmed our baby," I said. Because it would be. Then I took a few cautious steps back.

I asked my mom whether she thought the claims in the video were true. To my surprise, she responded with humility and quite a bit of skepticism. She said she didn't know if she could trust the people making the video, but that their skepticism of medical authority rang true to her experience. She reminded me that she'd lived through time periods during which long-standing conventional medical wisdom was later discovered to be wrong, sometimes disastrously so. We talked about how the opioid epidemic was an example of how the system could hugely fail the public. This was not direct evidence about vaccines (and I argued as much), but it helped me understand where her curiosity about the video was coming from. She also agreed with me that the video looked crazy, but here, too, she provided a broader perspective. For someone like her who was raised in a generation where eyewitness video was held up by the evening news as irrefutable evidence, the proliferation of fake video was baffling. I agreed with her that it's important to be a fierce advocate for my child. And I admitted that my growing up with YouTube gave us very different perspectives on digital realities.

A switch flipped; my mom and I were talking again. And the dangers I'd anticipated, of legitimizing garbage sources, fanning the flames of polarization, or being unable to counter the confusing and (sometimes intentionally) misleading claims in the video she'd sent me, turned out to be unfounded.

It matters here that my mom is not a "truther," a conspiracy theorist, or an anti-vaxxer. She was a reporter for a local paper before she had kids. She once uncovered a legitimate conspiracy in our small town's local government to hide the fact that they'd accidentally killed thousands of migrating monarch butterflies with a pesticide meant to poison mosquitoes.

It is also key that our relationship matters more to us than any of our more particular current philosophical views: in politics, parenting strategy, or our general levels of trust in mainstream media sources. We can disagree on the views, but we try to keep things in perspective. Indeed, one of the reasons why I want to have these conversations with my mom is because it helps us connect. I think I'd regret avoiding these conversations, because to really love someone you've got to periodically check in and try to understand where they're coming from. For us, disagreement is a way to build up the relationship we both care so much about.

We still talk often about politics, raising kids, and religion. But I've learned a lot over the course of our conversations, and I sometimes find myself changing my mind. So does she. And I have to keep reminding myself that it is good for us that she (sometimes) changes my mind. We can have the hard conversations as long as we remember that they're rooted in our relationship, and the respect and love we have for each other, and for the truth.

THE "TRUTH WARS" IN ANCIENT ATHENS

Sometimes you can turn fraught dialogue in a productive direction. But we also know that good life rhetoric is a real skill, something most of us need a lot of practice in. Sometimes a well-intentioned comment in a conversation can get you labeled a fascist, or worse. Plato was fascinated by the ways human minds can harmonize or clash miserably in joint attempts to pursue the truth.

If you pick up Plato's *Republic*, you might initially mistake it for a play rather than a philosophy book. Plato wrote entirely in the form of the dramatic dialogue; his works look and read more like scripts than scholarly essays. In most of these plays, Plato's main character was his teacher and philosophical mentor, Socrates. Sometimes Plato tries to portray Socrates's actual views and teachings. In the best dialogues, he simply uses Socrates as a mouthpiece for his own views. Later philosophers from nearly every tradition would all riff on Socrates as the archetype for any heroic figure willing to stand up to his culture in defense of the truth. The *Republic* features Socrates in his absolute element tackling more and more difficult variations of the question of whether we should want to really understand the world or just want to get along well in our current society.

Plato believed that everything, from starfish to justice to numbers, had an underlying nature, and that our highest purpose as humans was to understand these deeper natures. In his dialogues, he has Socrates interrogate everyone he meets, especially those who claim to be experts or to have some special knowledge of how things work. Socrates makes mincemeat of opponents who claim to know the underlying nature (or "form") of something but really have just been satisfied with appearances.

In the fourth century BC, debates about truth were having a big moment. Recall that ancient Athens was a direct democracy and any citizen—a status restricted to adult men—could attend any legislative session. If they felt so moved, they could stand up and give a speech about whatever law was under consideration. Laws were passed by simple majority, and votes were final. It was also fairly common for individuals to be sued or accused of the capital crime of tyranny. These cases would be argued in the Assembly as well. For a citizen in Athens, your ability to compose and deliver persuasive arguments could mean the difference between life and death. So it was a skill most Athenian citizens wanted to get better at.

The sophists were professionals who could teach you how to argue. They were self-proclaimed experts in rhetoric—the technical tools we use to persuade. Wealthy families would hire sophists to teach rhetoric to their sons. We can think of sophists as the ancient equivalent of debate coaches or college admissions essay tutors. They didn't tell you what to say and they didn't care about your personal reasons; they simply taught you how to say *whatever* you wanted to say more convincingly.

Sophists attracted many students, and those students became power players in Athens. Not everyone was thrilled with this result. Sophists were lawyerly, and some of them would brag about being able to convince an audience of outrageous falsehoods through rhetorical tricks. Harry Frankfurt, a contemporary philosopher at Princeton, has introduced the term "bullshit" into academic discourse to stand for the attitude of having no concern for the truth or a general indifference to how things really are. The best sophists were expert bullshitters.

Plato couldn't stand bullshit, and he thought the sophists—in teaching their students to argue without concern for the truth—were ruining Athenian democracy. If you came to a sophist and asked him to help you craft an argument in favor of a particular tax law, he would do it. If your friend came to the same sophist the next day and asked him to help craft an argument *against* that law, he would do that as well. (As long as you were both willing to pay, of course!) Sometimes, in Plato's dialogues, sophists are depicted changing their views midconversation to get a better audience reaction.

Accused of bullshit, the sophists would defend their profession, in classic sophistical fashion, by offering deflating arguments about the nature of truth itself.

First, they would often point out that they were just coaching students in a valuable skill, and that they shouldn't be held responsible for how the students use that skill. If I help train a boxer, showing them how to land a punch, is it fair to hold me responsible when that boxer later clobbers an innocent person? Logic and rhetoric are mere instruments. Truth is a personal problem. I've got mine and you've got yours.

Some sophists went even further. Eventually some of them started to argue that there was no such thing as *the* truth about anything. Arguments can be more or less persuasive, but, at the end of the day, "truth" is just a concept we use to generate attention or make our arguments seem important. Tabloids use this rhetorical trick, sometimes as clickbait, all the time: "The Real Truth about Area 51!" Or consider the actual title of this actual online article: "This Outrageous Truth about Green Gummy Bears Will Destroy Your World."* We bring in talk about "truth" and "reality" just because it makes the content seem more interesting and makes you more likely to agree with the conclusions. Noting this rhetorical power, the ancient sophists started to maintain that any appeal to "truth" was, itself, just a power move.

Plato thought that this sophistical attitude toward truth was poisoning Athenians' trust in one another and their institutions, making genuine and productive disagreements impossible. Plato frequently rails against the kinds of people this system is producing. In the *Republic*, he worries that when we stop desiring the truth, we just start cycling through increasingly bizarre desires. Here is how Plato describes the lifestyle of a "democratic souled man" who denies any objective truth. He spends the first day of the week drinking and listening to flute music. The second day of the week he is dieting and hitting the gym. Then he switches to lazing around, then he reads philosophy. He is always jumping into politics and "saying and doing whatever comes into his mind." In the aftermath of the 2016 election, on rereading this passage, Meghan had a

* Gillian Fuller, "This Outrageous Truth about Green Gummy Bears Will Destroy Your World," *Elite Daily*, September 3, 2015. (Spoiler alert: the world-destroying truth is that green gummy bears are strawberry flavored.)

sinking feeling in the pit of her stomach: Yeesh . . . that's us. That's how I behave on the internet—responding to crowds, searching out the inflammatory posts. That's how I am often directing my life—just moving with the loudest social cues.

BULLSHIT KEEPS US FROM THE GOOD LIFE

Plato's challenge was to figure out how to engage the sophists and convince them to care about truth, lest we become entangled in their web of reasoning. This is very hard, because often your own logical maneuvers just seem to feed into their systems of bullshit. How do you convince a whole culture that has become obsessed with spin—a culture in which a badly articulated argument can mean losing your property, your freedom, or your head—to focus on anything other than the art of persuasion?

Plato did not think that the solution was to argue the sophists out of their sophistry, but rather to convert them—to show them powerful images of what it is like to be a truth lover in the hopes that they would reactivate this aspect of their souls. Plato admittedly took this conversion program to the extreme. Most of the *Republic* consists of Plato's directions for building a rigid totalitarian utopia run by philosopher kings and queens identified in childhood. There is a lot of geometry and gymnastics, heavily censored poetry, and dire warnings of what happens if you let the wrong sorts of people have power.

On this basis, many readers have thought Plato is the chief example for why philosophers should never be put in charge of anything. The twentieth-century American philosopher Karl Popper thought Plato was even worse than the sophists, because his absolutism flowed effortlessly into totalitarianism: "Plato [became] the pioneer of the many propagandists who, often in good faith, developed the technique of appealing to moral, humanitarian sentiments, for anti-humanitarian, immoral purposes."

We'll happily agree that Plato does not have particularly great advice about how to set up a government. But his more fundamental insight is spot on: you can't make progress with arguments and reasoning unless everyone involved already cares about the truth.

If you find yourself in a bullshit standoff, you need to somehow remind the people you are arguing with (and yourself) why the truth is worth wanting. How can you do this?

The first step is admitting why sophistry is such a seductive lifestyle in the first place. Sophists accurately predict that persuasion *is* the primary aim of most of the people who try to give us arguments. Advertisers are an obvious case, since they often present claims purely in an attempt to convince you to buy some product. The adman doesn't care about whether you actually come to believe the truth about which soap is best, he just cares that you end up believing that it is his client's. This is true of many politicians as well. Indeed, because human institutions can be corrupted, it's more than plausible that there are those in academia, the media, or the government who would rather persuade large numbers of people to believe something they deem important than to help them seek after the truth, whatever that might be. So you might think that becoming a sophist yourself will help you avoid being a sucker for all of the sophistry surrounding us.

Sophistry also appeals to our egalitarian side. You might think it's offensive or arrogant to think that truth is objective, because this means believing that others don't have the truth. Consider the vast disagreements between cultures over time and across the world on the "good life." Should women work outside the home? Is it acceptable to eat animals? It seems implausible to think that, at most, *one* culture at *one* point in history knows the truth on these questions. It's even *more* wild to think that the one and only culture that acquired the truth happens to be *yours*.

On the other hand, if we think—along with the sophists—that truth talk is all just an attempt to persuade, then many people throughout history and around the world could have beliefs that are "true" for them. They won't believe our same truths, but that's okay. Different things work for different cultures, and so it is rational for them to be persuaded by different visions of reality. We shouldn't invalidate the beliefs of others, and we shouldn't arrogantly assume that we have sole access to the truth while everyone else just gets it wrong.

Are these justifications for sophistry any good? We don't think so. One insight we learn from Plato's depiction of Socrates and his dialogues is that the best way to rehabilitate a bullshitter is to encourage him to see how exhausting and unsatisfying it is to pursue the sophist way of life.

First, while we've acknowledged the fact that many will try to persuade without regard for the truth, this just means that truth seeking is hard, not that it's pointless. Think about the trade you make in going sophist. Sophists aren't any better positioned to resist unethical advertisements or carefully fact-check politicians' claims on the campaign trail. They can't claim that bias in academia, the media, or the government is a corruption of the truth. They have to go all in and admit that, while they might not like someone exerting power over them via argument, they aren't going to be able to offer any genuinely better arguments against such oppression. In a world without truth, every argument—and every attempt to uncover the "truth"—is just more bullshit.

Second, and somewhat paradoxically, the Platonic insistence on the objectivity of truth is often the more tolerant view in practice. Suppose someone from a different culture disagrees vehemently with a moral claim that you just made. Maybe you claimed that most teenage women should have the option to go to college, and your conversation partner comes from a culture that believes teenage women should marry young, forgo formal education, and raise families. There are two ways to engage in the disagreement. In Plato's scenario, you take their claim very seriously, and consider at length whether they are right. If they are, perhaps you should change your life significantly; perhaps you should convert to a different religion or radically change your parenting strategy. But in the sophist scenario, you don't need to care about their reasons at all, at least not as potential reasons for you. "That might be true for you," you could say, "but it's not true for me."

We think the first scenario is the more respectful, tolerant position. Most of us would want someone to take our good life claim seriously, even if they end up disagreeing, rather than summarily dismiss it without even hearing out our reasons. Tolerance is a virtue directed at people with positions, not positions themselves. The world isn't any better off if we just try to make every position, no matter how inconsistent, look true.

Finally, holding the Platonic view of truth need not entail arrogance or dogmatism. There's a distinction between believing, even very confidently, that some claim is true, and maintaining that you couldn't possibly be wrong. We can and should remain open to the possibility that we've made an error and that we believe falsely, or that we grasp some truth only partially or incompletely. This is what it means to take others' perspectives and experiences seriously, even when we disagree. It's to navigate the terrain together, jointly seeking the truth as our shared goal. In the opening of the *Republic*, Socrates urges his sophist opponents, "If you change your position, do it openly and don't deceive us." A good Platonist takes responsibility for bad beliefs.

It is tempting to think the sophists are "those guys"—the idiots on the other side of whatever political or moral battle we happen to be embroiled in. But Plato thought we each have a long way to go in developing concern for the truth.

WE EACH NEED TO ESCAPE OUR CAVE(S) . . .

In the *Republic*, Plato wants to emphasize how hard it is to live with the truth as a goal. So he has Socrates offer a parable. There once were some men living in a cave. Their legs and necks were fettered from childhood so they always remained in the same spot and could never move. Their captors would put on shadow puppet shows for the men—shadow trees, shadow animals, shadow sun: "Such prisoners would in every way believe that the truth is nothing other than the shadows of those artifacts."

What would it be like to escape from such a situation? Plato thinks initially the realization would be awful, but then become sublime. Imagine you are one of the men and you break free. You climb up out of your cave. At first you are blinded by the real (bright!) light outside. It is excruciating. Then your eyes start to adjust. You see . . . real trees! Real animals! Eventually you see the real sun, a kind of light you just had no clue was possible before.

The sun is Plato's metaphor for the truth. Think about walking from a very dark room into a brightly lit one. You don't immediately see more—you probably see less. Your pupils have to contract. Your brain has to process very different information. For Plato, this everyday visual experience is a guide to the more serious difficulty we face when we try to learn.

The hard question for Plato (for all virtue ethicists) is how we can move ourselves to see and love what's real. Do we want the sun or the puppet show? This is the core drama of any great education. You start off in the grips of one way of looking at things—fat makes you fat, physical objects are solid, the current economic system happens to be the best possible one. Your appearances are challenged by new evidence you let in. At first it is painful, disorienting, and alienating to try to see things in the new way. You argue with people back home about the best diet. You feel weird realizing that most of the physical world is an empty void. You are anxious about potential recessions that weren't even on your radar before. But if you get far enough along in your education, you come to value life on the other side. You value being closer to knowing.

We often have to deftly navigate when to introduce the truths into relationships. Parents worry about the right time to tell their children that Santa Claus is a fictional character. Harder still is telling others your hypotheses about what's a right way to live, about your religious outlook, about who and how you love. Remaining in the world of appearances can feel much safer.

The archvillains in the Platonic dialogues are the people who are unwilling to question whether they want the right things. For Plato, these are people doomed to cave life. Consider Callicles, one of the major sophists and an inspiration for Friedrich Nietzsche's philosophy. Callicles maintains that the good life is one in which your desires aren't questioned—they are just satisfied. Here is what he tells Socrates: "The man who'll live correctly ought to allow his own appetites to get as large as possible and not restrain them. And when they are as large as possible, he ought to be competent to devote himself to them by virtue of his bravery and intelligence, and to fill them with whatever he may have an appetite for at the time."

Technology, advanced markets, and a culture that values money and power make it easier and easier to fall into the Callicles version of the good life. We live in a world of one-click online purchases and the seemingly frictionless ability to change relationships, jobs, and projects. You can curate a persona on social media, making your life into an appearance. It can be a mighty struggle to not be seduced by the bullshit puppet show that you self-produce. Plato's realization, which certainly inspired Aristotle, is that the good life requires making yourself into someone with better desires. And that requires first desiring the truth.

Philosophers since Plato have returned to his symbolic cave over and over again to reflect the ways that a desire for truth can transform their lives and their societies. For example, in his apology, *Dusk of Dawn*, W. E. B. Du Bois invokes the cave to describe the feeling of intellectual escape from the grip of racist ideology in the United States and Europe at the turn of the last century. Du Bois was a Black New Englander, who studied first at a historically Black university—Fisk—before moving to Harvard. The prevailing sociological view at Harvard in the 1880s was that centuries of slavery had permanently damaged Black men and women, preventing them from ever achieving the levels of development enjoyed by whites. Du Bois recounts the experience of leaving Harvard, traveling throughout Africa, meeting Black men and women who were flourishing and for whom race meant something quite different from what it meant in the United States. These encounters convinced him that a big part of the problem was with how our theories and ideologies had, themselves, become limiting.

He imagines himself as a philosopher exploring the cave created by racism in the United States, trying to bring both Black and white Americans out: "It is as though one, looking out from a dark cave in a side of an impending mountain, sees the world passing and speaks to it; speaks courteously and persuasively, showing them how these entombed souls are hindered in their natural movement, expression and development; and how their loosening from prison would be a matter not simply of courtesy, sympathy and help to them, but aid to all the world."

This is a cave we still easily fall into. If you aren't part of a disadvantaged group, you see your shadows—your friends are mostly happy, the government deals with you fairly, and your plans more often than not seem to come together. You think to yourself, "Things aren't perfect, but we live in a basically fair society and everyone has a chance to live the good life." Then a Black friend shares with you that he doesn't feel like the local police are dealing with him fairly. An Ecuadorian friend tells you she thinks she is being passed over for job interviews because of her name. Maybe you remember a time when expectations about your weight, or your body, or your gender, or a disability unfairly held you back. In these instances, we hear a call from outside the cave, suggesting maybe our perception of fairness is off: "Hey, maybe this isn't the good life!" But it is hard to shake our desire for the particular life we have now and the social arrangements that made that life possible. You dig in your heels. You refuse to turn toward the light.

Du Bois shares the Platonic pessimism about the power of arguments alone to convince people to change this outlook on themselves and of the world. We're suffering a perceptual problem—when you are stuck in a cave, you definitely can't see what you are missing. Du Bois concludes, in true Socratic fashion, that the better tactic is to try to engage each other with questions, which have the capacity to help us see alternatives to false but gripping views. Most of the sixth chapter of *Dusk of Dawn* is taken up with a Socrates-style dialogue between Du Bois and a white supremacist named van Dieman. Du Bois asks van Dieman more and more probing questions about how whiteness could be the source of superior ingenuity, beauty, and so on. In the process, van Dieman starts to get tripped up by his answers. Du Bois insists that care for the soul requires this kind of confrontation and deconstruction: "Human beings are infinite in variety, and when they are agglutinated in groups, great and small, the groups differ as though they, too, had integrating souls. But they have not. The soul is still individual if it is free. Race is a cultural, sometimes an historical fact."

We bring our own souls and our own minds into the truth project. And when we do, we are not condemned to be cave dwellers.

WE ALL HAVE TO GO BACK INTO THE CAVE(S)

Socrates famously declared at his trial that he was a "gadfly," a desperately needed figure in society, using philosophy to drive his friends toward the truth: "As upon a great and noble horse which was somewhat sluggish because of its size and needed to be stirred up by a kind of gadfly . . . I never cease to rouse each and every one of you, to persuade and reproach you." This is an image that many philosophers have inherited, especially those who see their work as a direct challenge to social and systemic injustice. The philosopher George Yancy, for instance, describes the role of minority philosophers as being "gadflies" in the midst of structural racism; their job in part to lovingly "reveal whites to themselves—unconcealed and naked." In the "Letter from a Birmingham Jail," Martin Luther King Jr. describes the entire leadership of the civil rights movement as "non-violent gadflies," an army of Socrateses trying to move society to appreciate the need for justice and change, and then to make that change. The appeal of Socrates, for some of these philosophers, is the personal risk he was willing to shoulder on behalf of the good life—his burden resonates with philosophers who find themselves taking on a similar burden in their own flawed societies.

Plato thinks that once we have grasped the real truth, we are obligated to make the difficult journey back into the depths of the cave, let our eyes painfully adjust once again, and try to convince those inside of the truth outside.

This catches most readers off guard. After hearing about the harrowing journey of a prisoner who has just escaped, it strikes us that descending back into that dark place is the last thing the newly freed person would want to do. But Plato insists, "When they have made it and looked sufficiently, we mustn't allow them to do what they are allowed to do today . . . to stay there [outside the cave] and refuse to go down again to the prisoners in the cave and share their labors and honors, whether they are of less worth or of greater." There is no reason to think this will be easy. Consider how disorienting it is to go from the brightly lit room back to absolute darkness—you see bright splotches, you can no longer find the glass of water on the nightstand. It's much worse than that. Plato hypothesizes that anyone who goes back in the cave will be killed by prisoners who reject the sun nonsense.

For millennia, philosophers have struggled to explain why exactly Plato thinks you need to go back if your efforts are likely to be futile and if you have already achieved a key ingredient of the good life in getting yourself out. It is usually thought that you have some sort of duty to the people you've grown up with to save them from error. Paul's experience with his mom suggests that this is partly right, but that, in real life, cave escape is rarely an individual and linear effort.

On a simplistic reading of Plato's allegory, there's a single path of enlightenment. Education, philosophy in particular, leads an individual to a complete understanding of the world, and only then are they able to return to start their search-and-rescue mission. In reality, we're all trapped in a fairly complex network of caves, and it can be incredibly difficult to tell, as we traverse particular passageways, whether we're enlightened or just seeing things in the dark. This is threatening, especially for those who have made their "knowledge" of some area a core part of their identity.

But when it comes to something as complex as the good life, we need all the help we can get. Sometimes we'll be able to shine a light down a cavern that a loved one's been trapped in, and sometimes we'll have to admit that they've just done the same for us. Paul can help his mom decode moral arguments in op-eds with his specialized logical expertise, but he's got to be willing to accept that her understanding and life experience might shed more light on that argument's conclusion than his own. For Socrates and Plato, the mutual pursuit of the truth is a way of loving your friends and fellow citizens. It is the joy of solving a puzzle or learning a secret with a friend, but writ large. If you are the only one on the outside of your particular cave, you miss the best part of the escape.

From Plato we get a three-part vision for the role truth plays in the good life. First, he gives us an honest assessment for how miserable it is to stay in the cave, to become a thoroughgoing sophist. Sophistry makes us more gullible, less tolerant, and less humble. Second, Plato gives us an honest assessment of the other virtues we are likely to need to be people who care about the truth (courage, patience, good vision). Third, he gives us a stern warning against staying in our caves, even *if* we think our particular cave is closer to the truth. If you really love the truth, you should be able to maintain this habit even in situations that are threatening, confusing, and rife with bullshit. And that final skill is the crucial virtue for those of us who make good life decisions by deliberating with others.

This is why Plato's insights are crucial for the health of a democracy, even if he wasn't that big a fan of this system of government. In a democracy, a love of truth is the condition that makes discussions about what matters most in life possible. Without it, we're all just using words to exert raw power, attempting to harness rhetoric for our gain at the expense of the common good. It's also what underlies our respect for people who see the world differently. When we genuinely believe that our fellow citizens care about the truth, that they'll be responsive if we can find the right reasons to give them, we can see ourselves as members of a community, and one in which disagreements are opportunities for mutual growth rather than arenas of power struggle.

CORRUPTING THE YOUTH

This brings us back to November 9, 2016, in a very divided classroom, in a very divided country, with everyone fleeing to their nearest media caves. An hour before class, the teaching team huddled. We had to find a way to have a truth-seeking conversation about the election, and it needed to start with showing some curiosity about who was in the room with us. Students arrived at class and were asked to anonymously fill out a sheet inquiring about their political views, their reaction to the election, and the questions they had for those who supported other candidates. For example, we asked, What, if any, moral principles do you think "unite" the United States right now? What is your biggest fear and biggest hope for the political system we live in? We asked for views about the environment, abortion, and immigration. And we asked for anyone willing to share the stories of how they came by those views. We asked for stories about how politics was affecting our particular good lives.

We redistributed each of their sheets, and asked each person in the class to read the views of their anonymous classmate to themselves, and to spend a couple minutes in reflection. Then we broke into small groups and discussed what was surprising about the reasons on the sheets, what questions we'd have for the person behind those views, and what we learned about each other that we hadn't known on Monday. Students were not allowed to guess about the race or gender or background of the person who filled the sheet out. They were not allowed to initially assume that the answers were thoughtless or in need of reinterpretation. To set ourselves up for better, truth-seeking debates for the rest of the semester, we tried to understand what we did and didn't actually know about the people who live, study, and vote alongside us.

It didn't happen overnight, but in the weeks following, our conversations in class got more specific and personal, less comfortable, and much more interesting.

In our culture, questions often presuppose that the person asking already knows the right answer. In congressional hearings, questions are used to land political blows. A lawyer in a trial will only ask a witness questions to establish facts that bolster her case. Questions can be used simply to cast doubt, even about something the questioner himself is quite certain about. They can be used to confuse, obfuscate, or just change the subject. We might call these "prosecutor questions," because their entire point is to get something said on the record. For example, you might know that Fred is a vegetarian and want to point out the flaws in his moral views. To do this, you ask him, "Fred, don't you think it would be offensive to visit someone's house and refuse to eat meat at a dinner prepared in your honor?" Your question is philosophical in a sense—it has to do with morality. But you don't think you'll learn anything by asking it.

This is the way sophists use questions, as weapons to wield power or sow confusion. Philo-sophers—lovers of the truth—use questions differently. Suppose you really wanted to understand why Fred feels so strongly about vegetarianism. You might start by getting a bit of Fred's story—a bit of his apology. "Fred, have you always been vegetarian or was there a particular time in life when you decided to do this? What was your motivation back then? Is it the same motivation now?" You might also ask questions that probe whether you and Fred think the same kinds of reasons are relevant to your attitudes about meat eating. "Fred, if it turned out animals really couldn't feel pain the way we do, would you change your mind about eating meat? If I found out animals had deep emotional lives, I might change how I eat."

We might call these "dinner party questions," as opposed to prosecutor questions, because these open-ended questions are the kinds of prompts that tend to lead to great conversations. Asking them is an art form (and we are not necessarily recommending that you bring up vegetarianism at your next dinner party). Many of the great Platonic dialogues feature Socrates either on his way to a party or already at one, mostly sober but sometimes drunk. He'll engage anyone he meets with his questions: powerful political figures, cantankerous friends and family, even curious children. For Socrates, absolutely everyone—even the sophist!—is a potential partner in his quest to understand.

Now, obviously, this didn't always go well with Socrates's conversation partners. In some of the dialogues, his conversations with sophists end abruptly, when the sophist realizes that the truth in question isn't going to be favorable to his aims, and the sophist storms off. Eventually the politicians got fed up and put Socrates on trial, the chief charge being corrupting the youth with all of these questions. In forcing him to drink poison hemlock, Athens put a permanent end to his questioning, and inadvertently made him a martyred hero of philosophy professors everywhere.

In the time since Socrates's death, the charge of "corrupting the youth" has been appropriated by the philosophical tradition. It has become the official motto of GGL. Our class stickers, T-shirts, and hoodies are all emblazoned with the phrase "Corrupt the Youth!" and our student leaders have taken to signing off emails with "CTY!" It is a reminder that openly loving the truth has always been a bit counterculture, and good societies have always needed men and women open to this particular kind of "corruption" of appearances.

Truthcraft: Asking Strong Questions

Asking truth-seeking questions is hard. In order to do it well in conversation, you've first got to make sure that you are bringing the right motivations to the work.

1. **DESIRE THE TRUTH:** Pick questions that you are genuinely curious about the answers to. That way you are willing to follow the answers where they lead.
2. **CARE ABOUT THE PERSON:** Pick questions that might reveal something genuinely important, surprising, or meaningful in the conversation. Have faith that the person might have some genuine insight you are missing. That way you respect your relationship to the person you are asking.

Ideally, your conversation partner will agree to these conditions. Some people even find it helpful to verbally agree on them from the outset. Having explicit goals will keep you from slipping back to prosecutor habits. You'll both agree that, in attempting to answer these questions, you are partners on a team dedicated to uncovering the truth. But even if this isn't the case, it's always possible to make the attempt. Remember: Socrates used this method with the most powerful sophists and bullshitters in Athens, and—until the end at least—it often yielded incredibly productive results.

For example, here are some strong questions our students came up with to help us have a better conversation about race and the good life on campus, a perennially difficult issue:

- **STARTING POINT QUESTIONS:** When did you first become aware you had a racial identity? What do you think is possible to know about how other people experience race?
- **PHILOSOPHICAL GOAL QUESTIONS:** Would your life be better off without your racial identity? Would everyone's lives be better off without racial identity? Why or why not? How does this change what it means to live the good life? How should the history of your race impact your view of the good life?
- **MEANS QUESTIONS:** Given what we learned about our starting point and goals, what kinds of new habits might we want to try out? What would campus look like if we were doing a better job of promoting the good life for everyone (regardless of their race)?

Finding some silver-bullet policy solution won't make the dialogue successful. (We spend a fair bit of time in class arguing with students that writing a letter to the provost does not count as taking responsibility for an ethical problem.) Rather, the goal is to ping the walls of our caves, and see if together we can get pointed toward the exit. You'll notice the question categories mirror those in the apology assignment.

Sophists are good at prosecutor questions and other rhetorical techniques, and you might be tricked into believing some bullshit. To lower the stakes, practice asking questions with people you think you'll disagree with one-on-one instead of online or in front of an audience. Let your guard down. Humbly admit that you don't know everything about the topic in question, but insist that you're curious. If you find out your conversation partner is only interested in bullshit, listen politely, tell them you'll have to think about their point of view, thank them for sharing it, and move on to your next conversation.

Make sure to pick your questions carefully. Don't *just* focus on questions with clear answers. If it turns out that a disagreement will only be resolved when the two of you know some scientific fact out there in the world, that's fine—indeed: it's progress!—but you won't move forward by going back and forth about whether you think (without data) that this fact is true or false. Good *philosophical* questions tend to focus on topics we are capable of making joint progress on by listening and offering reasons.

If you aren't quite ready to practice the method of asking strong questions with loved ones on the opposite side of the political divide, start small and build up your muscle. Maybe prepare just one question that you think might be fun for your next dinner party. You'll be surprised how quickly it can start to transform your relationships.

2.

Live Generously

> Jesus said to him, "If you wish to be perfect, go, sell what you have and give to [the] poor, and you will have treasure in heaven. Then come, follow me." When the young man heard this statement, he went away sad, for he had many possessions.
>
> —Matthew 19:21–22

THE DEMANDINGNESS OF MORALITY

We open our class on moral obligations with a simple calculation:

> Tuition at Notre Dame costs roughly $28,000 per semester,
> divide this by 4 courses (the minimum load) = $7,000;
> the total cost of taking God and the Good Life

GiveWell is a meta-charity set up to evaluate the overall effectiveness of popular charities. In 2019, GiveWell estimated that the Against Malaria Foundation, an organization that provides bed nets to prevent the transmission of mosquito-borne diseases, could save the life of one young child in a developing nation for about $3,710.

Using the GiveWell math, our students could be saving the lives of about two children for every course they are taking this semester, including God and the Good Life.

The math makes a sobering argument, and we can gauge the impact in the thoughtful silence that fills the auditorium once we've walked through this exercise. It often comes up again in students' writing, and in spontaneous conversations during office hours or when we are in line to buy six-dollar lattes in the student center. "When we were talking about how one semester at Notre Dame could save however many lives," one of our students, Kat, tells us:

> I had a crisis. I called my parents. I can say that me being in college will help the world, but it's nothing compared with people actually *living.* And I understand the issues with a mathematical approach to morality, but I really do just have a hard time convincing myself that me being here is worth more than other people being alive. . . . If you really are concerned about being a good person, then you want to do the most good. You don't want to just feel good about yourself. It plagues me!

Kat is wrestling with a puzzle that philosophers call the "demandingness" of morality: living a morally good life might require radical changes in our current habits and desires. And while some moral quandaries only confront us occasionally, we manifest our financial virtues and vices every day. Financial habits are potent reflections of pride, shame, social pressure, and familial discord. All of this makes our financial lives the perfect subject for philosophical questioning. How much of the good life should be spent getting money? And how does a vision of a morally good life (for ourselves and others) guide us in earning and spending it?

Money can also be one of the most difficult topics to address in our philosophical apologies. For one thing, it is tempting to treat your finances as a way of quietly keeping score on the good life. How much you have in the bank can seem like a reflection of your virtue: how industrious or frugal you are. How much you give away can be seen as a reflection of your generosity and love. Pretty much as soon as capitalist economies developed in Europe, bank accounts were thought to reflect personal character and divine approval. In 1905, the sociologist Max Weber described how Calvinists and Methodists—looking for an earthly way to distinguish who God loved—developed a theory of flourishing that emphasized financial efficiency. Here is John Wesley, the founder of Methodism (quoted by Weber): "Those who gain all they can and save all they can should also give all they can so that they will grow in grace and lay up a treasure in heaven."

In this chapter, we'll think through two proposals for how to manage the earning and spending part of your good life. One approach, called effective altruism, is principle based and focused on the measurable, mathematical outcomes of your moral calculations.

The second approach, based in virtue ethics, is narrative based and requires situating your earning and giving in the context of your life story and the development of virtues. Using money as a case study, we'll also start to investigate in depth a philosophical debate that continues in other chapters: the debate between the consequentialists, who measure the goodness or badness of a life based on expected impact, and the virtue ethicists, who look instead to character and intention.

To date, none of the thousands of students who have taken GGL have heard the money argument and dropped out of Notre Dame to redirect their tuition to fighting malaria. But the argument forces us to put our assumptions about the relationship between money and other goods under the Socratic lens. The first step calls on you to examine the circumstances, explicit choices, and implicit habits that led you to your current financial state. We are willing to put our money where our mouths are, letting you in on the different ways finances have shaped our quest for eudaimonia.

In Deo Speramus
(Meghan's Apology)

I grew up in a family that (like so many) struggled financially. My mother has worked for forty years in various jobs supporting the family: as an office manager in a dental practice, an occupational therapy assistant, a house cleaner, a dog walker. My father put in his time as a cameraman, a local news manager, a manager at a china replacement company, a golf course starter, and an agent for a home health aide company. They have had a very happy marriage, with three very different, very loved children spaced (unintentionally) every seven years.

If you work in the kinds of jobs my parents have, you face cycles of unemployment. New bosses come in and cut staff. A wrist injury makes cleaning or dog walking impossible. We were often moving as kids, seeking better landlords and fresh starts.

I grew up the oldest child, and from preschool onward I have been a type A control freak. I resolved as a teenager to be very intentional about money. I went after part-time jobs: cashiered at the local grocery store megachain, moved boxes for the city council, cleaned up vomit in the playspaces of the local children's museum. I competed in speech and debate tournaments on weekends and sometimes won prize money. My parents shared access to my savings account, and more often than not my funds would leak out (voluntarily or involuntarily) to help with family needs.

In 2001, I won a full scholarship to attend college at the University of Virginia. I opened a new personal bank account and shared much less with the folks back home. I lived in dormitories for the next ten straight years, as an undergraduate at Virginia, then as a Rhodes scholar at Oxford, and then as a PhD student and graduate resident assistant at Rutgers. For most of my twenties, I shared a common bathroom with twenty other women. I cleaned up more vomit. I saved my housing money and scholarship stipends and invested in the markets. I had a decent war chest of cash when the 2008 recession hit. I scooped up cheap mutual funds from my laptop in the Rutgers library, taking breaks from writing a dissertation on the nature of time. I ate a lot of dining hall grilled cheese sandwiches. And I discovered the capitalist glee that comes with carefully configuring your Roth IRA, money market accounts, and tax mitigation strategies.

In the meantime, my family still struggled. My father lost his job working with a golf course in Florida. A year later and still unemployed and uninsured, he had a heart attack. He went to the emergency room at Martin Memorial Hospital on March 27, 2014, around 9:00 p.m. with what he thought was an intolerable case of the flu. Quick interventions from the hospital saved his life. Three weeks later he had triple bypass surgery. While he was in the ICU recovering, my mother and fifteen-year-old brother, Connor, were evicted from their apartment. Overwhelmed, they'd been unable to keep up with rent.

I flew down to Florida to help the family after the heart attack and was surprised by how rough our situation had become. I also had to finally face up to some hard questions about money, my good life, and the good of my family. My father survived, and as we all regrouped, the family rallied around a major goal: get my youngest brother Connor into an incredible college. The scholarship I'd received to Virginia had been my ticket to a new world. By then I was in my early thirties and getting established as a professor. I started putting money aside into a college investment fund. My parents and brother moved in with my grandfather. Connor attended the big Martin County Public High School.

My parents were relentlessly committed to the mission. When their car broke down, they put a gypsy cab company on retainer to pick Connor up and drop him off at County every day. Connor got to school before anyone else in the family knew how they would get to work. Our middle brother Patrick had dropped out of high school at tenth grade—he worked as a restaurant server and threw himself into being Connor's moral support team. Pat and my father would spend weekends with Connor at the library and Barnes and Noble, working on test prep books.

Of course, by that point I knew a lot *about how colleges worked. I was the family strategist. The summer after his junior year, Connor and I rented a car and drove all around New England visiting Yale and Brown, Wesleyan and Amherst. We took tours, bought T-shirts, discussed the essay topics on the Common Application. He fell in love with the ironic seventeenth-century-elitism-meets-hippy-culture at Brown. The crest has a three-century-old motto—*In Deo Speramus *(In God We Hope)—with a grinning cartoon sun over it. He decided to apply early decision, and I was so proud of him, mostly for taking the risk. We knew the odds were very much against a kid from County, however well prepared, breaking into the Ivies. I was just happy that he was willing to put himself out there, and worried we were all about to suffer the sting of rejection.*

But then . . . Connor's ticket came. He got in. In September 2016, my parents and I moved him up to Providence. I put on a brave face as we hauled boxes into Archibald Hall. The next morning on my way home, I locked myself in a women's bathroom stall in the Providence airport and wept.

It was a struggle (bureaucratically, but mostly emotionally) for my parents to complete the financial aid paperwork. Everything he didn't get from Brown's generous aid policy, I paid from that nest egg I'd *been growing, more than $50,000 in all. And as a result, in 2020 the world has another Sullivan with a BA (this one in History), who is currently unemployed and has moved into my guest room. Many of his classmates are in the same situation, neither able to earn nor to give, at least at the moment.*

The Against Malaria Foundation estimates I could have saved thirteen lives if I'd sacrificed the Connor College Dream. I know this, but I still believe that investing in Connor's education was one of the most significant moral accomplishments of my life so far. And none of that depends particularly on what he goes on to do next, though I very much hope it is something that he loves. How can this be? That we can give so much to someone we love, recognizing full well the greater good we could do for others?

And now I am goal-less again and wondering what to do. I get paid a pretty respectable but by no means blockbuster salary as a college professor. I am single and have the kinds of frugal tastes you'd expect from someone who lived in a dorm room for a decade. I own a two-bedroom, one-bathroom house in the Rust Belt. I'm hypercompetitive, overeducated, love solving math puzzles, love making investments, love planning for the future, and love winning. All of these habits and impulses—combined with a stunningly persistent market rally—have put me now, in my midthirties, with well over one million dollars in stock. In the background is another major economic crisis, with predictable cycles of unemployment (including for members of my family). I don't have the clear goals I had back in 2008 or 2015 anymore.

Philosophical apologies are not just useful for reflecting on decisions you've already made and now want to understand. Philosophy can also be helpful when you are trying to plot a new heading. And that's the good life puzzle I find myself in now—what am I aiming at with money? Admittedly a great puzzle to have, but by no means an easy one. In fact, I worry that the money will corrupt me if I just keep mindlessly hoarding it. And I worry that I will make a mistake in trying to spend it—I'll do something foolhardy or miss a critical opportunity. And I worry that telling people I don't care about the money will make them more likely to deal with me unfairly. Indeed, as a professional woman I find myself caught in the tension of wanting to be paid equally with men with similar talents and responsibilities, but adamantly not wanting my self-worth to be measured in dollars.

MONEY AND THE GOOD LIFE

Money's remarkable moral powers are its fungibility, measurability, and anonymity. Fungibility means we can easily trade money for many different things: food, medicine, art, educational services. It is an "instrumental" good—money gives us a powerful means for promoting many different kinds of goals. Compare how you can use money versus how you can use your time. Suppose you need a new house. You probably could spend a few decades learning construction techniques, drawing up plans, digging a foundation, and building it yourself. Or, you could spend your time earning money in a job you are already trained for, and use that money to pay a professional construction company to build the house. So long as you have skills someone values and a stable source of income, you can save yourself the trouble of becoming a builder. Money also helps you efficiently compensate for your lack of medical know-how, your difficulty preparing good Indian food, and many other good life goals that require skill to meet. Likewise, if you're trying to help someone else, it is often much more efficient for you to buy those goods for others to meet their needs than to try to produce those goods yourself. Money can replace skill and knowledge.

This links up to money's second exceptional power: it is measurable.

Money allows us to compare the value of very different kinds of goods and experiences. And as long as we can measure nutrition, health, beauty, and learning, we can estimate how cheap or expensive it is to promote different goals, and invest in the relevant market accordingly. Money creates a common scoreboard.

Third, because we don't have to spend our money in one-on-one personal transactions, fungibility and measurability enable us to use money as a largely anonymous way to do what we want in the world. You can choose whether your finances do or do not reflect outwardly on who you are as a person.

This anonymity gives us significant responsibility in figuring out how to combine money with care for our soul. In the *Republic*, Plato has us consider what would happen if an ordinary shepherd named Gyges found a ring that would make him invisible. Armed with a tool that allows him to intervene in the lives of others with complete anonymity, Gyges becomes a monster. He develops absurd, awful personal desires. He takes advantage of others whenever he can. He murders the king and coerces the queen into marrying him.

Plato thinks we should strive to be the kind of people for whom generosity, justice, and other virtues flow naturally. The kind of people who would take care of others just as well when we act anonymously as when it reflects back on us socially. But most of us are not even close to this point in our development, and with veils of anonymity, our moral lives get eaten by our desires.

Money serves as a real-life "ring of Gyges" in ways that we each have to contend with. With money, we can exert all kinds of power, and our desires—whatever they happen to be—will tend to be amplified by the amount of money we have. With one click, we can order exercise equipment, or a case of bourbon, or a case of mosquito nets for someone halfway across the world. And with money we can satisfy these desires in a private way while also controlling our public image.

As uncomfortable as it might be, it is important to take a sober look at our financial lives, and to ask whether and how we might use the self-knowledge this provides to help us make moral progress.

EFFECTIVE ALTRUISM

Peter Singer is a professor at Princeton, and one of the most influential ethicists of our time. Over the course of his long career, Singer has become a founding figure of effective altruism, a philosophical movement dedicated to giving people extremely specific advice about how money should factor into living an ethical life. In his recent book, *The Most Good You Can Do*, Singer tells the story of a promising young student, aptly named Matt Wage, in order to illustrate this way of thinking about ethics and money.

Matt Wage was an undergraduate at Princeton who took Singer's ethics class in 2009. Much like our students, he was unsettled by the thought that his money could be going to saving lives and easing suffering. But for Wage, this thought became *the* driving force in his career planning. After graduating from Princeton, Wage was admitted to Oxford's prestigious philosophy graduate program, a program Singer himself graduated from. But Wage turned the offer down. By then, Singer tells us, Wage had done a lot of thinking about "what career would do the most good." He accepted a job on Wall Street, so that he could donate almost half of his massive salary to highly effective charities. Within a few years he was able to donate more than one million dollars, all while still in his twenties.

Wage and Singer are part of the effective altruism movement, an ethical system guided by three connected assumptions about the role that money plays in the morally good life.

First, many effective altruists think that our primary moral obligation is to reduce suffering and promote happiness, and that we can measure the moral worth of our decisions based on how effective those decisions are at improving net happiness. Historically, this is sometimes called the Greatest Happiness Principle. It was fiercely advocated by a group of philosophers in Industrial Revolution England who are known as the "utilitarians." In 1789, the philosopher Jeremy Bentham introduced his "felicific calculus," a method for estimating the moral impact of your actions. For Bentham, the key to moral progress consisted in encouraging people to calculate the pain and pleasure for everyone potentially affected by a choice and pursue the options most likely to maximize pleasure. He even wrote a poem to help students remember their moral imperative:

> *Intense, long, certain, speedy, fruitful, pure*—
> Such marks in *pleasures* and in *pains* endure.
> Such pleasures seek if *private* be thy end:
> If it be *public*, wide let them *extend*
> Such *pains* avoid, whichever be thy view:
> If pains *must* come, let them *extend* to few.

Bentham's ideas were taken up and made even more systematic by history's most influential utilitarian thinker, John Stuart Mill. Mill's father, James, was friends with Bentham, and the pair immersed little John Stuart in the new philosophical and economic system. By the early nineteenth century, their experiment succeeded. Mill was a recognized public intellectual, publishing utilitarian arguments regularly in top newspapers and serving in the British Parliament. Twenty-first-century effective altruists, in the spirit of Mill and Bentham, think that a proper understanding of generosity involves developing a modern-day felicific calculus and spreading the message of moral optimization far and wide. Like Mill, they also tend to be very focused on converting others through publicly engaged philosophy.

A second feature of effective altruism is its intense focus on money's role in our moral lives. As we discussed above, money is unique in its fungibility, measurability, and anonymity. These qualities also make it a uniquely efficient means for promoting happiness and reducing suffering. Effective altruists like Singer thus give very direct moral advice on how to manage your financial life. Earn as much as you can. Then dedicate as much of your money as possible to the most effective causes for reducing suffering and promoting happiness. The effective altruists' slogan is the secular version of John Wesley's dictum: Earn to Give.

Third, the effective altruists think that we should make decisions about who to help and how by using data about which interventions are most effective at promoting happiness and reducing suffering. We should not make important moral decisions in ways that are primarily guided by emotions, history, or personal commitments. Everyone's needs are relevant—and morality requires us to consider the needs of strangers, of people who are very different from us, even of some nonhuman animals. The effective altruists vigorously warn against the availability bias, our tendency to focus on options that are most psychologically immediate.

Historically, this impartiality has been a point of pride for utilitarians. In the late 1700s, Jeremy Bentham used his felicific calculus to argue against slavery and the brutal colonialist policies of the British government. Mill advocated forcefully for women's equality in a time when cultural norms in Britain largely ignored and discounted women's ambitions. Utilitarians, in the spirit of Socrates, have long viewed the felicific calculus as a means for overcoming our prejudices and allowing reason to guide us to better outcomes. Through rational calculation we leave the cave of believing that our personal pain and pleasure (or the feelings of people we like) somehow count for more from the standpoint of the universe.

Effective altruists have a clear answer for how Meghan should handle her money questions. Operation Connor College was a well-intentioned mistake. Even though their situation was serious, Meghan's family was not facing the kind of life-threatening crisis that organizations like the Against Malaria Foundation work to mitigate. Tempting though it may be, she should resist the inclination to overvalue her family's well-being. Instead, her giving should be directed solely by expected impact. This may even mean investing it for many years while she gathers more data about where the money would be most effectively spent. Many utilitarians do not tend to make a distinction between happiness promoted now and much greater happiness promoted a century from now. Once uncertainty about the future has been taken into account, people in the future have just as much potential for happiness as people here and now. Indeed, a puzzle for pure utilitarianism is when to stop investing money and give it, bearing in mind that it tends to grow and compound over time.

Virtue ethicists reject this mathematical approach to questions about generosity. While effective altruism has the benefit of giving very clear advice about how to connect money to the good life, some of that advice is based on questionable reasons. Let's consider several puzzles with the approach: some mathematical, some emotional, and some concerning the ways in which we integrate morality with other dimensions of the good life.

TREATING PEOPLE AS "HAPPINESS RECEPTACLES"

The first puzzle concerns the Greatest Happiness Principle and the difficulty of setting primarily mathematical goals for morality.

Suppose you decide that you want to increase the average life span of your fellow man. There are multiple ways to do this. You could try to make everyone's lives longer via some intervention (like malaria nets). *Or* you could fund interventions that simply eliminate the really sick people. If we focus just on statistical averages, stopping sick people from existing will nudge the number upward just as much as making sick people well would. That second option sounds awful; it is the polar opposite of philanthropy—*philanthropos*, love of mankind. You can't love people and yet wish them away because they are hurting your bottom line. For this reason, it seems any mathematical approach to generosity cannot just focus on averages. It needs to be a *maximizing* morality—the effective altruists need to focus on pushing as much good out into the world as possible.

But this leads to another puzzle, a more abstract one that contemporary moral philosophers continue to fight over. Suppose you think the best thing to do would be to create a world with the highest total amount of happiness in it, distributed in whatever way gets our happiness metric highest. In the popular 2000s video game *The Sims*, you have the chance to create and manipulate digital people. Each person you add to your game comes with a thermometer above his head. If you treat your Sims well, the happiness thermometer fills up. If you lock your Sims in the house without any food, the thermometer gets dangerously low. This is not a bad metaphor for the way effective altruists frame your moral obligations. Other people (actual or potential) are vessels for happiness. Our moral goal is to get as much of that happiness into the game as possible.

One way to do this might be to try to make some fixed number of people as happy as possible. But another equally mathematically valid way is to just create many, many more people with barely happy lives. If we look at morality as a maximizing calculus, there is no significant difference between a lot of happiness poured into a few thermometers or a lot of happiness spread out in increments over many, many thermometers. We care about the amount of happiness, not the vessels.

These problems come about from efforts to abstract happiness away from particular lives. It seems like we can't aim for increasing statistical averages—that approach misses out on the value of lives themselves, even lives that are below the mean for happiness. And we can't aim to just pump as much total happiness out into the world as possible—that approach treats lives as just holding tanks for happiness. Virtue ethicists, in contrast, will argue that the good things worth spending money to promote are always components of valuable lives and the lives themselves are what have ultimate worth. This insight affects how we can measure generosity.

IMMEDIATE VERSUS MARKET-MEDIATED GENEROSITY

The commonsense view of generosity is that good people give freely to everyone they encounter in the course of everyday life. They put money in the Salvation Army bucket, buy birthday presents for coworkers, and pick up the check at dinner. They treat those in need as friends. Most of us think that an important aspect of generosity is *immediate*—noticing a need in another person and meeting it personally, directly, and sometimes in inefficient but relational ways. Compare this with the vision of the ideal philanthropist in effective altruism. The perfect effective altruist uses mathematics to abstract from the immediate. Because of the unique powers of money and the extraordinary need across our world, all of their generosity inevitably becomes mediated by the markets.

This might seem like progress, but the reliance on market mediation leads to another round of problems. The effective altruists want us to measure the moral value of our actions based on the scope of the consequences of our decisions. But it is a matter of both extraordinary luck and unjust privilege whether any particular person has power in the economic marketplace. Just consider again how Matt Wage, the Princeton student, was able to choose a profession that enables him to systematically accumulate more than a million dollars in personal wealth and then decide how to give it away, all while still in his twenties. Wage is very privileged indeed. But why should something as important as morality depend on variables you have extremely limited personal responsibility for?

And even if you are lucky enough to have money (or the capacity to earn it), a bit of economic reasoning also raises questions about the preferred market-based means. The effective altruists' emphasis on personal finance does not seem well supported by their emphasis on reducing as much suffering as possible. Malaria is an acute problem in so many nations because corrupt officials refuse to implement adequate public health programs. The market itself can value human lives in morally problematic ways—HIV drugs cost 520 times as much in Philadelphia as in Nairobi. Effective altruism combined with unquestioned acceptance of the markets would suggest that whether your life is cost-effective enough to merit saving depends on grossly arbitrary features like where you happen to live. And even more arbitrary facts about you as a worker—your gender, your race—will often affect how much you are able to earn. Those college students advised to adopt the maximize-earnings-to-redistribute good life strategy deserve an explanation for how market pressures can line up with the actual value of actual human lives. Effective altruism tries to redirect capitalism to more moral ends, but perhaps unphilosophically accepts too much of its existing structures.

Of course, as individuals trying to lead good lives, we have even less power to foment the anticapitalist revolution than we do to earn money and give it away. (As Paul can attest, it is hard enough to lead a revolution to stop the sale of a municipal golf course.) This means that if you are centering your moral life around the effective altruism goal, you might also start to worry that nothing you do morally matters. It's hard to know what an effective altruist could say to someone stuck on the following argument:

1. My actions only have moral value insofar as they lead to better overall consequences.
2. But my capacity to bring about such consequences in the world is extremely limited, and my ability to know whether my actions are bringing about such consequences is even more limited.
3. So, for any given decision I'm considering, I don't really have any reason to think that one action I perform will be morally better than any other action I could perform.

Conclusion: So nothing I do really morally matters.

We shared this argument with a friend who is a top hedge fund manager, and he took the second premise as a challenge. "I bet I could earn even more and make a huge difference!" Some of us might have access to this level of financial capacity, but most of us are in the far more modest tax band. For those of us who are financial mortals, we must look beyond maximizing impact to find our moral agency.

Virtue ethicists are sometimes accused of advocating a self-centered morality, one that overemphasizes how your spending and giving affect you, the giver, and your pursuit of eudaimonia. Shouldn't morality be about other people—about selflessness? But the effective altruists are selfless in a way that few of us can stomach. Their approach makes it very hard to see where there is any room to grow as a person with moral accomplishments and commitments. We see this as well in the disconnect between the advice that Singer and some other effective altruists offer as visions of the good life and the lives they actually choose to pursue. Singer is a philosophy professor at Princeton University who discourages aspiring philosophers from further study—you wonder why he doesn't himself pursue a more lucrative hedge fund job while advocating for effective altruism on the side.

And when it comes to other potential components of eudaimonia, the effective altruists struggle to capture what many of us deem essential to the good life. Consider the tortured ways they talk about the value of parenthood and family life. On the one hand, as we've seen, it makes mathematical sense for effective altruists to create new people if they will have positive well-being. More people mean more nodes for happiness in the world. But the effective altruists also know that most of us can't decide to have children and then not make incredibly inefficient investments in their flourishing. Most of us can't bring ourselves to give our children the cheapest health care or most cost-efficient education. We take valuable time off from earning money to spend it nurturing them. We buy them toys and piano lessons. We invest in their whims.

In *The Most Good You Can Do*, Singer reports on the reasoning of a couple trying to decide whether it is morally acceptable to have a child.

Ultimately they decide that they would be personally so miserable without a child that they would be worse in the long run at their altruistic projects. Here is Singer's take on their decision: "Effective altruists are real people, not saints, and they don't seek to maximize the good in every single thing they do, 24/7. . . . Typical effective altruists leave themselves time and resources to relax and do what they want. For most of us, being close to our children and other family members or friends is central to how we want to spend our time."

For Singer, having children and investing in them in all of the inefficient ways love seems to require is something you do because you are morally imperfect. So is buying a birthday present for your friend or volunteering for inefficient charities. You might do these things to satisfy your contingent psychological needs. But these actions aren't worth much moral credit. They don't fit into the "optimization" paradigm. Rather, your children, neighbors, and friends compete with your moral obligations for your attention. This theory, we'd argue, struggles to explain the central moral role that relationships play in the good life.

Having Kids in Grad School
(Paul's [and Shayla's] Apology)

In 2015, I was a second-year PhD student at Notre Dame. I was in the middle of brutal comprehensive exams and starting to think about writing my dissertation. My wife, Shayla, was teaching thirty-five second graders in an underfunded public school and creating and selling curricular resources on the side. I'd deferred my college loans, but we had been chipping away at her student loans for years. Because she taught in low-income schools for so long, she'd just received forgiveness for the last three thousand dollars of it. (Thanks, Obama!)

When it comes to money, we have never been that interested in maximizing. As long as we've had enough to pay our monthly bills, buy a few luxuries, and keep enough saved up for emergencies, we've been pretty happy. Insofar as we invested our money, it was in things like paying down our loans or saving up for a house without several dozen mice living in the basement. Six years ago—around the time we were launching God and the Good Life—Shayla and I started talking more seriously about having kids. I'm sure we had less than ten thousand dollars in our bank account when we began having those conversations, but that fact quite literally never crossed our minds. In our relationship, financial considerations have always been balanced against a range of other factors in conversations about our family life.

We obviously wanted to pay off our debt and keep making our house payments, and we knew that it's important to start saving for retirement early. But we've found that the things that matter most in our home life—how we live as a family, how we give our kids the experiences we want them to have, and how many of them there will ultimately end up being—are all things we're willing to adapt our financial lives around. Our kids wear hand-me-downs, Shayla has a preternatural gift for "garage saling," and we can visit virtually any state we can drive to with our tent and our minivan.

I realize, of course, that this way of thinking and planning is itself a kind of financial decision; a way of investing in certain kinds of wealth that manifests our personal "economics of attention." I also realize that I'll most certainly start caring a bit more about other kinds of wealth as I start doing the work-years-to-retirement-fund calculations a bit more carefully. But, for now, money plays a relatively small role. I would much rather spend my time and attention caring directly for the tiny humans in my life (we currently have three), even if there's some monetary opportunity cost in doing so.

Does this make me a bad person? The effective altruist seems to think so. Indifference toward maximization and donation, plus creating tiny money pits, then focusing obsessively on them at the further cost of productivity and philanthropy, are all things the effective altruist would count against my character, even if they're ultimately understandable. But this seems totally false to me. At the end of my life, I think I'll look back on those things as virtues. I could be wrong, but I think I'll be glad that I was more invested in the personal economics of my attention than in . . . actual economics. The biggest good life question on Shayla's and my horizon is not whether I should quit my philosophy job to go into investment banking, but whether we think we should adopt a child at some point. We've talked seriously about doing this, even adopting a kid with special needs, and virtually none of those conversations have centered around the potential financial costs.

GETTING YOUR FINANCIAL GOOD LIFE IN ORDER

"Essential goods" are the virtues, resources, or circumstances that are required for eudaimonia. Moral life is about pursuing these goods for ourselves and others. For most virtue ethicists there are multiple essential goods we need for the good life, and while we may not need all of them or need to have them all at the same time, they also cannot be reduced to a single good. For virtue ethicists, close relationships are a paradigm of an essential good.

In one respect, we think effective altruism gets something right about morality: it recognizes that reason-based generosity is demanding. But it makes sense of this demandingness in the wrong way. Morality isn't hard because there's a limitless demand to convert money into longer lives and incremental reductions in suffering. Instead, from the virtue ethics approach, morality's demandingness is that it requires intense engagement with other people and their idiosyncratic needs. If we think that the good life demands much more than pleasure, and we think moral virtue requires us to link up our own flourishing to other people's flourishing, then it follows that we owe others much *more* than help with pleasure and suffering. We owe them companionship, education, spiritual fulfillment, art, and much more. Morality is demanding because eudaimonia itself is so demanding. People have a lot of needs!

So virtue ethics is a self-centered philosophy, in the sense that your moral goal is to develop moral virtues like generosity within yourself, not to use yourself as a mechanism for promoting some selfless external moral objective. And the ultimate sources of value in the world are selves—lives—that are integrated and purposeful. But that doesn't get you off the hook for thinking seriously about how and why you give. If anything, it should make us even more anxious about our financial lives; these habits are shaping our souls.

If we take the virtue ethics vision of the good life seriously, we have to figure out a way to link up our finances to eudaimonia—both our own flourishing and that of others. And we have to view our finances as an extension of our rational capacity, our power to make plans based on good reasons that will move us closer to being the kind of people we want to become.

Virtue ethics also encourages us to take a person-centered and story-centered approach to generosity rather than a calculation-centered approach. Your personal financial history, and that of those whose lives you share, will help you understand what generosity might look like in your own life. You can and should reflect on how capacities like generosity change based on your circumstances—the same virtue can be expressed one way by children sharing toys, another way by a hedge fund manager, another way by a parent or a friend. Someone like Bill Gates can radically pivot from superearner to supergiver by understanding that the same underlying talent can be directed toward multiple ends.

Your present budget and your capacity to earn are powerful variables in the story of your life. The essential goods of eudaimonia are the sort of goals that can be budgeted for and that financial lives can be arranged around. They are the targets that philosophical reasoning reveals to us. Some are obvious: we need to secure health and physical safety. Others are fundamental but require reflection: we need opportunities to learn and spread the truth. What else belongs on the list—love, courage, faith, contemplation—these will be the themes of more philosophy in the chapters to come. To varying degrees these goods can be framed as opportunities for financial investment. How should we make those choices?

Meghan has been wrestling with the challenge.

In the course of writing this book, I've been reflecting on essential goods, not only the goods I need to invest in for my own life but also the goods that I might have a special capacity to promote for others. Thinking about the role money plays in the good life has been a way to make this concrete. My personal needs are relatively simple. I think it is worth keeping up an emergency fund for myself and my parents' needs. It is worth investing in my retirement account, so that I have the capacity to care for myself and my family even when I can't work anymore. It's worth paying for health insurance. I think it is worth keeping a gym membership; that's where I meet my friends. I'm part of a church that needs to keep the lights on and candles burning, and needs funds to make sure that people who are suffering are cared for. I'd say I need at most three thousand dollars per year for books, movies, hiking trips, and a kind of fancy bike. The "good life" area where I need to work the most on at the moment is my contemplative life, the cheapest virtue of them all to develop.

It hasn't helped that it has been an incredibly volatile season for markets. I could slow down on the earning/investing race and carry on, just with less intensity. But I feel a sense of pride when I "lean in." I also like thinking about the tax codes. I love pursuing opportunities to do more and love the idea of pursuing economic opportunities to help others. I'd feel bored and miserable if I tried to ignore the way my own life fits within the capitalist system that I occupy and that shaped so much of my story until this point. And I have those strong moral views about women's pay being equal to men's for similar work.

I've recognized that building up a capacity for generosity means forcing my investments to be less fungible. I know myself, and I know that without some external coercion, I won't be able to resist buying a hot tub or simply hoarding the money and using it as part of some screwed-up internal "good life" scorecard. With this in mind, in 2020 I started donating 20 percent of my income to an irrevocable charitable fund called a donor-advised fund.

Setting aside the money was easy. Harder was the question of when and where to donate it.

I'm an educator by vocation. It is part of my story: I see my life so far as one that has flourished because people provided me with the educational opportunities I needed. Investing in educational initiatives is also a chance for me to practice the skills I have developed personally and professionally in the past fifteen years. So it seems like the thing to do is find a meaningful way to connect these resources and the extra money I continue to earn with projects that promote education as an essential part of the good life. I'm interested in programs that are effective, that respect knowledge as an essential good for all of us, and that help make my life more meaningful by connecting it with the lives of others.

I am not quite sure what fits the bill yet. Investing in helping other promising and needy young people like Connor launch into the Ivy League? Investing in programs that help adults like my brother Pat get a high-quality education even when they have been off "the track" for a while? Equalizing the playing field for many of my neighbors who deserve good schools as much as anyone else? Making educational infrastructure possible for women in Somalia or Afghanistan or other regions where structural injustice is keeping people from this essential good?

All of these are routes to growing in generosity, but I am not yet sure which one is most "live" for me. And I'm on the hook to steward those funds until I can find the generous way to use them. I also think, for reasons that will become clear in the next chapter, that my intentions matter when I give. I am not going to liquidate half of my savings because a website recommended a particular charity; I am going to be confident in why I am giving to some specific cause. If you don't deeply understand why you are giving, I would argue that it isn't generosity.

Something that has helped me plan through these issues is thinking about other virtues in my life. For instance, I was moved by love to help Connor and my parents. How can I start to see strangers I might help in the same way? Just what is so great about education if the economy is a shambles? And what exactly makes a risky venture, like an investment, a live or dead option for me? The picture is getting clearer, but I am not quite there yet. Money questions drive us into more philosophy.

Soulcraft: Invest to Flourish

If you want to practice investing for eudaimonia, the first step is the hardest . . . and it is one where virtue ethicists and effective altruists share a common mission. Risking all of the shame and anxiety (and greed and ego, too), you need to take a look at your finances. Reflect on the story of how you got here, the episodes you have controlled, the episodes that just happened, the episodes that showed other people's virtue in your life, and even the episodes that showed how you benefit from injustice, greed, or other people's vices, too.

Here are several concrete steps you might take.

Ask yourself strong questions to elicit the role money plays in your approach to the good life. These can fall into the three typical philosophical apology categories:

The Starting Point: Are there events in your life in which you tend to use finances as an indicator of your good life? If you are willing to push a bit further—what does it mean to you to have "access" to money as a means to do things in your life and in the world?

Goals: Reflect on the essential ingredients for your good life, which hopefully you'll continue to do as you work through this book. It may be that you conclude after the last chapter that the opportunity to get reliable and trustworthy news is high on your list. Or that it is an essential good that you have the opportunity to be in a community that engages in deep, truth-seeking conversations with other people. As you read later chapters, you may decide that parenthood or marriage or religious life is the core component of your good life. Or you might see your moral good life calling out for particular involvement with confronting racial injustice.

Once you have your list of essential goods, split them up into components of eudaimonia you need to invest in in your own life and the essential goods you think you might be situated to promote for others. There are different ways to promote the truth as an essential good. For instance, you might decide that needing better news means you need to invest in subscribing to (and reading) at least four different newspapers. You might decide that confronting race-based injustice means financially supporting initiatives to desegregate schools.

Then the fun part.

The Means: There is a powerful potential good life tool at your disposal: you can make a financial plan that reflects not only your financial goals but your good life goals, projecting into the future in a way that makes sense given your ability to see how far out your story goes. Maybe you set up that fund to donate to causes that develop better educational communities. You set aside twenty dollars a month for the good news subscriptions. You put money into a college plan for someone you love. You craft a very detailed, tax-responsive donation strategy to unload half a million dollars to fight malaria. You decide to take a pay cut at work to spend more time deepening a relationship with family members. The approach is not Earn to Give, but rather Invest to Flourish. And the investment is part of a bigger vision of what you need to become. Crucially, unlike Earn to Give, Invest to Flourish might very well at times require you to hit the brakes on developing your finances.

Like any investments, good life investments will also carry some significant risks. They will require the kinds of virtues that help us take responsibility for our moral lives, determine who to care about, and determine how to manage uncertainty. And it is to these topics we now turn.

3.

Take Responsibility

> Principles that are mistakenly high and strict are a trap; they may easily lead in the end directly or indirectly to the justification of monstrous things.
>
> —Elizabeth Anscombe, "War and Murder"

A SINKING LIFEBOAT

In the first weeks of the GGL course, we present groups of our students with a classic moral dilemma:

> *The Lifeboat:* You and your group are on a sinking lifeboat and the only way to stay afloat is to select someone to throw overboard to their death. No one has volunteered to jump, so you're going to have to vote, and execute the group's decision by force. As a group, discuss your options and vote on who must die for the good of the group.

In early versions of the activity, we simply gave students a list of the passengers on the boat, along with their ages and occupations. Discussion would wrap up in just a minute or two. Walt, a seventy-seven-year-old retired Vietnam War veteran, was quickly voted off the lifeboat. We assigned points for this exercise based on whether the reasoning showed engagement with ethical theories. We'd see answers like this: "Walt won't increase the overall good as much as others in the boat, and—as the oldest occupant of the lifeboat—he has already had the most time to make something of himself and his life (and likely has the least time left). So it is best that he should be the one sacrificed."

In the fall of 2019, however, our undergraduate discussion leaders wondered what, if anything, would change if hc had the other students dramatically enact the scenario, bringing to life each of the characters in the lifeboat, and filling out their biographies a bit more. Walt, along with the others, was given a voice and a backstory. After meeting Walt and the others, students still had to justify their decision. Students learned that Walt was on an anniversary cruise with his wife when the ship went down, that one of the other occupants of the lifeboat coincidentally happened to be a nurse who had treated him at the VA, and that he still has plans and aspirations, things he wants to accomplish in retirement.

Nearly every group still voted to kill Walt. But what was remarkable was how much more *difficult* the decision became. Groups would start asking if they could refuse to throw anyone overboard, or would beg one of the occupants to volunteer to jump out of their own free will. The reasoning they'd give after the decision had been made wasn't so straightforward. They'd agonize about it, and then sound like they were rationalizing their choice after the fact. Many groups had dissenters, and even those who voted Walt off would express regrets and characterize their actions as something they were being forced to do rather than something they willingly chose.

This was a deeply interesting development for us, because it illustrates a debate that's divided moral philosophers for at least the past seventy years.

In one prominent camp are the consequentialists—philosophers like the effective altruists who hold that moral credit and blame is a matter of weighing up the consequences of our decisions. Sometimes the consequences are weighed in lives made happier or made worse, sometimes in lives saved or ended. Other times the consequences are weighed in quite complex ways: Do your actions promote more widespread access to rights or enhanced human development? Crucially for consequentialists, moral improvement is a matter of trying to make yourself into the kind of person who causes the most good (however you measure good effects—consequentialism is a big tent). The morally good life is one of calculation and efficiency.

Virtue ethicists see the situation differently. Sometimes we make horrible decisions that, luckily, don't result in disaster. Sometimes we try to do heroic, loving, or generous deeds but don't make any difference in the world. Moral improvement is a matter of improving your intentions, developing your character, and better understanding why you are aiming at particular morally important goals. And the good life is one that can be captured in a certain kind of story, one that depicts your own moral development accurately, and incorporates other people and the ways you support them in their pursuit of the good life.

In the first version of our lifeboat exercise, our students instinctively felt the appeal of consequentialist reasoning. It turns out that such reasoning is much easier when certain personal details were left out. When decision makers had to look at the whole picture and direct their reasoning to Walt, the ethical dynamics of the situation shifted. This raises a key question: Were students who completed the earlier version approaching the scenario more rationally, arriving at the right decision through cool calculation, while students in the latter situation were clouded by morally irrelevant (but real and powerful) social pressures?

If the second interpretation is right, then one lesson we could all take away from the students' responses is that moral decisions should be made as impersonally as possible. This would have social and political implications: if personal details obscure moral judgment, then we should train leaders, set up institutions, and create policy in a way that removes decision makers as far as possible from the personal lives of those who would be affected by their decisions.

On the other hand, some of our student fellows felt strongly that the personal encounter was critical to arrive at the right moral decision. Some of them drew an analogy close to their own lives: one reason people treat each other horribly online is because the interaction is so depersonalized. Most of the insults we hurl anonymously would be unthinkable for us to say to someone face-to-face. The depersonalizing nature of the internet *distorts* our moral judgment.

Our experience with our small-scale lifeboat exercise parallels research that is now being done in psychology and neuroscience on the profound effects of personal interactions on moral reasoning.

TROLLEY-OLOGY

Over the past decade, Harvard psychologist Joshua Greene and his colleagues have been conducting experiments to try to figure out what's going on in our heads when we make moral decisions. Underlying the research is a suspicion that our emotions regularly cloud our judgment when it comes to moral decisions, and that the first step in eliminating this kind of bias is understanding where it comes from.

To test this suspicion, Greene asks subjects who visit his lab to consider variations on the "trolley problem," a classic of ethics textbooks that has a similar structure to the lifeboat thought experiment. A trolley is careening out of control down some tracks, on a heading to strike and kill five workers. But you can pull a lever, redirecting the trolley to a different route. On the new route there is a single worker who will be struck and killed. Do you pull the lever to redirect the train? If it is okay to pull the lever, would it also be okay to push one bystander onto some train tracks to stop the trolley from hitting the five workers (killing him in the process)? In another version you're asked if it's okay to pull a lever that would lower the bystander onto the tracks; in yet another you can use a remote to open a trapdoor and drop him from afar.

The philosophical assumption that Greene and his team are operating under is that these small causal differences can't possibly make a moral difference as to what the subject should do in the case. If one person dies in every scenario, why should it matter that she was pulled rather than pushed, killed by moving a lever versus falling through a trapdoor? The surprising discovery is that subjects do have different reactions to these variations. The more "person-to-person" the trolley problem is, the more reluctant someone was to act. So people are more likely to pull a lever to change the tracks, much less likely to push another person to their death.

Greene's subjects are drawn toward the consequentialist reasoning when considering the case abstractly: Are five deaths worse than one from the standpoint of the moral universe? Judgments change when you ask subjects to locate themselves *in the situation.* Imagine pushing with your own two hands. What if that were your brother, or your mother, on the train tracks? What if one of the workers had just brought his newborn home? Emotions are now involved, which makes the decision gut-wrenching. To Greene, the variation suggests that our moral judgment is shot through with bias.

Instead of seeing these differences of judgment as irrationality, the virtue ethicist sees this variation as a natural result of our well-functioning, person-wired moral detectors—our consciences. As we saw in the introduction, Aristotle asks us to make moral decisions by bringing philosophical principles up against the details of the circumstances and the person we are bringing to the decision. And if the right thing to do isn't captured by some perfectly rendered abstract principle, that's just because morality can defy such principles.

This issue of conscience is part of the core debate between consequentialism and virtue ethics. Paul Bloom, another consequentialist psychologist, argues in a similar vein that our emotions make us innumerate, and as a result we make bad decisions about how to help others: "[Empathy] does poorly in a world where there are many people in need and where the effects of one's actions are diffuse, often delayed, and difficult to compute." Bloom, like Greene, thinks psychological de-biasing can help us improve morally by muting these empathetic instincts. He even titled his book *Against Empathy.*

Consequentialists are certainly right that we feel a great deal more emotional involvement when it comes to friends and family members. It is hard to feel as much about a statistic like twenty-four anonymous malaria patients as you do about individuals with names and stories that you understand. And whether you happen to know or like someone is no deep reason to upgrade the value of their lives and downgrade the worth of strangers. The question is whether this concern for reason should cause us to be suspicious of our moral emotions.

Virtue ethicists take a different view—we think we should be skeptical of any moral advice that is incapable of appropriately connecting to our emotional lives. Virtue ethicists have long held that cultivating appropriate emotional attitudes is a key part of learning to live well and act virtuously. Here again is Aristotle: "[Emotions and pleasure] may be felt both too much and too little, and in both cases not well; but to feel them at the right times, with reference to the right objects, towards the right people, with the right motive, and in the right way, is what is both intermediate and best, and this is characteristic of virtue."

For the virtue ethicists, feelings like love, pity, and empathy motivate us to care about others. That's a psychological claim, and one with exceptions: many of us also can bring ourselves to do what is right even when we have a hard time summoning the right feelings. The philosophical heart of virtue ethics is that in the *best situation* we should want our feelings and actions to line up. We want to be the kind of people who give for good reasons, feeling love for the recipient and pride in ourselves. And acts of giving and feeling are morally significant insofar as they nudge us closer to eudaimonia.

In the *Nicomachean Ethics*, Aristotle draws an extended distinction between continence (doing something merely because you understand that you have reason to do it) and genuine virtue, which is being moved naturally—without calculation—to do the right thing. All of us, he thinks, start out like the child who shares toys merely to avoid punishment. And just like such children, we become better people when we are more likely to be moved by the opportunity to be generous to another person. The exact same act—sharing toys—is a developmental milestone when children do it because they are moved by generosity.

Notably, both virtue ethicists and consequentialists agree that our moral reactions should be guided by reason; we shouldn't just respond with knee-jerk reactions to emergencies or *purely* emotional appeals. And we have to be equally careful about biases and errors in our calculations. Consequentialists must admit that we fall prey just as much to statistical biases; sometimes the numbers are not what they seem. A massive one-time donation to an antipoverty program might appear to be the best course of action, but in the long run that same program could destabilize the economy for the very people it means to serve. For virtue ethicists, we have to reckon with the fact that our emotional lives tend to be parochial, causing us to ignore important sources of value. Most of us know from personal experience that sometimes it is emotion keeping us in our particular cave.

Importantly, the debate doesn't center on whether you should try to bury your emotions or juice them up when it comes time to make moral decisions. The debate is over whether being a good person is more about serving some overriding principle as consistently as possible or developing your mental and emotional life so that you can reason creatively and attentively when you find yourself faced with particular nuanced moral decisions. This brings us back to the trolley problem. In real life, it turns out that sometimes distancing and emotional suppression can do irreparable damage to our moral and emotional lives.

MORAL INJURY

If you drive about forty-five minutes northwest from the Las Vegas Strip, you will hit Creech Air Force Base, where an increasing number of military personnel execute Overseas Contingency Operations. In civilian-speak, this means that hundreds of men and women in the armed forces run missions out of Creech, often in support of U.S. ground troops, targeting enemy combatants with armed unmanned remotely piloted aircraft (RPA). In recent years, as demand for these missions and the manpower to run them has skyrocketed, these troops have a key case study for military psychologists.

One reason why the military has so enthusiastically embraced the use of RPAs is because it allows soldiers to bypass the very natural aversion to killing in direct combat. The history of military weapons technology is sometimes told in terms of the increasingly sophisticated ways we've been able to put distance between ourselves and the enemy. You would think, given Joshua Greene's studies, that serving as a drone pilot would help both strategically and morally. By detaching yourself from the urgency and danger of direct combat, soldiers are able to calmly calculate about their life-and-death decisions. Depending on how the numbers look, they can also execute their mission without the "biases" that Greene thinks tend to cloud our moral thinking. But things are not nearly this simple.

Although RPA pilots face no imminent *physical* danger, a significant percentage of these remote pilots show symptoms that mirror the PTSD of troops who have seen physical combat, like long-term behavioral and emotional disturbances. Here's how one pilot recounted his experiences after the first mission in which he'd killed someone:

> I went home that night and couldn't talk with my wife. She knew something was wrong. I couldn't get that image . . . out of

> my mind. Then about four days later I started thinking about a kid growing up without his father that I had killed. The humane thing is to let him live, but this guy was trying to kill Americans. Finally, about two weeks later I broke down. I couldn't hold it in anymore and I had to seek help. . . . I wanted to know if God was OK with what I was doing.

In a paper devoted to categorizing and finding ways to treat these symptoms, the researcher Brett Litz and his coauthors argue that dominant models of PTSD cannot adequately capture what these remote aircraft pilots are going through. Most definitions of PTSD connect it to the terrifying fear experienced by someone *in a life-threatening situation*. But RPA pilots are never in any life-threatening danger, nor do they report feeling abnormal levels of fear before, during, or after their lethal missions.

For Litz, and for an increasing number of thinkers both inside and outside of the military, the more appropriate way of categorizing these reactions is as "moral injuries": the "lasting psychological, biological, spiritual, behavioral, and social impact of perpetrating, failing to prevent, or bearing witness to acts that transgress deeply held moral beliefs and expectations [about oneself or the world]."

All of this casts Joshua Greene's research in a new light. Suppose that we can change our most basic moral reactions simply by putting more distance—physically, emotionally, or mentally—between ourselves and someone whose life hangs in the balance. For Greene, the consequentialist, this distance creates the space we need to think more logically; to calculate appropriately without the ethical noise of potentially messy personal interactions.

But now suppose that this distance itself creates more distortion in the part of our psychology designed (biologically and socially) to be our moral positioning system. That is, suppose that the messiness of moral reasoning is a feature and not a bug; that simple calculations based on totalizing principles are actually less likely to lead us to do what we come to view as the right thing. If this is right, then the effects of creating distance between a soldier and her target may be debilitating to the soldier and add bias, the kind of bias that comes from forcing a decision maker to ignore relevant details.

For Marc LiVecche, who teaches ethics at the United States Naval Academy, these questions urgently need to be addressed in his classroom. He describes his students, navy midshipmen, as needing a moral framework that allows them to wade into the messiness of life and death scenarios "in a desperate way." To do the work that is required of them, to make the decision to kill, he says, it is necessary to dehumanize someone. This distancing is familiar in other fields. To do his job, the surgeon has got to think about his patient as "the liver in room three"; the first responder has to think of an accident victim as "male, midforties, head trauma."

But *how* you make decisions in that scenario, and how you survive the process, depends on your ability to make fine-grained distinctions. If you help the midshipmen dehumanize the enemy through brainwashing or prejudice, you're setting them up for bad decisions in military conflicts. Why distinguish between a civilian and a combatant if they're all the same and none of them are human? And if you teach them to abstract the particulars away, you are setting them up for problems down the road. What to do with the shame or guilt they feel when they recall personal details from an attack? How will they know whether to see this moral injury as a sacrifice to the cause they have dedicated their lives to, or something for which they should seek forgiveness? Soldiers flourish by attending to the details; they cannot just turn these off after combat.

LiVecche is humble about the role he plays in such training. He says his students pick up much of it, in the best case, from their parents, churches, and the broader culture growing up. He builds on their conceptions of the good life in class as much as he can, using virtue theory, immersive activities, and discussions of complex real-life examples. He puts his students in touch with older, more experienced veterans. His role is to help these young people sort through where concepts like justice, peace, and forgiveness fit into their lives, and how they'll inform their decisions going forward.

He hopes they can build a culture of moral resilience, knowing that the next theater they have to fight in will likely look different from past wars.

A WAR AND ITS CONSEQUENCES

Some of the most important developments in moral philosophy have followed in the wake of major wars. This was certainly true of World War II. In England in the late 1930s, many of the most prominent philosophers at Oxford and Cambridge—almost all of whom were men—began to be conscripted into military service. Some were sent to Japan, others to Italy, often to interview prisoners of war who were sometimes being tortured in the hopes of extracting lifesaving information about the strategy and combat plans of enemy forces.

These philosophers were observing the deadly clash of ideologies (Nazism, communism, and liberal nationalism) firsthand, and many returned with a very pragmatic, consequentialist approach to ethics. Suddenly everything was a cost-benefit analysis. Torture, for instance, could be justified by the value of the information it affords and by the lives it might save downstream. Such thinking likely became common, at least in part, because the global scale of the horror made depersonalization seem like the *only* rational way to navigate the complex ethical terrain. And perhaps the cause was partly psychological, too: we already know that focusing on numbers rather than the suffering of particular people can make otherwise paralyzing choices seem tractable.

At the same time, another intellectual movement was growing in England. As the men began disappearing from academic life to serve in the military, the proportion of female students and professors was quickly growing. Before the war, in 1936, the women of Oxford were outnumbered five to one, but by 1940 this was down to just two to one. The period marked the beginning of the careers of a cohort of extraordinary women philosophers who shared a vision for what their profession could contribute to the postwar world. It also spurred a revival in virtue ethics.

These philosophers paid special attention to the details of human life and experience, inspired by that Aristotelian idea that doing ethics well requires a special sensitivity to human action in its *particularity.* One of the philosophers involved in this movement, Mary Midgley, saw these intellectual developments as directly connected with change in the intellectual climate. The reason why so many well-known women philosophers emerged after the war, she claimed, is that they were given the space to develop an alternative to the "brash, unreal style of philosophising . . . that was current at the time." For her, "it was clear that we were all more interested in understanding this deeply puzzling world than in putting each other down," and that this made for more than a mere difference of style.

Elizabeth Anscombe was another one of these "Oxford women" (as they came to be called). Anscombe attended both Oxford and Cambridge as a student and was eventually given a faculty position at Oxford. She was a committed Catholic and a devotee of both Aristotle and the revered medieval Catholic philosopher Saint Thomas Aquinas, but was also famous for purportedly humiliating C. S. Lewis in a debate at Oxford on the nature of miracles. Anscombe disdained what she considered to be intellectual shortcuts in arguments offered in support of religious faith. She was the kind of philosophy professor that perhaps seems a bit hard to imagine now: a highly orthodox Catholic, an outspoken feminist, an activist who spent plenty of time researching dead medieval philosophers and the logic of adverbs. In a telling story, Anscombe was once stopped at the door of a Boston restaurant where she was told that women wearing pants were not allowed to enter. So, without missing a beat, she took her pants off.

And when Oxford decided to grant Harry Truman an honorary degree, Anscombe went to battle.

It was the 1950s, and Truman was being hailed throughout the Western world for having brought World War II to a decisive end. By dropping the newly developed atomic bomb, he was seen to have punctuated a horrific and seemingly endless global conflagration; in the eyes of many, he had used a weapon proportionate to the size of the conflict. For Truman's defenders, the consequentialist calculus of the number of lives lost versus the number of lives that *could* have been lost came out in Truman's favor. The end, in this case the literal end of a brutal war, "justified the means."

This was not how Anscombe saw things at all.

For Anscombe, there was nothing admirable about the U.S. president's decisive action. Writing in a time before the scope of the devastation of the bombing was widely known, Anscombe already saw in Truman's decision a deep moral corruption that she feared was characteristic of consequentialist thinking more generally. Aboard a ship crossing the Atlantic Ocean, Truman was sent the news, by wire, that the weapon had been completed. He replied immediately that it should be used, leading some to speculate about whether he had ever really stopped to think about what he was doing. There were nearly two hundred thousand civilian casualties as a result of the U.S. bombings.

In a pamphlet that she self-published and distributed ahead of the Oxford ceremony at which Truman was to be honored, Anscombe opened her case against Truman: the laws of war prohibited the targeting of civilian populations; it was well known that this bomb would kill innocent civilians; and the Japanese had already indicated a willingness to surrender.

Her colleagues reacted with equal measures of indifference, embarrassment, and disgust. After she proposed a vote on the matter ahead of the ceremony, she reported that the faculty of one of Oxford's colleges were simply told "The women are up to something in the Convocation:

we have to go and vote them down." Some dismissed Anscombe's stated reasons for her opposition as a mere emotional appeal with no real philosophical basis. Skeptics wanted a more decisive argument, one that could satisfy even the consequentialists that what Truman had done was morally wrong.

Instead, Anscombe responded in true philosophical fashion by writing a book, *Intention*, which came to play a crucial role in advancing virtue ethics. *Intention* wrestles with the question, How do you appropriately bring yourself into ethical arguments?

STORIES OF ACTION

Intention starts with a surprisingly simple observation. What we do can be described in all sorts of ways, but some of these descriptions are more important than others. Suppose that a man is pumping water into a house from a well a short distance away. And suppose that the following descriptions are all, at some level, true of this man and his action:

- The man is moving his arm up and down.
- The handle of the well is tapping out a recognizable rhythm.
- The house, into which he is pumping the water, is filled with commanders of an occupying force.
- The water that the man is pumping is actually poisoned, and the gradual effect of this poison will be to kill these commanders.

If we ask right now whether what the man is doing is flat-out right or wrong, Anscombe thinks we are making a mistake. This is because we haven't yet figured out the *story* of what's happening. Who is this man? Is he a fascist sympathizer or a member of the resistance? And what's the broader context of his life, his relationship to these officers, their cause, and the community he lives in? Without these narrative details, we don't know enough about the man, what he knows, and what his motivations are, to evaluate what he's doing. Consider the difference between the following two stories:

> *Story #1:* This man's house has been recently taken over by commanders of an occupying force who are intent on genocide. The man has been ordered, by these commanders, to cooperate with their efforts by pumping water into the house so that they can drink. The man pretends to submit to their request, but laces the well with an undetectable chemical compound. He knows that, if he's caught, he'll be killed, but he cannot allow these soldiers to kill his friends, neighbors, and fellow citizens.
>
> *Story #2:* When this man noticed commanders of an occupying force making their way through his city, he invited them into his house and asked them to use it as their base. He has long sympathized with their genocidal efforts, and wants to help their cause in any way that he can. While they are working, he notices that they're thirsty and so offers to pump water into the house in order to keep them well hydrated. Unbeknownst to him, a toxic chemical has seeped into the water supply, and he is contributing to the downfall of this occupying force by providing them with the poisoned water.

The key events in each story are the same, as are the actions that the man literally takes and their consequences. What matters is that the stories bring out radically different descriptions of the man and his actions. Whether the man's actions are heroic or despicable, virtuous or vicious, morally good or reprehensible, depends on which of these stories is true.

And this isn't just true in extreme cases. Think back to the last time you treated a friend with contempt or indifference. Perhaps you didn't think to warn them that you were running late and you made them wait for an hour to be picked up from the airport. When you finally do arrive, they'll expect a story, and how they react to you will depend on whether you can tell a certain kind of true story. "I got caught in traffic because of an unpredictable accident and my phone died" is one story you could tell. If true, it shows your friend that your lateness wasn't due to indifference.

Unfortunately, there won't always be such a story available. Sometimes the true story is just "I was selfish and I didn't manage my time well." You might rationalize—well, there was traffic, too. You might even tell your friend the traffic excuse. If she knows the true story, her reaction will be very different. And it should be. Your lateness reveals a kind of indifference. Your attempts to explain it away amount to rationalization. The right thing to do in such a case is to tell the true story, making no excuses, and accept responsibility for your action.

THE SKILL OF AGENCY

At this point, we recognize that the consequentialist has a good objection: ethics can't depend on the stories we tell about our actions. This is too subjective and opens us up to all kinds of bias! We humans are constantly confabulating and rationalizing, the stories we tell are as much a product of our imagination as they are a reflection of how things are. And, even more worryingly, we can do this in the worst of circumstances. A great novel can make the villain into a hero. Great propaganda makes a dictator into a savior.

We should admit that there's danger in overemphasizing storytelling in ethics. Suppose you are thinking of taking your family to Walt Disney World during a major virus outbreak. The truth is, your plan is probably risky, imprudent, and callous. But if you are dead set on the trip, you might instead frame the vacation as a madcap adventure—everyone was wearing a hazmat suit! We were so courageous and fun-loving, and we rode Space Mountain four times in a row! The story overemphasizes morally irrelevant details to deflect moral criticism.

On the other hand, sometimes we take too much responsibility. A few years back, Paul noticed that almost all of the stories he told involving failure framed him as an innocent victim. To correct for this, he started to tell stories in which he tried instead to take responsibility for serious problems. He started to suspect that he'd overshot the mean when one day, after confessing to complicity in global warming (he hadn't turned the lights off when leaving the apartment), factory farming (he'd eaten some highly processed chicken nuggets at a friend's house), and war crimes (because he hadn't more actively protested Obama's program of drone strikes), he was told by an incredulous priest, "I don't think those are all *your* sins."

Stories, just like claims, can be more or less true. And we are apt to tell *false* stories about our actions—just like we can use statistical data or out-of-context quotes—to lie. That brings us back to Plato. Growing as moral actors means learning to identify and correct for our moral bullshit, which we are often the most prolific authors of. But better storytelling means more attention to finding the detail rather than less. Moreover, think about what we give up if we refuse to tell each other stories about our motives and actions. For one thing, we're not able to hold each other accountable. We're not able to fact-check political narratives, or to call someone out when they try to gaslight us.

For Anscombe, the key to figuring out which descriptions of an action in a story are true is to ask the "Why" question. Here's how the method works, as illustrated by an imagined conversation between Paul and his son, Solomon:

> P: "Solomon, what did you do?"
>
> S: "I knocked over the glass of milk."
>
> P: "Why?"
>
> S: "Because I was mad."

The true description of Solomon's action is that he spilled milk because he was angry. This entitles us to infer that he ought to apologize and clean it up. Alternatively, he might have responded differently to the "Why" question: "Because I didn't see it!" In this case, the correct description of his action—the true story—is that he mistakenly knocked over the milk. Maybe he should still clean it up, but we're not going to blame him (or parent him) in the same way we otherwise would. Learning how to tell the true story, and becoming disciplined enough to do it, is how we develop the skill of personal agency. It's how we learn to take responsibility for our actions.

For Anscombe, ethics is all about intentionality, and the way to be more intentional (and in the right sort of way) is to make sure that you're checking in on the stories that you're telling about yourself, your actions, and your life as a whole. When you told your friend that you arrived late because of traffic, was that true? Why do you plan to make a donation in public rather than anonymously? Is it because you're really more interested in the reputational boost than you are about the charitable work being done?

These questions can take on even more significance when we start thinking about the ways we relate to each other in society, and to our social and cultural history. Consider just two examples.

We often tell ourselves the story that with a bit of hard work, some frugality, and a smidgen of common sense, each of us has complete control over our destinies. Leaving out the facts of inequality or deemphasizing the role that systemic obstacles can play in holding an individual back (or even actively oppressing them) is a failure to respect the truth that approaches propagandistic bullshit.

Likewise, we often construct narratives about our past, our community, or our personal relationships that glorify our efforts—or the efforts of those we trust and respect—and discount the suffering of others. The philosopher Alasdair MacIntyre—a virtue ethicist and major proponent of the storytelling approach to ethics—calls this phenomenon "heedlessness." It's easy to dismiss the needs and suffering of the person you pass on your daily walk if you characterize them as an "addict."

This is one way we refuse to engage with the sometimes life-altering problems our fellow citizens are dealing with, by casting them as stock characters: "rednecks" or "hillbillies" who are too ignorant to be trusted to make their own decisions, let alone vote on issues that affect ours; "snowflakes" who find themselves simply incapable of facing up to reality outside the safe spaces they've created for themselves. Likewise, setting our stories about others in "rough neighborhoods" or "bad schools," or against the universalizing backdrop of "privilege," "entitlement," or "laziness," might tend to have a soothing effect on our consciences.

And so we can use the "Why" question to make sure that we're not getting caught up in false stories that make us look better than we are, and that we're being intentional about the action we plan to take in the future.

For Anscombe, the first important ethical question to ask about Harry Truman was: What was Truman (the man, the character, the "doer") aiming at? Here are a few hypotheses. In directly ordering that bombs be dropped on Hiroshima and Nagasaki, Truman was

- trying to bring a world war to an end;
- establishing decisive military victory for the United States and Allied troops;
- bringing about unconditional surrender on the part of the Japanese; and
- killing innocent civilians in order to accomplish these military goals.

Because consequentialists are so focused on the *consequences* of an action, and not on its intentional nature, they are free to pick and choose which of these descriptions they want to emphasize. Anscombe's point is that we don't get to pick and choose, and that the consequences an action has are only *part* of the story.

For Anscombe, any true story told about Truman's action has to include what it looked like from the inside. And, it matters in this case that there's no way of telling the true story of how Truman ended the war that doesn't include his intending to kill innocent civilians in order to accomplish military goals. To Anscombe, who defines murder as "the intentional killing of innocents," this meant that Truman could not escape being a mass murderer, and the conclusion that he ought not to be awarded an honorary degree quickly followed.

Even if you don't agree with Anscombe's moral evaluation of Truman in this case (for the record, one of us thinks Truman is a murderer, and one of us judges him a tragic figure), we think the broader point still stands. To fully appreciate whether and how to hold someone responsible, to ask of a person in a particular situation what he's really doing, we need to know something about the situation, something about his action, and something about his mind. Stories that are limited to cause and effect, and that treat people like billiard balls on the pool table of life, will not be informative enough for us to draw conclusions. They won't be the whole story.

TELLING "MORALLY THICK" STORIES

Virtue ethicists, from Aristotle to Anscombe, realize that learning to tell the truth (the true stories) of your decisions is often easier said than done. Storytelling is a skill that requires careful attention to the details of life. It requires developing a "morally thick" vocabulary that brings out the nuance in our intentions. Instead of thinking about our decisions in simple terms like "right," "permissible," or "inexcusable," we need more expressive language to capture our situations and our responses to them. We're sometimes "cowardly" even when we do the right thing. We can be "selfishly motivated," or "generous." Virtue ethicists think an important part of the moral life is encountering such "morally thick" stories, and then learning to tell them about our own lives. It is also a crucial skill for our relationships, as Plato taught us in the allegory of the cave.

Think for a moment about stories you like to tell about yourself when you are making new friends. Maybe you love to tell stories about misadventures at work or about winsome antics of family members or about how you stood up to an authority figure. All of these stories are meant to reveal something about your virtues to someone you want to get to know. And the stories can be more or less true and more or less informative about who we are. It is a genuine art to get these stories to be both true and "thick," they have the morally significant personal details included. One recommendation for getting better at telling the philosophical truth is to spend some time reflecting and refining your "friend pitches."

Another recommendation is to carefully attend to the stories of *others*, and to encounter as many life stories as you can, in order to hone these skills and to figure out how you want your life to resemble these biographies. These might be classic "lives of the saints" or "great men of history" types of resources you draw from. Or it might mean asking story-eliciting questions of those close to you, and listening for the philosophical detail.

For virtue ethicists, there's something crucial about listening to the story of someone's life *as a story* and noticing the particulars that make the story what it is. One way to do this is to put yourself in someone else's shoes; for example, ask yourself, "What would I have done in Truman's shoes, and why?" or "How would I have responded to massive disappointments in my own career or family life?" This gets us thinking about feelings and intentions. The arts also help, since novels and films can often provide us with more psychological detail and a wider variety of situations than we're able to get in simply observing one another, or in collecting the reports of those in our immediate social circles.

Of course, all stories take place against a setting—structures, relationships, rules, and forces that shape what we are and are not able to do. In the next chapter we'll consider the challenges we face when we try to harmonize our good lives with the communal systems that shape us.

Storycraft: Explain Yourself

If you're ready to explore how morally thick storytelling can help you in your quest for the good life, try telling a story about something for which you'd like to take more responsibility. How did you tell the story back when it was happening? And how might you tell it differently now? Make sure to include details about what you were thinking, what emotions you were feeling, and what circumstance you were responding to. In retelling the story, try to find a word that describes the virtue or vice in your scenario. Were you "cowardly" or "courageous," "generous" or "small"? Look for the right terms to capture your intentions.

Consider using these prompts for generating ideas:

Starting Point Prompts

- Tell a story of a time when you did something you're now incredibly proud of.
- If a stranger knew only one story about your life, what would you hope it to be?
- Tell a story about a time when you did something you're now ashamed of.
- Tell a story of a time when you discovered something surprising about yourself.
- How do you think the figure you most look up to would tell the story of your life right now?

Questions to Uncover Goals and Means

- What, if any, moral principles or ideals does this story illustrate?
- What virtues are in play? How might you build on these virtues?
- What vices does the story (or your telling of it) reveal about you? How might you change your habits as a result?
- Do you think that you're a "reliable narrator" of your own experience most of the time? What are your most common blind spots?

We find this to be one of the most private activities of an apology, since it can feel incredibly risky to open up your moral life for scrutiny. Still, even if these stories aren't something you're comfortable sharing widely at this point, it's important for your soulcraft. A key tenet of virtue ethics is that our moral lives are tended by this kind of storytelling.

4.

Work with Integrity

When I consider how my light is spent
Ere half my days, in this dark world and wide,
And that one Talent, which is death to hide,
Lodged with me useless, though my Soul more bent

—John Milton, "Sonnet 19: When I consider how my light is spent"

COMMITMENT CULTURE

Notre Dame, like many universities, starts sending its students to career fairs just a few weeks into their freshman year. The promise at the mouth of the educational cave is not just enlightenment but also a great job. For adults just starting out, that job is *the* good life goal, and understandably so: a great job can seem to provide many of our other essential goods—friends, confidence, self-sufficiency. More than ever, twenty-first-century workers with options believe that their employers are highly responsible for their spiritual and mental well-being.

As a workplace, Notre Dame takes great pride in the high numbers awarded in its own annual staff engagement surveys. The statistics we monitor are relatively anodyne: 85 percent of Notre Dame staff report that their manager "cares about them as a person." (It's perhaps more troubling to think that 15 percent of our coworkers do not report thinking this.) But some modern workplaces set even more aggressive engagement goals.

Brian Chesky, the cofounder and chief executive of Airbnb, has long taken pride in creating an intense, holistic "commitment culture" at his company. New employees are screened for empathy. Belonging is the core of the corporate mission statement, and Chesky frequently mentions belonging as calling out for love. Under Chesky's leadership, Airbnb bills itself as a family: "the Airfam."

Predictably, such a culture has myriad business benefits. You'll be motivated to work long hours for people you consider "family." You will make significant sacrifices if you think it's in the interest of protecting your "home." But by all accounts Chesky was earnest in his attempt to create such a culture at Airbnb. And his employees bought in. There was a sense that they had a common mission, which built on the excitement of seeing their company grow and have a real impact on the world. Viewed one way, Airbnb is running a relatively unregulated rental brokerage firm. But in a different narrative, employees saw themselves as helping strangers connect globally in one of the most intimate and trusting ways imaginable, sharing a home.

Airbnb's story sounded inspiring and triumphant in the boom years of the 2010s. Then in 2020 a global pandemic suddenly eviscerated the gig rental industry. You can do everything right to set up a happy and profitable firm, but if travel preferences shift unexpectedly, you will have a difficult time operating as a business. Within a matter of weeks, Airbnb's revenue dropped off a cliff and the company was forced to cut a quarter of its workforce (almost two thousand employees), on top of many more of its precariously employed contractors. Chesky cried on the video call as he announced the layoffs.

The New York Times profiled Airbnb's leadership team during the tumultuous time, asking the central philosophical question: "What happens when a company that has positioned itself as family to its employees reveals that it is just a regular business with the same capitalist concerns—namely, survival—as any other?"

One immediate consequence, as reported by many of the laid-off employees, is a feeling of existential whiplash. Kaspian Clark, a customer support specialist for the company, said that, because he had bought into Airbnb's mission so completely, he "felt denial and grief when he was let go. 'There are a lot of people who feel very betrayed by this,'" he said. "I deeply hope that Airbnb is able to remain the thing that I believed in."

Losing your job is one thing; being abandoned by your family is something entirely different. Did Clark make a mistake as an employee in putting his faith in Airbnb? The highly engaged workplace is meant to be a bulwark against a potent reality of twenty-first-century work life: employee burnout. Burnout seems to elude a precise definition. Many psychologists roughly characterize it as a general state in which you feel exhausted, cynical, and hopeless from prolonged workplace stress, lack of appropriate support networks, or lack of control. The opposite of employee burnout, you might think, is employee eudaimonia. If your workplace could help you care for your soul—if the place where you spend the majority of your waking hours could help you flourish as a person—wouldn't this be a capitalistic win-win? With the right design, we theoretically should get happier, more productive workers doing better, more efficient business. As we'll see, it isn't quite this simple. Integrating the good life with good work requires a fair bit of philosophy.

THE VALUES-BALANCE-IMPACT FRAMEWORK

Most popular, white-collar-oriented business advice about work and the good life is framed in terms of personal values, work-life balance, and expected impact. If you want to fit work into your good life, the advice goes, you just need to calibrate these three ingredients. Let's consider each facet—and its philosophical limits—in turn.

First, you are supposed to make sure that you're living out your personal values. This might mean picking a company to work for with a mission that strongly resonates. Some career decisions require settling major facts about your ethical outlook—for instance, you shouldn't work for an arms dealer if you're a pacifist. Often the challenges are more narrow—you shouldn't work in the sales department if you think its particular marketing tactics are deceptive. And in the long run, you'll risk burnout if you take a demanding job doing work you can't bring yourself to care about. For most jobs, there are typically many ways to harmonize your values with your means of earning. Good managers help frame your work in such a way that activates your personal values. This advice assumes that you come to your work with your values preloaded; it falls short because we know that our work can also influence the kinds of people we become.

The "work-life balance" dimension of the common advice suggests that these are two mostly separate worlds, and you've got to know how and when to commute from one of them to the other. This might be as simple as turning off your phone in the evening or taking vacations at regular intervals. With this approach, you try to measure eudaimonia as a ratio of the hours spent in workland to the hours spent in homeland. The advice falls short when we realize there often is no such clear boundary in our life; it assumes narrow and rigid concepts of "work" and "life" and ignores our drive to "join the circles."

Finally, the way we typically define "impact" assumes meaning in your work can be measured. The advice holds that you should identify your passions and then find a job that allows you to *optimize* your ability to realize them. Do you think clean water and renewable energy are keys to the health of our planet? Don't just recycle; found a clean energy company. Perhaps your passion lies in helping those who faced a challenge that you, too, faced and overcame. The goal in this case is to find a way to reach more of these people and optimize the impact you have on each of their lives. This advice falls short for all of the reasons consequentialist thinking falters, as we saw in the previous two chapters. There is more to your moral life than your outputs.

And even if we just take the values-balance-impact framework as a rough guideline, we will realize there are many cases where it simply cannot guide us on what to do.

Consider the following thought experiment. Jim is a recent college graduate. He majored in engineering, and has always been drawn to deeply personal social causes. He spent much of his free time in college volunteering at the local homeless shelter, and even found creative ways to bring his passion for engineering to bear on his time working with the men and women he got to know there. Now that he's graduated, he's presented with two options. His father, a military contractor, offers him a position at a facility researching nuclear weapons. Jim's father tells him that if Jim doesn't take the job, he's going to offer it to Jim's friend Kim. Jim is deeply conflicted. He abhors the threat of nuclear war. Still, he feels like he has to weigh at least two major considerations in coming to a decision. First, Kim is an excellent scientist and has no qualms about nuclear war. She would perform her duties at the facility with extreme competence and vigor, and could contribute to a major breakthrough in nuclear weapons technology. Jim reasons that, if he were to take the job, he might be able to perform the duties in a minimally competent way, not actively sabotaging the project, but making sure that he did everything he could to slow the team's progress, and perhaps help avoid such a breakthrough. Jim also knows that the job would pay much better than any alternatives he's considering. As director of the local homeless shelter, for instance, his engineering skills would go to waste, and he'd make a measly salary. Sure, he could personally help ten or fifteen individuals per year in this role, but think about how many more lives he could change by making a six-figure salary and then donating most of it to more effective charities run on a much larger scale.

What should Jim do?

The values-balance-impact framework can't answer this question, because it doesn't have guidance on how to weigh the trade-offs across categories.

If Jim works for the homeless shelter he has a huge *impact* on a few lives, but forgoes an even bigger impact overall (potentially saving hundreds of thousands or even millions of lives). And how should his *values* inform his decision? Should we always refuse to work for an organization with a mission that conflicts in any way with the values we hold? Or is it sometimes okay to take a job in the hopes of steering, shaping, or guiding that mission into greater alignment with the values we think are most important? In terms of *balance*, the best thing might be for Jim to take the job at the nuclear facility, punch the clock from nine to five, and use his vacation time judiciously, rather than committing himself to a somewhat structureless endeavor that will require long hours and might entail a somewhat erratic schedule to serve the needs of his clients who are homeless.

Consequentialists will argue that Jim should solve the problem by reducing his decision to just the impact variable. Jim should take the nuclear weapons job. As virtue ethicists, we don't think it's so obvious what Jim should do with his life, but we do think one thing is obvious: Jim shouldn't take the nuclear weapons job for the reasons he's considering. These reasons—whether or not the nuclear facility makes a breakthrough, whether his skills could be monetized in a more market-efficient way—don't have anything to do with Jim at all. And worse: deciding to take a job just because it would maximize the amount of money he could redistribute as part of the market mechanism would be for Jim to "objectify" himself—to treat himself as a mere money-redistribution instrument.

The British philosopher Bernard Williams came up with the original version of this thought experiment in 1973. Williams, like Elizabeth Anscombe, was an Oxford-trained virtue ethicist. Unlike Anscombe, he was committed to liberal politics, in both the social and the more classical senses. He served as a minor bureaucrat in various civic institutions and moved to Berkeley to protest the election of Margaret Thatcher. Two qualities Williams and Anscombe do share, however, are their commitment to evaluating people in the particulars of their circumstances (for Williams, history and narrative were indispensable tools for the ethicist) and their deep antipathy toward reducing every decision to its impact.

Williams argues vigorously that to think about one's job in the way Jim is forced to think in a consequentialist mind-set is objectionable in large part because it doesn't respect our *integrity* as individuals. It doesn't take seriously that we are trying to lead our own good lives with our beliefs, values, and desires. Overemphasizing the consequences we could bring about in making such decisions alienates a worker from himself.

INDIVIDUAL GOODS AND COMMON GOODS

Virtue ethics is focused on the good of the individual. In this case, we're encouraging Jim to think about what's good for *him*, how *he* should live out *his* values, and what impact this work would have on *his* pursuit of virtue. The focus is on Jim aligning his work with care for his soul and the essential goods he needs. As with debates we considered in earlier chapters, it can seem like virtue ethics is too self-centered. But these criticisms miss the mark.

Not all essential goods are individual goods. We can start to see this difference if we consider forms of "commitment culture" that are much older than Airbnb. Consider the Trappist monks of New Melleray Abbey. These monks have lived in community for 161 years. Originally founded in Ireland, their home monastery is now based in Dubuque, Iowa.

Any religious order like a monastery functions as a single unit, and the good of the community is always the guiding intention. The monk at New Melleray asks community permission for small things, like whether he can take a day or two off. But he also takes direction on major life-forming decisions like the sort of work he'll be doing for the next ten or twenty years. In fact, monks in some communities take a vow of obedience to do whatever is best for the community, even if that means packing up in the middle of the night and moving across the country to start a new church or brewery. (Trappist monks have, for centuries, been master brewers.)

It can be hard to wrap our minds around the idea that men and women, even today, choose to join monastic religious orders. But part of our human function is to seek out communities—families, clubs, churches, workplaces, and so on—that share a common good. Being excluded from such communities is one of the most painful deprivations we can experience, as many of us learn in childhood or adolescence.

Virtue ethics starts by asking each of us to think about what we are aiming at in our lives—what's the overarching goal? Answers vary, but clear patterns emerge. Cultivating interpersonal virtues like generosity, curiosity, and love are essential goods. So is being in a position to know the truth. And, of course, for both intellectual and interpersonal virtues, a certain amount of health, wealth, and physical comfort are needed. These are all primarily individual essential goods.

However, learning to flourish as a rational *social* animal means learning how to connect up our individual happiness with the goals of social units we are part of. This, in the broadest sense, is our work.

The Trappists of New Melleray Abbey spend half of their waking day, literally up to eight hours, in prayer, which makes sense given their religious priorities. But the other half of the day is spent working. One of their particular rules is to "live by the work of their hands" rather than on donations, and so this requires them to produce something that people are willing to pay for. After trying out several ventures, one that stuck—partly because they owned land with plenty of high-quality lumber on it—was making caskets.

They see the work as fully integrated with their religious mission. As

Brother Felix, who has become a master craftsman in the abbey, puts it: "The prayer life flows into the work life." He explains: "There's a certain amount of precision [in the work]. It's a nice routine. I can keep in God's presence."

The community has hired a layman, Sam Mulgrew, as their business manager. Mulgrew characterizes their plan as a very "modest approach to business" and explains that they don't have any interest in making the operation "any larger than it needs to be." Indeed, sometimes they completely reject the laws of supply and demand. When a pandemic ravaged central Iowa, they started giving the caskets away.

Refusing to respond to market demand and seeing something other than maximization of profit as the determining factor in the size of the organization is not a consequentialist approach to work. Still, there is a goal directing all of this, a goal directed at the souls of the monks and their relationship to their God and the broader community.

When the time comes for evening prayer, the monks simply turn off their industrial equipment. They walk to the chapel. The abbot, as the head of the organization, explains, "Okay, you've got your work. And if you don't complete it today you complete it tomorrow."

While the monks present a relatively extreme example of what it looks like to prioritize your work community over its work products, we can find more ordinary examples even among our own family members. Shayla, Paul's wife, worked for many years for underfunded schools. She and her colleagues regularly found themselves investing their own money in classroom supplies and other vital resources for their students. Obviously, they weren't doing this because they thought it would get them ahead, or because it would somehow maximize efficiency in the long term, but because they saw a need in their community and were moved to meet it. Setting aside bigger questions about whether teachers should have to pay for such expenses out of pocket, the example illustrates how invested they are in the flourishing of their students, and in the common good of education that their work exists to promote.

BURNOUT, ALIENATION, AND INTEGRITY

Consider someone in the grips of a genuine crisis of meaning about her work. She finds herself unable to get out of bed because she just finds her work overwhelming and meaningless. When pressed, she's able to explain that the problem isn't just mental or physical exhaustion (fixing those would be as easy as asking for a couple weeks off). Instead, the value she formerly found in her work has been drained entirely; it's that she sees her job as eight hours of robotic activity that she's utterly unmotivated to do. The tasks appear pointless.

Could we help such a worker just by changing her mind-set? It is tempting to think of burnout as a psychological phenomenon—one that can be treated by altering the way we experience work day to day. Many well-meaning workplaces are trying this strategy. Consider the rise of consultancies like Ritualist, who come into existentially drained corporate environments and devise rituals to try to improve office culture and morale. The rituals borrow from some of the same traditions that guide the Trappists but are designed to make workers feel more meaning regardless of the goal of their work. Ritualist designs quasi-religious practices for helping teams grieve when a project fails, for blessing new domain names, and for celebrating being incorporated as an LLC. Like many design-minded tethics initiatives, firms like Ritualist do not "touch the running code." Their goal is to make the work feel meaningful regardless of what it is actually achieving.

We've known since the dawn of the Industrial Revolution that such interventions are doomed to fail. Karl Marx is undoubtedly one of the most controversial and politicized philosophers in modern times. Readers of any political persuasion might be surprised by how closely aligned their views are to some of his most basic insights, and by the way those insights have been incorporated into left, right, secular, and religious philosophies of work and the good life.

Central to his theories of labor is the idea that we are frequently doing tasks that are radically disconnected from the people whom our work is meant to serve. To take a stock example: In a barter economy, you might make a table that you could give to a friend. You might fix your neighbor's cart in return for a basket of eggs. Maybe we could spend our lives in an ongoing exchange like this: each working to ensure the other's well-being in the work we do for the common good. But today, you might log in to work remotely on a series of spreadsheets that's used to service a software application for millions of people you will never meet. You might not even understand what the software does. Maybe no human totally understands what the software does. And, even if you did understand, you might not care that it is providing that particular service for that particular segment of the population. If the prospect of this kind of work strikes you as a good life problem, then you're starting to identify the feeling Marx refers to as "alienation."

Of course, we all feel alienated now and then. Making tables or fixing carts can feel detached or unexciting. Sometimes we actually have lost sight of the goal or forgotten our answers to the "Why" question. The problem for Marx is that in some social and economic systems people experience a constant state of alienation. And such working conditions are fundamentally incompatible with a good life. Why?

Here's where we can kick it back to Aristotle.

For Aristotle, some of the goods required to flourish are held in common, a result of the groups we are drawn into. We naturally form households, villages, and political societies that strive toward self-sufficiency, and these in turn develop our individual conceptions of happiness as their members. For work to be meaningful, it must complement our social nature. It should shape the true stories we are able to tell about our lives as social beings. Importantly, it also means seeing your work as contributing, in some direct way, to these common goods. Aristotle worried, prefiguring Marx, that markets unchecked by a vision of the good life will confuse us with the soul-crushing illusion that our goal is solely "getting goods."

To further understand this, consider the good life puzzles that involuntary unemployment creates. When the global coronavirus pandemic struck in 2020, Paul's brother James was laid off from his job as a car salesman. James found himself in the unexpected position of making more money on unemployment than he did working forty to sixty hours per week. When his car dealership reopened, and James was offered his job back, the math didn't quite add up. He could continue to receive unemployment for another few months, not working and earning thousands of dollars more, or he could return to work and take a net loss over that same period. "I think I'm going to go back," James told Paul in a phone call. "But I don't understand. Do I work for more than just money?"

Aristotle's answer to this (and one that Marx himself was sympathetic to) is a resounding: "Yes!"

To flourish in life we need meaningful work that doesn't alienate us. At minimum, this will mean that any work that objectifies and dehumanizes you in ways deeply at odds with your values is out. But when we ask how our work should go beyond these minimal conditions, we find ourselves right back at the Airbnb problem.

One key difference between Airbnb, or *any* corporation, and a genuine community like a family or even a Trappist monastery is functional. Genuine communities have an interest in the common good that transcends a financial interest. You can't fire family if they're not bringing in enough revenue (though family firms are a whole different story); you can't report on a family's well-being by looking primarily at its members' net worth. Firms can be created with profit as the singular aim, but this will inevitably lead to alienation for the simple reason that money is not an essential good. And no amount of effort to make working conditions better will thwart alienation if, ultimately, the group is not aiming at a genuine common good. We can go badly wrong if we let the illusions created by "commitment culture" try to fill up this very natural human need.

Firms are increasingly trying to frame their goals in terms of stakeholders (employees, government, local community) rather than financial return to shareholders. But as we learn from the market-based challenges to the Airbnb experiment, we're likely to come up against conflicts, some potentially irreconcilable, when we attempt to expand the goal of our collective work. You can't just frame *whatever* goal your work happens to be pursuing as an essential good (that's bullshit). You need workplaces that are actually formed to pursue a genuine common good. And the common good needs to be one that that group is plausibly connected to. It would be unintelligible for Brian Chesky to make the monks' goal—promoting the Kingdom of God—into the mission of Airbnb. Airbnb must do the hard work of discerning what essential goods a rental company can promote. And even for common-good workplaces, we must wrestle with how impersonal capitalist demands will compete with the personal and common goods. That raises two more good life questions. The first is individual and practical: How do virtue ethicists advise you about reconciling your work life and good life? The second is communal and structural: How much responsibility do we have for creating (and solving) our problems with alienation, and how much of our struggle is a function of the market itself?

A PHILOSOPHY OF WORK

Which brings us back to the puzzle of how to give good life work advice. To approach the individual question, we need to add some philosophical depth to the values-balance-impact framework.

1. *Values:* To flourish as individuals, we need to find work that allows us to connect our views about our essential goods (individual and common) with the work we do on an everyday basis.

This will look different for each of us, which is exactly as it should be. If all of us recognized and were motivated to meet the basic human need to eat, we'd have an abundance of restaurants and no hotels, schools, or artists. Just as you have the freedom and responsibility to choose which essential goods to promote through investments of time and money, you have the freedom and responsibility to identify essential common goods you promote with your work. This might mean changing the way you do your job and the intentions you bring into your work.

None of us have the privilege of choosing any career we like, but many jobs allow for us to join up our circles: to connect up our efforts with the good of those we serve. When Meghan worked as a resident adviser in a college dorm, she could see her vomit-cleanup duties as a way of caring for her residents or merely as a means for extra beer money. The former intentions make her work part of her good life. So we recommend doing what you can to make this the case. In modern organizational theory, this is sometimes called job-crafting—using your values to nudge the direction of your day-to-day work. But the direction you point your work in should be one influenced by your philosophical theory of what humans in fact need. And there needs to be genuine value at bottom. Jim's work for the nuclear arms dealer might just have no rock-bottom common good behind it.

An account of work and the good life also must recognize that work comes in many forms throughout a single life and in different kinds of lives. Virtue ethics gives us the capacity to see work far more expansively than, say, the effective altruists. The work of an activist might be organizing to help groups exercise political agency. The work that an adult with Down syndrome performs might be serving the common good through being a loving member of a family. The work that a deployed soldier does is serving the good through a 24/7 commitment to protecting national security. And in a good life, we revisit these stories and change them in new ways all the time.

2. *Balance:* To flourish as persons, we need to find the right balance of work to leisure.

The different forms work can take also require us to rethink what we mean by balance. It simply does not make sense to separate workland and homeland on this expansive conception of work (think of the time demands on an Army Ranger or a full-time parent for that matter). Importantly, for virtue ethicists, "balance" is not (and cannot be) an hours-based calculation. There cannot be a perfect number of hours that the average person should work per week, partly because the "balance" here has little to do with hours spent *here* versus *there*. Instead, each of us needs to understand the extent to which working for the good of ourselves, our families, and others is consistent with the kind of leisure we need to flourish. "Leisure" means something specific for virtue ethicists. As the Catholic philosopher Josef Pieper puts it, leisure isn't just time spent outside of workland, since it's "not the inevitable result of spare time, a holiday, a weekend or a vacation." For Pieper, true leisure is "an attitude of mind" or "a condition of the soul." It's the time we protect to be with ourselves and those we love. It might include indulging our hobbies and passions, even if these are quite strenuous. Instead of simply "vegging out" and taking time away from our place of employment, it consists in giving ourselves the space in our lives to develop love, wonder, and other essential contemplative virtues.

3. *Impact:* Our work should have real, recognizable impact on the good lives of the people it serves.

Far from "maximizing impact" in the way some philosophers recommend, we think—with Marx, Aristotle, and the great monastic philosophers like Saint Thomas Aquinas and Saint Benedict—that impact should be measured in human terms. Do you know the names of some of the people that your work serves? Have you seen how their lives, in a particular and personal way, have been changed for the better because of something you've done? Is your work contributing to your individual good, your needs as a person, and the common good of the communities you find yourself a part of? If your answer to these questions is yes, then we think you're on the right track in terms of impact. Your goals should be focused more on mastering the relevant virtues in your life through this work.

BUT WHAT ABOUT THE COMMUNIST REVOLUTION?

We can't conclude a chapter on work and the good life—especially one that incorporates the insights of Karl Marx—without raising the more difficult question. Most simply, this question is:

> Are there social and economic structures under which humans are regularly and systematically prevented from flourishing?

And, of course, the corollary (and gut-wrenching) question: Are these structures our own?

To see why this question is so pressing, consider a not-too-distant way in which circumstances beyond someone's control could make good work impossible.

Suppose a vast segment of the population of some society is in a position where, to survive, they must work in jobs that are inconsistent with their own flourishing. Wealth inequality is bad and getting worse. Economic conditions for the poorest 40 percent of the population mean that they are working for subsistence. And suppose that the economic realities of, say, a partially free market mean that the only jobs available to those in this society are deeply alienating (counting beans, working on a digital assembly line, or—worse—exploiting themselves in ways they abhor).

Much of philosophy is in the business of social critique—telling us (unsurprisingly) that this scenario is bad. But virtue ethics is in the business of trying to give us reflective agency; so what does our philosophical framework suggest you should do if you worry you are part of the oppression scenario? For Marx, the answer is relatively straightforward: hope for a revolution in the economic and political structure, and do what you can as an individual to join with others in solidarity to promote it. This revolutionary plotting is itself a form of work. Marx also thought revolutions (and the roles we play in them) are fully determined by the structures themselves and facts about history. So in the end he thought we won't really have any meaningful choice when it comes time to change our work.

The ancients are much more divided on the role of revolution in the good life. Plato seems to think we should exit the cave as quickly and efficiently as possible, even if it means burning the old world to the ground. Much of the *Republic* and his later writings concern describing how these revolutions will unfold.

But the Aristotelians tend to think there is value in moving toward a better life through cultivating habits and through perfecting our intentions and characters, often more gradually. You can acknowledge that the common good compels us to build a society where everyone has the capacity for meaningful work. And you can acknowledge our starting point: alienated social and rational animals, faced with frequent tradeoffs, and with a tenuous philosophical grip on our individual and communal goals. Any means to get us from here to the common good for work will have to be harmonized with all of the other dimensions on which we are pursuing the good life. And as with any morally significant act—including trying to transform society—we need to understand the new goal enough to properly intend it.

One thing we can say with certainty is that a good life in the twenty-first century will not be complete without reckoning with such structural issues. And the promise of virtue ethics is that it is possible to meaningfully shape an individual good life against the background of these forces.

Workcraft: Telling Your Work Story

Just as learning to tell the true, "morally thick" stories is central to understanding our moral lives, learning to tell true, "common good" stories is central to understanding our work. Here's a simple activity you can use to practice this kind of reflective planning. (You can also try it with people you work with.)

1. Write down a list of everything that you believe falls within the scope of "your work." Consider the balance of instrumental activities (e.g., working for a paycheck, studying) to activities you consider meaningful and important for their own sake.

For some of us, this list will consist mostly of the things we do under the title in our email signature. For others, we might include the time we spend volunteering or caring for dependent family members. It might include reading philosophy books, crafts, sports, or other hobbies. When we asked someone who we thought of as a real estate agent what she considers to be "her work," she responded that she was a ceramicist. Her main work was what she was able to get done in the pottery studio between showings and caring for her school-age children. As an afterthought, she said, "Oh and I also sell houses."

2. Think about the people you're working *with* and *for.* Write down some of their names and describe how you're working together and what you're aiming at together. Think also about the people you'd like to work with and the common causes you might share.

Remember, in life we're aiming at both individual and common goods. It is easy to think about how you'd like to linearly progress through a career but more philosophically rewarding to think about whom you will progress with and how they will affect your development. As Aristotle reminds us, we are rational, *social* animals.

3. Next, think about the ways in which your work develops your particular virtues now and the virtues you'd like to grow in. What story could you tell about how your current pursuit of the good life connects to those common goods?

A key strategy for avoiding burnout-like alienation is making sure that you're connecting the things you do on a day-to-day basis with what you find important and meaningful. Great mentors and bosses make sure these through lines exist and that others can see them. Maybe you handle billing for a dental office. How would you tell the common-good story? You work with an office team whose livelihoods depend on your accuracy and strategic thinking. And when your office is functioning well, the patients are healthy and cared for.

4. Now write up four things you could do tomorrow, next week, or in a month to make your work story one that is even more tied in with your philosophical apology.

Some of these might be simple ("I'm going to eat in the cafeteria with people I've never met"); some might be riskier ("I'm going to ask my boss to change how she holds meetings with me" or "I'm going to propose a project and ask to take significant ownership over its completion"). If you think that the only work story available to you at the moment is bullshit, maybe it is time for a more radical change. Remember, virtue ethics is supposed to be action oriented, and if you're not trying experiments—some of which are very low stakes, and many of which will fail—you're not getting the experiential data you need to keep moving forward and growing as a person.

This exercise may lead to big surprising insights, or it might just inspire a few good life tweaks. If you're really in a period of intense introspection, think about keeping a "work journal" for a couple weeks. Notice patterns in your entries, revisit some of these prompts, and see if you're able to use this information to continue the hard process of integrating the various good things in your life.

5.

Love Attentively

> He was beginning to think that death was finally upon them and that they should find some place to hide where they would not be found. There were times when he sat watching the boy sleep that he would begin to sob uncontrollably but it wasnt about death. He wasnt sure what it was about but he thought it was about beauty or about goodness. Things that he'd no longer any way to think about at all.
>
> —Cormac McCarthy, *The Road*

LOVE AND THE GOOD LIFE

There is a recipe for a standard-issue romantic comedy. Two attractive protagonists, each distracted by something (a demanding job, a badly matched relationship, an illness/death/divorce). Then a fateful encounter. A seemingly chemical reaction that leads each to discover, in the other, what's been missing from their respective lives. Fate conspires to almost ruin it, but then brings them together at the end. A closing kiss in the rain.

These stories tend to leave us with the impression that romantic love is the Platonic form of love, the purest and most complete version of the virtue. It is a virtue most eloquently expressed in the start of an exclusive relationship, stereotypically by young and beautiful people. This impression is, of course, mistaken. Love infuses our lives in many different ways—romantic love is just one dimension of that—and loving relationships themselves transform and develop over time.

This raises an important question: If love is so central to the good life, can philosophical reflection make us better at it, the way philosophy aims to improve other virtues?

Ancient virtue ethicists thought that our philosophical goals ought to play a central guiding role in our love lives. In particular, many of the ancients thought we should only love people who are helping us toward eudaimonia and who themselves have acquired the virtues. *Philia* is the Greek word for the love we have characteristically toward our friends, a love we can direct and cultivate. The Greeks distinguished it from other kinds of love, like erotic love, or the instinctual love we might have for family members, or the spiritual love we might have for gods. Philia can, of course, sometimes accompany these other forms of love. In modern life, we expect to be friends with our lovers. Certain conceptions of religious faith encourage friendship with God.

Aristotle thought there were three main types of philia. In the first category are friends we choose for pleasure. In the second category are friends we choose because they give us an advantage in life. And in the third category are those we properly love, friends whose souls we care about for their own sake. Many of our friends fall into the first category—we love them because they are hilarious, fun to drink with, or tell good stories. Callicles and the other sophists we met in the chapter on truth thought all of our relationships ultimately boil down to the second category—the people we aim to get something from. Aristotle thought the third category to be the most rare—the people we choose to love for the sake of their virtuous souls and on whom our good lives most fundamentally depend.

What does it mean to love another person "for their own sake"? For

Aristotle, true philia seems to mean that you spend time reflecting on the ways your friends care for their souls. You also admire the distinctive ways your friends are honest and generous, and how their styles of virtue complement your own. At his most poetic, Aristotle tells us that in the closest third-category friendships, your friend becomes "another self"—the virtuous person lives out not only his own good life but somehow the good lives of his loved ones as well.

Aristotle's virtue theory of love was both popular and controversial in its own time and remains so today. It faces (at least) three problems.

First, if we love people for their virtues, and find the same virtues in someone new, presumably we ought to love them too. Or at the very least, there would be nothing wrong with swapping out one of your current courageous/generous/wise friends for another one with the same virtues. But we don't think of our loved ones as swappable in this way. Also, Aristotle's theory of love seems to reduce the people in our lives to walking virtues rather than full-fledged, colorful selves.

Relatedly, if we love our friends for their virtue, and we discover that there are more virtuous people out there, presumably we would feel pressure to upgrade our friends. But we tend to think that loyalty and shared history should lead us to maintain love even when the friend isn't an obvious fit for our ambitions. We admire people who stick with their friends from the "old neighborhood" even when they make it. We take it as a sign of moral progress when teenagers stop rapidly cycling through relationships and settle down.

The third problem is perhaps the most direct. Aristotle says that we love our closest friends for their virtues. But most of us don't even *like* moral overachievers, let alone love them. In fact, sometimes what binds us most to our friends are shared vices. When Meghan was a student at Oxford, she was surrounded by aspiring moral saints. This is especially true in the Rhodes scholar community, whose completely unironic motto is "fighting the world's fight." Some of the time this was inspiring, but sometimes it was also exhausting. For a few months, Meghan and her friend and fellow Rhodie Nick adopted a policy of only being willing to "officially" befriend people who would share a cigarette with them. It was a petty, unhealthy, and short-lived friendship test. But surrounded by paragons of virtue (and perpetually overwhelmed by school), they wanted a system for weeding out stressful, unlovable Dudley Do-Rights.

Maybe the conclusion to draw is that love is immune from philosophical guidance. But that would be surprising, since love *is* such a central part of our good lives. It is a part of life we seek advice on from our other people, from trashy magazines, and from ancient traditions. For the writers of the New Testament, love isn't just a virtue, love is *the* virtue. The "greatest commandment," as it appears in all four Gospels, is to love God unconditionally, and to "love your neighbor as yourself." Saint Paul spills plenty of ink advising us on the topic. Love, for these and so many other thinkers, is the most important part of our soul we can develop on the path to eudaimonia.

To understand love in terms of virtue ethics, we need to think about how our capacity to love connects with our distinctive function as humans. And we think the place to start is to consider how virtue ethics frames one of the most profound forms of love—the love parents have for their children.

OUTSOURCING PARENTAL ATTENTION

In 2017, at the dawn of the Christmas season, Mattel rolled out advertisements for a $350 "smart" baby monitor. Marketed as the Aristotle, it promised to bring the internet of things into nurseries. Parents already dependent on Alexa to update grocery lists and Apple Watches to count their steps could now also keep track of their infant's sleep patterns, feedings, and even bowel movements with the same ease and efficiency. Aristotle could automatically soothe a restless infant with lights and white noise. As the child grows, Aristotle could provide her with stimulating music and word games. Aristotle could respond to verbal commands and was inhumanly tolerant of requests to play *Frozen* songs. You could even set Aristotle to require the child to issue commands with "please" and "thank you," to develop good manners. Better data, more sleep, and a cognitive and social edge for toddlers—what could possibly be the downside?

The product imploded before arriving at a single store. The website Jezebel ran a review: "Mattel's New Baby Monitoring Device Is Creepy as Hell." Privacy advocates raised alarms about the security of the data being collected. Unlike an adult on Facebook, a two-year-old cannot consent to trade her information to sophisticated marketers. But even beyond the privacy worries, there is a much deeper question here: Are there some aspects of parenting that just shouldn't be outsourced, no matter what? It may be good in the short term for a child to get better sleep or calibrated cognitive stimulation. But in the long run, shouldn't the parent-child bond be forged in poop and tears and sleepless nights?

Addressing how this new technology would affect parenting, Mattel's chief products officer was refreshingly frank—"Honestly speaking, we just don't know," adding, "If we're successful, kids will form some emotional ties to this. Hopefully, it will be the right types of emotional ties."

Real Aristotle, in his teachings on love, had a lot to say about the correct ways to parent. You wonder if any of the Mattel execs even skimmed his books before choosing their product's name. Real Aristotle holds the parent-child bond to be one of the most morally significant in our lives: "By nature, friendship seems to be inherent in a parent for offspring and offspring for a parent." Particularly relevant to this debate, he considers whether objects can replace people in our most important relationships: "Friendship is not spoken of when it comes to loving inanimate objects, since in that case there is no reciprocated love or wish for the good of the inanimate thing."

He also warns us against thinking that the most important ways of loving another person can be made more efficient. While some of our relationships are aimed at making us feel happy in the short run, our most important relationships are about growing our personalities together. An excellent parent-child relationship has exactly this power, just as an abusive relationship can nearly destroy someone.

Of course, we might think Aristotle had an outdated view of just what it is to be a well-functioning human. Technology is just a much bigger part of our lives than it was for the Greeks. Some modern philosophers have embraced just this stance.

According to defenders of the extended mind hypothesis, the thinking part of a human organism (e.g., the gray matter between your ears) can be "linked with an external entity in a two-way interaction, creating a *coupled system* that can be seen as a cognitive system in its own right." Here is a straightforward test for telling whether a part of your physical brain is part of your thinking mind. Consider all of the things you can do because of your thinking system now. If you incapacitated a part of your brain—say you shoved an ice pick through your frontal lobe—would there be tasks you couldn't do anymore? If so, the frontal lobe is part of your mind. The trouble is, this test seems to work well for technology that we've become dependent on. If your iPhone is destroyed, could you still competently drive from South Bend to Chicago? Remember your appointments? Calculate fractions? Many of the actions and behaviors we take responsibility for depend on "thinking" that happens because our brains are connected with technology. Extended mind philosophers say: Exactly—your iPhone is part of your mind. The U.S. Supreme Court seems to agree. A 2014 ruling determined that police cannot search your cell phone without a warrant, because, according to Chief Justice Roberts, "modern cell phones . . . are now such a pervasive and insistent part of daily life that the proverbial visitor from Mars might conclude they were an important feature of human anatomy."

The extended mind hypothesis relies strongly on the computer analogy—you are like a computer, your phone is a computer, and when you link two computers in the right way, you get another better computer. A hyper-sophisticated baby monitor is just an extension of the parent. But virtue ethicists think there is a dimension to *your* mental life that isn't about computing, and isn't just about performing cognitive tasks efficiently. And this dimension of your mental life is crucially important to your capacity to love.

THE ATTENTIVE MIND

Iris Murdoch was a contemporary of Elizabeth Anscombe and another one of the "Oxford women" we met in the chapter on responsibility. Murdoch attended Somerville College in the years before World War II, and the two women later became much closer as graduate students in philosophy at Cambridge. At one point, Anscombe and another friend made fish soup in Murdoch's apartment while she was away, straining it with Iris's chiffon scarf. The disgusting smell and unruly subletters got Murdoch evicted. Still, Murdoch admired Anscombe for her fearless, defiant wearing of pants to Mass, and for getting arrested at 5:00 a.m. for roaming the streets with her hair down (and then refusing to give police her name). Their complicated friendship itself is evidence that people with very different lifestyles can sometimes be drawn together. Anscombe was a conservative Roman Catholic, a mother of seven, who spent her spare time leading the aforementioned campaign to get Truman dishonored and to encourage the outlawing of contraception. Murdoch was at turns curious and wary of religious practice, curious and wary of existentialist philosophy, equally likely to write a novel or an essay, and while happily married to fellow writer John Bayley for forty years, had affairs with both men and women throughout her life. Murdoch dedicated her magnum opus, *Metaphysics as a Guide to Morals*, in part to her "old friend-foe" Anscombe.

What united them was a love of the truth, and the conviction that virtue ethics deserved to be taken more seriously in their rarefied academic circles. Both women contributed in their own ways to that revival.

Murdoch, much like Anscombe, decried the "behaviourist, existentialist, utilitarian" worldview she saw pervading British life in the postwar period. For Murdoch, the views were behaviorist because they thought all there was to having a mind was being able to do certain tasks; existentialist because they thought the entire goal of our mental lives was to perform the tasks; and utilitarian because they thought the main moral value of our decisions lies in the good or bad consequences brought about by those tasks. Where in this theory, she lamented, could we possibly make space for virtues like love and contemplation?

Murdoch argued for a critical distinction between our "outer world"—the dimensions of our good life that involve action—and our "inner world"—the dimensions of our good life that involve how we think, how we narrate our lives to ourselves, and—most crucially for love—how we work to see others. "Surely there is such a thing as deciding and not acting?" she wrote. "Surely there are *private* decisions? Surely there are lots and lots of objects, more or less easily identified, in orbit as it were in inner space?"

We've already seen this same kind of distinction in previous chapters—we have responsibility for our intentions, for the reasons we take to be guiding our decisions and the stories of our character that those reasons shape. We "make up our minds" in a crucial way before we are capable of acting. We are also capable of wondering about our own thoughts—wondering if we are telling our story correctly. And moral progress over the course of our lives partially involves progress in understanding events and people in the right light. Murdoch was inspired by Plato's allegory of the cave—we all must learn how to see the world and ourselves correctly. Her genius was connecting this idea of intention and "seeing" with our capacity for love.

In her essay "The Idea of Perfection," Murdoch gives the example of a mother-in-law who outwardly acts as though she loves her daughter-in-law but inwardly despises the young woman. She also realizes that she ought to love her daughter-in-law. The mother carries on a dialogue with herself internally: "I am old-fashioned and conventional. I may be prejudiced and narrow-minded. I may be snobbish. I am certainly jealous. *Let me look again*." She keeps asking herself to reconsider her daughter-in-law, and over time she makes progress; she learns to tolerate and then, eventually, love the woman. And that, for Murdoch, is a significant moral achievement for the mother that doesn't involve acting at all. She learns to love her daughter-in-law by learning to look at her the right way.

There is a temptation to think love is all about how we act. You love your friend if you go out of your way to arrange a surprise party for her. Paul's love for his children is expressed in hugs and snuggles. When we want to encourage people to improve their love lives, we typically give action-oriented advice. Our action-oriented lives can seemingly be optimized and made more efficient, especially with technological off-loading.

But for Murdoch, love is a virtue we cultivate by working on our capacities for attention rather than action. How do we improve on this dimension?

36 QUESTIONS THAT LEAD TO LOVE

One of the most read *New York Times* stories in 2015 was not news at all, but rather a list of questions: "36 Questions That Lead to Love." The article described an exercise proven to cultivate intimacy between two people, including complete strangers. The exercise was based on a provocative study by a team of social psychologists at SUNY Stony Brook led by Arthur Aron. Aron and his team were trying to come up with a task that could help relative strangers "simulate" the intimacy of a close relationship in a lab setting. They discovered the key was to find a structured activity that encouraged "sustained, escalating, reciprocal, personal self-disclosure." Participants in the study were chosen to be paired with strangers who were told ahead of time that (1) they shared the same outlook on daily life (e.g., about whether smoking is okay, or how to dress) and (2) they were likely to like each other. They were told explicitly that the goal of the experiment was to provoke feelings of closeness with the other person. Some of the pairs were male-female and some were both female.

The questions started off light—"Would you like to be famous? In what way?" But they got increasingly serious, ending with high-vulnerability questions like "If you were to die this evening with no opportunity to communicate with anyone, what would you most regret not having told someone? Why haven't you told them yet?" (The control groups were given only easy questions to stimulate ordinary small talk.) All of the experimental questions were "strong" in the Platonic sense we described in the chapter on truth—in that the participants were not very likely to know how their partners would answer. The exercise ended with participants staring into each other's eyes for four minutes.

The results were significant. After the experiment, partners were surveyed on their feelings of intimacy. When asked to think of their most important relationships, participants typically rated their intimacy around 4.65 out of 7 on the scale. After performing the forty-five-minute question test, 30 percent of the experimental subjects gave their partner a score at least this high. The mean score was 4.06 (compared with 3 for the small-talk groups). Moreover, when asked what they thought about participating in the study afterward, the vast majority of participants indicated it was highly enjoyable. One of the original experimental pairs eventually married.

Of course, this is an exercise for promoting feelings of intimacy, not long-term relationships. Still, it works, and Aron and his coauthors support what Aristotle, Murdoch, and other philosophers in the virtue tradition have long hypothesized: Self-disclosure and self-expansion are the first steps in establishing feelings of intimacy. Sharing our "inner worlds"—not just acting—is a crucial building block of love. Aristotle puts this point beautifully in his lectures on friendship in the *Nicomachean Ethics*:

> Perceiving that one lives belongs among the things pleasant in themselves, for life is by nature a good thing, and to perceive the good present in oneself is pleasant. . . . Accordingly, one ought to share in the friend's perception that he exists, and this would come to pass by living together and sharing in a community of speeches and thought—for this is what living together would seem to mean in the case of human beings, and not as with cattle, merely feeding in the same place.

One of the most remarkable features of the human mind is this capacity for attention. We can become utterly absorbed in a colorful bird outside the window. In a joke or a memory we enjoy completely privately. In the sheer joy of being a conscious existent. And—and this is Aristotle's point—through attention we can be a part of our loved ones' "inner lives."

This passage helps us see why it is probably unfair to attribute to Aristotle the view that friendship requires us to look at people as just walking virtues. You can't read virtues just off behavior. This process of attention is inherently particular—it takes time, the right kinds of attention, and the capacity to get absorbed in the weird distinctiveness of another person's inner good life. And this is why our friends are not easily replaceable or upgradable. When we love someone, we are not just loving what they do, we love the thoughts they give us access to. These inner lives are so unique that they avoid easy substitution or comparison. And even getting access to them in the first place requires commitment and trust.

Love and Questions
(Paul's [and Shayla's] Apology)

When Meghan first sent me the link to the "36 Questions That Lead to Love" article ahead of our class session on love and friendship, my initial reaction was, "Oh, Shayla and I did this!" Of course, we hadn't participated in the original study, or even used the same prompts, but structured question-and-answer sessions played a big role in the early episodes of our love story.

When I first told my family that Shayla and I were dating, my sister Katie went to her bedroom closet, pulled out a huge binder of photocopied articles and worksheets, and handed it to me. In it was everything she'd amassed in her time leading couples through marriage-preparation classes at her church, and she assured me that it pretty much covered everything we needed to figure out before deciding whether or not we were meant to build a life together.

I'm a bit intense. On our first date, I asked Shayla—hypothetically—if she'd be willing to marry a professional philosopher. (She laughed, but said yes. Hypothetically.) I took Katie's binder full of love worksheets very, very seriously. The day after I received it, Shayla and I drove the three hours from my hometown to hers. I told her I figured we could make it through about half of the material if we skimmed a bit. Each section had strong good life questions:

- *In your family growing up, who generally paid the bills?*
- *How important is it to you that your children are brought up in the religion you were raised in?*
- *How far away from your immediate family would you be willing to live?*

It took a bit of time to process, but working through these questions changed us in two important ways. First, they brought our differences out into the open. While dating, we naturally tended to spend our time reflecting on similarities and common interests, and the questions surprised us—in very good, though sometimes difficult, ways—by reminding us that we brought different beliefs, experiences, and expectations to the table. Probably the biggest surprise came when we simultaneously revealed the number of children we expected to make up our family, and found a difference of three kids.

Second—and I've got to assume that this at least partly explains the effect observed in Aron's study—the questions gave us the raw materials to start thinking together about how our good lives could become our common good life. We started thinking about ourselves and our relationship very differently when we had to answer concrete, future-directed questions like "What do you think is most likely to change about our marriage in the next forty years?" and "Would you be willing to move for your partner's major career opportunity?"

JOINING MINDS VERSUS JOINING LIVES

The attention theory insists that love requires coming to see another person's mind: their intentions, their desires, and the unique ways they think. But we might worry that this philosophical approach makes love far too brainy—too much of an intellectual accomplishment. It requires tremendous cognitive capacity to be able to monitor even your own thoughts. Very few of us would seem to have the ability to keep track of the thoughts of our loved ones at the same time.

In a tragic turn of events, Iris Murdoch succumbed at the end of her life to Alzheimer's disease. When she died in 1999, she had been married for more than forty years. Her diary entries tracked her decline, growing shorter and less coherent each day. She stopped being her usual charismatic self. She began declining food and drink. She told a friend in 1997 that she was "sailing away into the darkness." Murdoch stopped speaking, communicating by kissing the hands of her friends or bowing with her hands in the prayer position. Almost as if she were a child again, she spent her final days with a teddy bear named Jimbo by her side.

The attention theory of love would seem to imply that Murdoch at the end of life (and any cognitively disabled individual) wasn't capable of love. We think this is the wrong approach to the theory. It is true that a seriously cognitively disabled person cannot do much by way of reasoning, calculating, choosing, acting, or storytelling. But crucially, they can still be thoughtfully absorbed in other people's minds. At her philosophical height, Murdoch thought this absorption capacity is also one of the distinctively human capacities for love. Murdoch's authorized biographer reports that in the final stages of her illness, Murdoch was utterly absorbed in her surroundings: "There was a sense that she was experiencing a new way of knowing."

That said, we need to develop the attention theory still further, because we need to be able to distinguish good love from the kind of absorption that comes with pathological obsession or even hatred. Loving attention must take a particular form. For Aristotle and Murdoch, learning to love also requires learning how to "unself" (Murdoch's term); it requires joining up your own inner life with others', taking on their good lives as your own. This is where virtue comes back into the discussion. When we are lovingly absorbed, other people's pursuits of the good life successfully merge with our own.

The legendary Roman statesman Cicero wrote more than two hundred years after Aristotle, but he knew and admired the theory of virtues that came from Aristotle's school. This is how Cicero describes the value of friends in his essay *De Amiticia*:

> And great and numerous as are the blessings of friendship, this certainly is the sovereign one, that it gives us bright hopes for the future and forbids weakness and despair. In the face of a true friend a man sees as it were a second self. So that where his friend is he is; if his friend be rich, he is not poor; though he be weak, his friend's strength is his; and in his friend's life he enjoys a second life after his own is finished.

The chief benefit of love for Aristotle and Cicero is its unique capacity to let us in on "second lives." It is a bit of a twist on the extended mind hypothesis discussed earlier—somehow from our first-personal attention, our loved ones help us live extended lives. You still have your own particular goals, and your loved ones have theirs. But love has the capacity to make their lives like extensions of your own. And in some cases, as when Paul and Shayla committed to literally merging their two lives, it can help us envision a third: a good life shared with a spouse, children, friends, or family. Moreover, someone's willingness to be part of your weird inner world—that is one of the surest ways we know we are loved.

This, too, raises a puzzle, one debated even in Greek and Roman times. How do we accomplish this "unselfing"? We have our own lives, with their own integrity, to lead. More than that, the good life requires taking responsibility and control over your "inner life"—but we can't make up any mind but our own. To start to understand how this works, it is helpful to think about the practical ways we try to get "inside" our loved ones' good lives.

Fins
(Meghan's Apology)

When I was eleven, I was part of a competition at my school called Furs, Fins, and Feathers. It involved choosing an animal to dress up as and delivering a monologue as the animal. As soon as the project was announced, I knew immediately what I needed to be: Great White Shark. What more perfect spirit animal for a painfully shy, physically awkward fifth grader? I had undiagnosed vision problems, which my teachers interpreted as ineptitude. I was afraid of them but also wanted more than anything to finally impress them. I had very short "boy cut" hair; ate only yellow foods; my favorite game was Lego pirates; I was starting to grasp the horror that would be middle school.

I dreamed of walking onstage completely enclosed in a full-body shark suit, life-sized (fifteen feet!), with sharp teeth and cold, predatory eyes. And fins. I drew schematics—where I'd need holes to breathe, how the toothy mouth would open. I shared them with the one person on earth I knew would understand the urgency of this mission.

Liam Sullivan is not what you would call a "crafty dad." He would patiently, gleefully explain the rules of tennis, golf, or football to any elementary schooler. But none of his children shared his interest in sports. Much of his parenting has involved trying to be part of the alien worlds of his three very different progeny.

Here's the pragmatic thing to do when presented with an eleven-year-old's detailed colored pencil drawing of a full-body shark costume: laugh, post it on the fridge, and then see what the local party store has in terms of fish masks. My dad took a long look at the drawings, furrowed his brow, and then thought . . . upholstery foam. He bet we could get the head big enough and light enough if we carved it out of upholstery foam. He called a friend and we found ourselves early on a Saturday morning in an industrial park where cushions are manufactured. His friend helped us construct a four-foot-tall foam cylinder (after negotiating the costume's scale). There were armholes and breathing holes and a tapered, sharky-looking mouth—we followed the specs of the drawing as best we could. We spent the afternoon back in our garage carving intricate teeth into that mouth, turning plastic Easter eggs into the merciless eyes, gluing dorsal fins, spray-painting everything bluish gray, adding a dribble of blood. We worked on the monologue, which contained some shark facts from Encyclopaedia Britannica, *some ruminations about being fierce, some of the directions from the assignment. We practiced being loud enough to be heard from under the layers of upholstery foam.*

Liam Sullivan has never felt the urge to eat the other children in his elementary school. He doesn't have any direct experience with what it is like to be an awkward preteen girl. His love is the capacity to understand enough what the world looks like from his daughter's vantage, and to see it being a perfectly good use of a weekend to make her dream his own.

We don't want to live our loved ones' lives for them. The "second self" theory involves being able to see our loved ones' goals "from the inside," see why they are working toward them, and to participate in the process of them becoming the person with those virtues. In this case, it means seeing that your daughter needs confidence and courage, and that a uniquely effective way for her to develop these virtues is to get to be a shark for a little while.

The second self theory also helps us to answer the Dudley Do-Right worry for virtuous love. We typically resent the moral saints in our lives for one of three reasons. First, we might reject the saint's moral code—it isn't our own, or we are not sure it is true. Perhaps we don't understand their intentions or we aren't sure whether they are admirable. For example, we might dislike a supervegetarian because hanging out with her raises a question we genuinely aren't sure how to answer: Is eating meat wrong? The solution to this is to try to work on our own moral development—and probably to engage her with some strong questions.

Second, we might accept their moral code but fail to identify them as a second self, maybe because they are way too far ahead of us (a view Aristotle considers at length). We love ourselves, despite our imperfections, partly for the people we aspire to become; for the virtues we are cultivating but don't yet have. We could try to do the same for saintly friends. Likewise, we find ourselves loving others who are at a similar stage of moral development not *because* of their vices but because we can relate to where they are on the path to virtue. And one of the ways we can love and care about them is by paying close enough attention to their lives to help them keep moving forward on that path.

Third, we might simply lack the ability to pay attention to the saints, at least enough attention to see them as a second self. Maybe they won't share their inner worlds with us—they are cold and detached or so mechanical in their saintliness that there isn't a world to access. Maybe it's that we aren't prepared to share ours with them.

Importantly, attention is also a virtue we can work on—we can build up our capacity to see other people.

CULTIVATING LOVING ATTENTION THROUGH LITERATURE

Loving someone for the sake of their own soul requires the ability to see someone's life from the inside and to empathize with the particular ways they are pursuing eudaimonia. It requires getting access to inner worlds. But it is admittedly difficult and rare to find a friend, a child, or a romantic partner who is both willing and able to bare their soul. Most of us develop such relationships over long periods of time. Until the real thing comes along, one way we get practice occupying the detailed inner lives of others is through literature and art. Excellent stories describe action "from the inside out."

Cormac McCarthy's *The Road* seems, at first, an implausible plot for a book about love. It is the antimatter to romantic comedies. The novel takes place in a postapocalyptic southeastern United States. A father and his young son are traveling from the mountains to the sea, desperately searching for food and avoiding cannibal tribes. There is absolutely no reason to believe they will be safer by the ocean. Early in the book, we learn that the boy's mother has killed herself, seeing no hope of a good life. She urges the father to do the same, but knows he will try to live as long as he can because of the boy.

As with Iris Murdoch, vision plays a critical role in how their love is portrayed. "He saw the boy watching him. He was what the boy thought about. Well should he." The son, for his part, persistently asks the father what they (collectively) are in the world. Are they the good guys? Are they robbers? There is no question that their moral fates could be anything but intertwined. And this keeps the father going.

A persistent theme in the book is the father and son discussing how they are "carrying the fire," a metaphor that recurs in ancient virtue ethics. For example, the Stoic philosopher Marcus Aurelius uses this as a metaphor for holding on to what's truly valuable (good souls) even in catastrophic circumstances. In his review of *The Road*, novelist Michael Chabon characterizes this kind of horror novel as a form of Stoic virtue ethics "with a taste for spectacle."

There is no more efficient way to ruin a wonderful book than to critically dissect it. So we'll just report that the experience of reading *The Road* and occupying the father's world for however many hours was a small but powerfully effective way for us to learn what it is like to love as a father. McCarthy's beautiful depiction of the relationship between a father and his son made Paul start to see fatherhood as an essential part of his goal in life. For Meghan, the experience of reading the book was like opening a new mental door: Oh, that's what it must feel like for dads like mine.

How exactly literary stories are able to do this is contested, though the history of literary criticism and commentary leaves no doubt that literature does succeed in this way. One recent and growing research project in neuroscience offers us data and a potential model that is hard for the follower of Murdoch to resist: brain scans of readers, and of those witnessing the actions and episodes of another, reveal that the same parts of our brains light up when we envision another perform an action as they do when we perform it ourselves. Vividly watching a friend chop an onion activates "mirror neurons" that allow us to process this as if it were our own action. As one group of researchers puts the point, "John grasps Mary's action because even as it is happening before his eyes, it is also happening, in effect, inside his head. . . . Mirror neurons permit an observed act to be directly understood by experiencing it."

Similarly, seeing a character experience heartbreak in a film induces a miniature version of the experience in ourselves. Neither Murdoch's nor Aristotle's philosophical theory of love is offered as a scientific explanation, but the connection here is illuminating, and this research points to physical mechanisms that might underlie the ability to "unself," or to experience the story of another as one of "a second self." If we are fortunate enough to have access to rich stories in our lives, via the experiences of our friends, or through classical or contemporary literature, we can experience, in an indirect way, the most powerful and most human emotions, without, or before, having to encounter them firsthand.

Lovecraft: Strong Questions That Lead to Love

As we've seen throughout this chapter, love can be forged or enhanced through a meeting of the minds. In order to find a second self, we've got to know more about that person's inner life. This includes understanding what drives them to do what they do and also about the way they see the world and their life in it. Learning how to share our own "inner lives" also helps build up the open-mindedness and vulnerability that love depends on. So here's your love-based soulcraft experiment.

Find a friend or a partner you'd like to know more about. Explain, in your own words, the attention theory of love, and why philosophers like Iris Murdoch and Aristotle thought that seeing a person, and understanding their inner life, plays such a vital role in genuine friendships. Then tell them what their friendship means to you. For instance, if you take joy in what's good for them for their own sake, tell them that. Then work through the following list of questions. Take turns answering. When you're listening, pay close attention to your partner's answers and ask follow-up questions as they arise:

1. What's something that most people don't know about you?
2. Can you describe a time when you did something that was right, even though it came at a great personal cost?
3. What are you most looking forward to in the next six months?
4. What's one thing you've always wanted to change about yourself or your life?
5. How do you think you'll most change as you get older?
6. In a single word, what is the thing you value more than anything else in the world? Explain.
7. What's the single biggest thing someone could do today to help you become the person you want to become?
8. Can you think of anything that's held you back in life, but that you're too afraid to let go of?

9. Do you have anything you've always wanted to tell someone but haven't?

10. If we wanted to become even better friends, what's one thing I'd have to know about you that I don't already?

Now comes the weird part. Sit together in silence for two minutes, making eye contact the whole time. Then take turns sharing, for a few minutes each, your answers to the following questions: What do you think motivates your partner? What are their best qualities and strengths as a person? And what advice would you give them in their pursuit of a good life? As each person shares, the other person can sit and listen silently. Afterward, you can ask each other questions and clarify what you meant, but the point is to approach these descriptions from a place of curiosity.

II.

God and the Good Life

6.

Wonder about God

> For I do not seek to understand that I may believe, but I believe in order to understand. For this also I believe—that unless I believed, I shall not understand.
>
> —Saint Anselm

In a recent profile of comedian Stephen Colbert, *GQ* reported that he used to have a note taped to his computer that read "Joy is the most infallible sign of the existence of God."

When considering the deepest questions of philosophical theology, a comedian might be a surprising figure to start with. But Colbert is well known for his religious convictions. He's likely the only major talk show host to have recited the Nicene Creed on cable television (at least twice). He's at ease joking about his faith on air, but he's opened up on the topic in a more serious way on multiple occasions.

Colbert's life has been shaped by tragedy. When he was just ten years old, his father and two of his older brothers, Peter and Paul, died suddenly when Eastern Air Lines Flight 212 crashed while attempting to land in Charlotte, North Carolina. The subsequent investigation showed that avoidable crew errors led to the accident, which killed seventy-two of the eighty-two people on board.

Colbert was the youngest and the only child living at home at the time. He took on the role of keeping his mother's spirits up. In a widely watched interview with Anderson Cooper on CNN in 2019, Colbert opened up in a raw and emotional conversation about that chapter in his life and its philosophical significance.

Cooper wonders how such a tragedy wouldn't destroy any confidence that God exists, and Colbert (somewhat surprisingly) replies with what sounds very much like an argument for God's existence. He explains that his basic disposition toward the world is gratitude. "I'm very grateful to be alive," he says. "And so that act, that impulse to be grateful, wants an object. That object I call God. . . . That's my context for my existence, is that I am here to know God, love God, serve God, that we might be happy with each other in this world and with Him in the next." Colbert is quoting this last phrase directly from a version of the Catholic catechism.

What should we make of Colbert's argument? Clearly, this way of thinking has had an impact on his life. The response had a visceral effect on Cooper, who was grieving the recent loss of his own mother at the time of the interview. But the human mind finds comfort in many things. There is a world of difference between a psychological rationalization that helps with trauma and a rational, truth-seeking argument.

And yet . . . suppose we take Colbert at his word. Perhaps the argument goes something like this: When he looks out at the world, he is filled with gratitude and wonder. And it's not the naive enthusiasm of someone who's never experienced pain or suffering. It's battle-tested, a feeling that arises in *response* to the frailty and brokenness and imperfection of human life rather than in spite of it. Paraphrasing a view that J. R. R. Tolkien offers in a letter to a fellow author, Colbert often asks: "What punishments of God are not gifts?"

Suppose that like Colbert you have this unshakable feeling of gratitude and you want to know why. You consider the possibility that thankfulness is just wired into you biologically—maybe social creatures like us do better in evolutionary races if we are instinctively grateful when people share food, resources, and family life with us. But as Colbert sees it, this gratitude isn't something that you can limit to particular aspects of life. If you are grateful for life, you feel compelled to be grateful for all of it: the whole messy enterprise. As he tells Anderson Cooper, and as he's said in other interviews on the subject, his suffering has taught him to love the thing he "most wish[es] had not happened. . . . [That] it's a gift to exist. With existence comes suffering." He's grateful for a life that includes the plane crash, because he's grateful for his life itself. That gratitude is looking for a target, someone or something personal and responsible. What's a better object of cosmic gratitude than the being we've traditionally referred to as God?

Colbert's reasoning parallels arguments for God's existence that have been offered by some of the most influential philosophers and theologians in the Western tradition. There's a hint of Saint Augustine, who confessed, "Our hearts are restless until they rest in you"; Saint Anselm, who claimed, "God is that than which a greater cannot be conceived," the most likely candidate for any cosmic excellence; and Saint Thomas Aquinas, who identifies God as Aristotle's "prime mover," the cause and source of all things in the world, including our good lives.

The philosophical tradition in virtue ethics revved up almost at the same time as the wisdom tradition in Judaism. There are virtue ethics traditions that aren't particularly concerned with whether a personal, all-powerful, morally perfect god exists (Aristotle, the Stoics, the Confucians). But from at least the sixth century BC onward, when the author of the Book of Job was freaking out about the capricious suffering in our lives, the questions of how and why and whether to add God to our picture of the good life have been a central topic of philosophical concern.

In the second half of this book, we now turn to these concerns. We come at these questions as partisans: we're both religious Catholics, but with somewhat different experiences of the faith. Paul is a cradle Catholic, was in seminary training to be a priest for years, became disenchanted with his faith, and then, after a struggle, found it renewed. Meghan grew up with some familiarity with Catholicism but became a convert somewhat abruptly as a college student, after the 9/11 terrorist attacks.

Adding God into the mix makes some of the philosophical issues we've already discussed much more tractable but others much more difficult. Philosophical arguments for and against the existence of God can play central roles in how we join up the circles of our personal good lives with existential considerations that influence our goals.

We don't think that they will decisively convince you to add or subtract religious faith from your good life, for reasons we'll explain in coming chapters.

But we do believe that the arguments can help you *understand yourself* in relation to God (or in relation to a universe without any god). As we saw in the chapter on responsibility, the art of the philosophical life is learning to tell the right story of why we are here and what we are doing. Just as intention shapes our moral lives, it can shape our spiritual lives. There is a world of difference between setting a candle on a table in a dark room and lighting it to create the mood for a romantic dinner and setting that same candle out to pray for a friend who has died. The difference is not just in the outward consequences, but also in the person doing the lighting.

Finally, when faith is an important dimension to your good life, the arguments can help you understand the god you love. As we've seen, a crucial part of the virtue of love is sustained attention to the unique character of those you love. An intriguing and frustrating aspect of our relationship with God is how much philosophy it seems to take to grasp him, how much that attention is rooted not in blind faith but in a love of knowledge.

BELIEFS ABOUT VERSUS BELIEF IN

To start, we should consider the sometimes uncomfortable relationship between religious life and philosophical questioning. We might think that religious faith isn't rational unless it's based on a scientific or logical proof that God (with a capital *G*) exists. As truth seekers, this demand for proof seems like a natural approach to any hotly disputed or confusing debate. Is gluten unhealthy? Are vaccines dangerous? Show me the evidence!

If we need conclusive evidence to settle the God debates, then conditions don't look particularly good for rational religious life, since many philosophers (even religiously inclined ones) will admit that we don't have arguments nearly strong enough to settle a question as big as God's existence.

Given this challenge, we might swing to another extreme and take the view that belief in God is an irrational attitude, a form of wishful thinking. This might lead us to look at religious believers the same way we look at Plato's prisoners who refuse to leave the cave: religious people just don't have the strength to face the cold, hard facts about our universe.

Paul and Meghan both love the 1990s indie band They Might Be Giants. Years ago, the band put out a children's album aimed at stoking scientific curiosity. The lead song—"Science Is Real!"—encourages kids to enjoy fun stories about "angels, unicorns and elves" but to turn to science when they want to know the truth about the world. The song emphasizes to the elementary school audience that no reason-seeking process will need to concern itself with angels or anything else in religious traditions. But why grant that assumption? Why not think instead, with Socrates, that reason can be applied with curiosity and strong questions to absolutely any subject?

There are some people who think religion of one sort or another is a useful ingredient in the good life—we should just cut the "truth vulnerable" historical and metaphysical assumptions out of the picture. That will get rid of any apparent tension between faith and reason, because religion becomes a purely practical matter. In the introduction we discussed Martin Seligman's research in positive psychology that "being religious" tends to correlate with higher reports of well-being. Some years back, *The New York Times* ran a piece about a group of millennials who are atheists attending seminary that flipped the "spiritual but not religious" dynamic on its head. Though the millennials don't buy into any of the metaphysics, they find something irresistible about the liturgy, history, community, and structure that religion provides.

What is it to "be religious" in this sense?

Maybe it means being part of a devoted community with a relatively comprehensive teaching about the good life, a teaching you can immerse yourself in as a practice.

If that's all it takes, then some pretty surprising activities come to count as religions. Paul and Meghan both go almost every day to a local CrossFit-style gym in South Bend, called Primal. The name makes the gym sound more hard-core than it is. Primal is run by Coach Chris, our very kind (and very shredded) neighbor. The clientele is an even mix of Notre Dame professors and students, stay-at-home parents, retirees, teenagers, even a sitting justice on the Supreme Court. The gym meets downtown in a space wedged between a financial planner's office and a homeless shelter. The median Primal member has been at the gym for more than three years. Primal brings people together to work for a common good. And it sets goals to structure every day. Some goals are personal: after years of work, Meghan can now bench ninety pounds, and Paul is inching closer to the goal of benching his body weight. Some are communal: there is a whiteboard where we might keep a tally of all burpees the gym as a whole has done in a day. A large part of the gym's appeal is its "liturgy": showing up each morning to listen to a well-curated pump-up playlist, stretching together while we gossip, and then doing something challenging and healthy and transformative in the company of close friends. And because of the peculiar Notre Dame clientele, there is typically a vigorous side discussion of philosophy, theology, and politics in between sets.

Are we part of a Primal religion? Chris would love to market his gym that way, but the answer seems emphatically no. Exercise affects our day-to-day life, but the *scope* of the good life vision Primal offers is still pretty limited. It answers some of the "Why" questions that drive our pursuit of happiness. Why warm up before you run? So you don't get a knee injury. But Primal just assumes you know the answers to others, like how important it is to be physically strong. Other kinds of good life questions, like what you ought to do with your money and who you ought to love, might get dealt with in conversations at the gym but not in the gym program itself. Finally, we're good friends with Chris and we know he cares about us as individuals, but Primal is a business, and the training regimes and advice it offers are importantly shaped by its capitalist goals, not any "chief good." God tends to come into the good life picture, as we've seen, because we need something or someone big enough to be this "chief good."

Perhaps this is why it seems so difficult to subtract the question of God from the question of religious life.

We have other options for understanding how to draw philosophical connections between religious believers and a being like God.

For instance, we can distinguish beliefs *about* God that come from philosophical arguments from faith *in* God. To appreciate the difference, imagine that you were describing your best friend to someone you had just met. Your friend is kind and loving, able to comfort you in times of distress and guide you in your journey toward becoming a better person. Now suppose your new acquaintance stops you. "This friend sounds lovely," she says. "But I have a question. How do you know that she exists?"

Well, you've seen her. You've spoken with her. You have a relationship with her. . . .

But your conversation partner is insistent: "You could have imagined all of those things. Hallucinated your interactions and dreamed up your phone calls. What proof do you have that can establish, without a doubt, that your best friend exists?"

There are many things you might say in your defense—you know a whole lot more about yourself and your friend than this random acquaintance does. And we all take some things for granted in the pursuit of knowledge. We assume we aren't just living in a vivid dream. We trust others and what they tell us.

For many religious people faith in God is much like the faith we put in other people. It *presupposes* certain things—their existence, at a minimum. The tricky point is whether demanding proof of God's existence is unduly skeptical and overly philosophical. Are religious people rationally licensed to take God's existence for granted in their pursuit of eudaimonia?

God is a singular case, and it's not difficult to see disanalogies between the role God would play in our lives and the role our friends play. God doesn't call you on the phone; only the very lucky or very special allegedly get to encounter him face-to-face in this life with any clarity. An argument for God's existence would be handy for a few different reasons. For the people who mostly take God's existence for granted, it would be a source of comfort in those inevitable times when the skeptical worry gets its grip on them. Some religious traditions demand that believers be able "to give a reason for their hope." For atheists, the arguments about God's existence can provide a shared language for talking with theists about their conception of the good life. Knowing Colbert's gratitude argument tells you a lot about who he is and what drives him, even if you don't share his metaphysical assumptions. And for everyone involved, the arguments help give us some clarity on what it is we've been arguing about—what exactly the stakes are in debates about religion and the good life.

"WHAT IS GOD?"

Thomas Aquinas lived in Italy in the thirteenth century AD. Think big stone towers and knights on horseback. He was born to a wealthy family (his father actually was a knight), and, as was the custom for a noble family's youngest boy, educated by Benedictine monks in the hopes of placing him into a prestigious clerical role. Thomas was a precocious boy, and, in a telling bit of lore, was said to have walked around the halls of the monastery at the age of five or six asking the monks, "What is God?" We don't know what his teachers said in response, but—whatever it was—it seems not to have fully satisfied him.

Around the time he was to start his university studies, Aquinas decided to become a Dominican, much to the chagrin of his family. Dominicans, at that time, often studied the liberal arts, like philosophy and theology, to become teachers and preachers, not archbishops or abbots, the powerful clerics his noble family was hoping he would emulate.

Aquinas lived during an extraordinary time in the history of philosophy. For almost a thousand years, the European world had lost touch with Aristotle. Christian philosophers, like Saint Augustine and Saint Anselm, knew the Greek master very indirectly through some of Plato's original works and traditional commentaries on these. But Islamic scholars were studying and commenting on the *Nicomachean Ethics* throughout this entire period. They knew Aristotle's logical and scientific systems and had developed ingenious and systematic interpretations of his philosophy. Aquinas was part of the first generation of European scholars, one that included the influential Jewish philosopher Moses Maimonides, to rediscover Aristotle and have his texts translated into a language they could read (Latin). The texts, and the commentaries from Middle Eastern scholars that came with them, made a huge impact on young Aquinas. He decided to make it part of his life's work to reconcile Aristotelian virtue ethics, logic, and science with the doctrines of the Catholic Church.

Throughout his life, Aquinas wrote a truly staggering number of texts on topics ranging from physics to astronomy to theology. But his crowning achievement is the *Summa Theologica*. The *Summa* is a monumental work that aims to answer quite literally all of life's most important questions. It starts with questions about the nature of God, the natural order, and reality, before moving on to a comprehensive theory of human nature, rationality, and ethics. The structure of each section seems strange to modern readers. Instead of chapters, the work is organized into particular questions (like "Is God perfectly good?"). Aquinas asks the question and then entertains the opposite of the answer he takes to be true ("No") so that he can consider all of the best opposing arguments before giving us *his* answer and the reasoning behind it. Some questions go through dozens of objections before getting to the main point. This strange (to us) format reflects how philosophers taught in the Middle Ages. Professors would stand in the classroom, or in the public square, state the disputed question of the day, collect any objections that the crowd or professor might think of, and then respond to the question with a theory, followed by answers to each of the objections just raised. (The professor's job was much harder back then.)

The overall structure and format of the *Summa* is as meaningful as the answers and arguments it contains, because it shows how Aquinas fundamentally thought about reality as a rationally structured, comprehensible thing. There were no questions too big or too small to ask or answer. Nothing was off limits for debate. And answers were there to be had.

On the question of what it means to live a good life, Aquinas became, unequivocally, a follower of Aristotle. He calls Aristotle "The Philosopher"—as though nobody else on earth deserved the name. (Take that, Plato!) Like Aristotle, Aquinas thinks our intellectual lives distinguish us from animals. The purpose or function of life is to use reason to acquire the virtues in the pursuit of flourishing.

He takes this Greek idea and runs with it. He wonders: Clearly we are capable of appreciating that there is more to life than mere happiness. Reason suggests to us that our ultimate goal lies in something beyond this life. Reason can even guide us to know things about God—it is just harder and much more incomplete work to do if, like Aristotle, you don't have the benefit of divine revelation, the Bible, tradition.

For Aquinas, faith is not—and can never be—incompatible with reason, though it might sometimes venture beyond what we can know just by our own philosophical smarts. Still, for Aquinas, faith is a different sort of knowledge, closely related to the virtue of love. Love is a deeply intellectual virtue, requiring attention and understanding. But it is a different way of understanding than understanding something impersonal and theoretical (like the Pythagorean theorem) or understanding how to do something practical (like how to buy and sell stock). Love is interpersonal understanding—it requires absorption as well.

For Aquinas, this is our fundamental relationship with God. He thinks we can know that God exists through rational argument. We can know that God is omnipotent, perfect, and the source of all truth. We can know that God has these *properties*, and that this is the kind of being that God is. But the important stuff—the stuff of faith—requires a deep understanding of the person of God that can only be acquired through prayer, contemplation, meditation, and worship.

That doesn't mean we shouldn't also philosophize about him.

A PROOF FOR THE EXISTENCE OF GOD

In the *Summa*, Aquinas actually makes five attempts at proving the existence of God (famously known among philosophers as "The Five Ways"). In class, we start the unit on Aquinas by hyping up the auditorium: we're about to *prove* the existence of God. A proof purports to be rationally compelling. As the philosopher Robert Nozick says, the best kind of argument is one with true premises so strong that, if you continue to disagree with their conclusion after seeing them, you *die*. The success or failure of these God arguments feels deeply significant compared with the more brain teaser–like logical arguments we also teach (e.g., "This sentence is false." Is that sentence true or false?).

The usefulness of Aquinas's proofs for modern readers varies. To understand his "Argument from Causation," for instance, you need to understand a very particular, ancient notion of what it is for one thing to "cause" another. But some of the arguments are more approachable. For instance, Aquinas's "Argument from Necessity," the third of the so-called Five Ways, appeals to relatively benign—if somewhat mind-bending—metaphysical premises.

In order to understand this argument, you need to know two things. First, the argument takes the form of what philosophers call a reductio ad absurdum. This is just the Latinized way of saying that the argument "reduces to absurdity" some assumption, by showing that taking that assumption to be true would lead to irrational results. Philosophers typically just shorten the move to "reductio," which makes it sound like a Harry Potter spell. We make these reductio arguments all the time in the course of everyday life. Meghan wants to prove to Paul that the coffee shop next door is closed. Paul is resisting. "Okay, well, assume it is open. Would they really be open but have all of the lights off, all of the chairs upside down on the tables, and nobody behind the counter?"

Weighing the mounting absurdity of his Open Starbucks hypothesis, Paul relents and admits it makes more sense to believe it is closed. Aquinas is going to use this kind of strategy, but the target is the hypothesis that there is no God.

The second thing that you need to know is that Aquinas isn't trying to give us a proof that delivers the full-blown God of Christianity (or Judaism or Islam), with all of the history and qualities and personality attributed to him in the scriptures. The argument doesn't say anything interesting about what did or didn't happen in Jerusalem two thousand years ago. It doesn't even entail that there is a loving god in the universe who has any particular concern for you. Aquinas realizes that this would be biting off more than he can chew.

Instead, he picks just one property that he thinks everyone would agree only God would have and attempts to prove that "a being with this property must exist." What's the property? In the Third Way it is the property of *necessarily existing*, and this is contrasted with the property of existing contingently. This gets us into a topic we've mostly dodged so far in this book: metaphysics, the branch of philosophy that deals with the most fundamental categories of reality.

Meghan exists contingently, and so does Paul. So does every human on the planet. To say this is simply to acknowledge that we all exist (we're real), but it is possible for us to fail to exist. How do we know? In our case it's simple: there was presumably a time before we were born when we didn't exist. And there will be a time (hopefully in the distant future) when we will die and then fail to exist. We are contingent beings, not necessary beings. But unlike us, if there is a God, he has always been there . . . somehow.

Enough with the warm-up. Ready? Let's do this.

Aquinas starts his argument by asking the atheist and agnostic to agree: if I can prove to you that a necessary being exists—a being who exists now, has always existed and always will, and who cannot fail to exist—then I will have proved that "God" exists, since a being with this property is one we all would agree should be called by the name "God." Let's set aside any skepticism about this assumption, just for the moment, and see how Aquinas attempts to deliver, step-by-step.

1. Assume that there is no necessary being.

This is what he hopes to reduce to absurdity.

2. If there's no necessary being, then all beings are contingent (like Paul and Meghan and all existing humans).

This just follows from the definitions of necessary and contingent beings. In a world without necessary beings, every being that actually exists must be contingent.

3. Assume that the past is infinite, that there was no time at which time itself began to exist.

This is getting a bit trippy, but stay with us.

4. Given an infinite amount of time, if all beings were merely contingent, then there would have been a point at which literally nothing existed.

Why is this true? Well, given an infinite amount of time, all possible configurations of beings will be realized. And one possible configuration is one in which all contingent beings simply fail to exist. So, if our assumptions so far are all true, then there would have been a point in the past where there was absolutely nothing that existed.

5. But if there had been a point at which absolutely nothing existed, then there would be nothing now.

Why? Because nothing comes from nothing. If there's ever a self-evident principle, this is perhaps it. In order for something to be caused, created, generated, or whatever, you've got to have something to cause, create, or generate it.

6. But this is absurd: there are clearly things that exist now.

We exist, the world exists, electrons exist—you get the point.

7. So we have to reject our initial assumption, that there is no necessary being. Our conclusion is that **there is at least one necessary being**.

Reductio!

8. And such a being, Aquinas claims, everyone agrees should be called "God."

What do you think? Whenever we finish this argument in class, the room descends into a hush while our students squint at each of the premises, letting them sink in. Most students, especially if they came in skeptical of the possibility of "proving God," feel like they've just seen a magic trick or heard the pitch of a snake oil salesman. Nobody dies. They point to various premises, and try to find a way out. Some of these are legitimate objections. How do we reconcile premise 5 with what cosmology tells us about the big bang? We now know from the theory of general relativity that time itself is a thing—so does premise 4 have the wrong concept of time? Our students are pretty smart and Aquinas promised this process would work with science!

We can scrutinize the individual premises, and this will require even more reasons. But we can also return to the overarching methodological question: What should we *do* with such arguments for God's existence?

It's hard for us to see a scenario in which an agnostic or an atheist walks through each of these premises, nodding in acknowledgment of the truth of each, and is ready to be baptized by the time they've reached the conclusion. And it's equally hard for us to imagine a world in which we present arguments for God's existence one by one, have them debunked by an atheist, and as a result scratch off attending Mass on Sundays from our calendars. Does this mean that we're all, basically, unable to be moved by rational appeals to evidence when it comes to matters of faith? Does it mean that such arguments are somehow fundamentally misguided?

We don't think so.

As Aristotelians, we—along with Saint Thomas Aquinas—think that reason is what sets us apart as humans, and that pursuing and contemplating the truth is our function in life. We're convinced that if you can prove a belief to be false, you should give that belief up. Refusing to do so, engaging in wishful thinking, is a recipe for frustration and unhappiness. Arguments for God's existence may not land the death blow to one side or the other, but they can play a crucial regulatory role. When they work, they reassure believers that their faith is not *irrational*. They also provide a way for the religious person to reasonably engage with peers of different religious outlooks, providing reasons that we believe we all deserve in our search for truth.

And if the philosophical arguments don't convert very many people, they certainly help to deepen and integrate the project of trying to join up God and the good life. This has certainly been Meghan's experience.

Finding God in 9/11
(Meghan's Apology)

I started college at the University of Virginia two weeks before the 9/11 terrorist attacks. September 11 was a framing event in my adult life, but in an unexpected way. I was an ambitious nineteen-year-old who had grown up in a largely irreligious family. We weren't card-carrying atheists—there are very few of them in the South and among the working class—more just a burdened family without much time or interest in organized religion.

College was my ticket to professional life and security. I'd loved debate in high school, loved logic, and had a personal style that my friends to this day describe as "aggressive and exhausting." So I planned to be a lawyer. I had long imagined myself living in a high-rise in New York, working somewhere like the World Trade Center. I watched the second plane hit the tower on live television in our dorm common room. It was surreal.

On the first anniversary of 9/11, I read a news story about parents who were working in the Trade Center on the day of the attacks, including details about some children who had lost both parents. Reading that story, I just couldn't get over the idea that people with my ideal life could show up to the office on an ordinary morning and then lose everything. Tied to that was a more recent, nagging worry that the seemingly ambitious goals I was setting for myself weren't the right ones—they weren't wrong, just kind of . . . shortsighted. And what exactly was the point of achieving my goals in a chaotic senseless world like this one?

The same day I read the news story (September 11, 2002) was when I first started down the path of religious conversion. I was feeling sad and philosophical. I called my mom at her office. We usually didn't talk on the phone except on weekends, and even then our conversations were usually limited to family gossip or dinner plans. But that day I unloaded on her: telling her how much I loved her and our family, and how short life is, and how we have to take time to care about the right things. She was pretty confused at this point (and she's at work, dealing with a line of complaining dental patients). "Sure, of course. Are you okay?" In the back of her mind she's wondering if I am experimenting with drugs. She recommends I give my dad a call. After a few "love yous!" I hung up and realized however much I loved my mom, her insight was not really what I was looking for.

Months earlier, down the street from my dorm, I'd noticed a Catholic church, St. Thomas Aquinas, run by a group of Dominicans. I'd been curious about religion in a general and intellectual way since arriving at college. I read books about different traditions. I had a kind of awkward, secret, mild jealousy of some of my classmates who were deeply involved in faith groups. And I had a vague idea of what going to a Catholic service would amount to—I'd been to some as a kid. All three of us kids were baptized as infants. It was an important family ritual.

I figured since it was the anniversary of 9/11, the pastor or whoever would give a big speech making sense of catastrophes like that event. The special skill of religious practice, as I saw it, was infusing daily life with meaningful context. Or at the very least religious people offered the rest of us an occasion to be sad and light candles in public spaces, performing outwardly in a community the care we couldn't find appropriate ways to show by ourselves.

So I looked up the afternoon Mass time and I went. And there were no speeches about 9/11. It was a totally ordinary Wednesday service. Me, a few old ladies, and the priest. A couple of readings, the ones that the Church buries in the middle of the week because they are boring. Communion. Many prayers and responses that I didn't know the words to. The whole event should have been embarrassing and awkward.

But it wasn't. Even though it wasn't at all what I expected, I felt an incredible sense of peace and belonging there. I started going back. Week after week I'd return on Wednesdays, hungry to reconnect with that sense of peace. After a month of this, a priest kindly suggested that if I liked Wednesdays, I'd love Sundays.

My third year of college, I took a course on theology offered by the parish and started the process of officially joining the Catholic Church.

I told my parents and friends that I was going to be confirmed about a month before Easter 2004. Most people in my life at that time thought it was weird and out of character. When they asked me why I was doing this, the best I could say was: it is somehow helping me see where I'm going. And now, of course, the story of this decision is part of many other stories in my life—my choice of where to work, my views about charities, my thinking about love and death.

It's never been easy. Some people talk about religious conversion like a switch flips for them—they are blind and now they see, lights on, full intensity. I graduated from Virginia and went on to study philosophy in graduate school. The vast majority of professional philosophers are atheists. I knew there were hard philosophical problems for rational belief in God (The problem of evil! Coming in chapter 8!). I also worried that becoming religious put the burden on me to explain to my peers and colleagues how evolution and cosmology worked with God in the picture. These all struck me as great questions, ones that my bachelor's degree and a single year of spiritual direction didn't remotely equip me to answer.

It took nearly a decade, some patient spiritual mentors, and most of graduate school to get comfortable being open about the ways my faith life influences the philosophical questions I ask. I wish I had more people in my life back when I was nineteen who could have given me the "Socrates talk"—that it is okay to not have all of the answers right away as long as you are willing to hold fast to the questions. As a Christian, I gravitate to the stories of the disciples, spending time right in the presence of God, but most of the time bumbling through their lives, trying to make sense of what they are seeing and hearing. They always seem to be jumping out of boats, staring up at the sky like children, scratching their heads about why God would command them to feed the poor in one breath but in the next yell at them for trying to sell the perfume. I feel like we often undersell the importance of philosophy for helping us hold the God questions in our hearts.

I still get the "Why" question all the time. Why Catholicism, with its long and complicated history? And patriarchy? And the bread that's really a body and bodies that will die and then come back? From the outside, my kind of conversion seems abrupt, psychologically motivated, and weirdly specific. How do you get from a terrorist attack in a far-off city to a church pew in Charlottesville? The dots don't connect. This itself has been a major part of my philosophical life in the past fifteen years—trying to make sense of how God could fit with everything else I am learning. But seen from this angle, the mysteries aren't a threat to religion and the good life—figuring them out is the next phase of it.

Some of us move in a different direction, having a critical meaning-making experience from *leaving* a religion we were brought up in. Sometimes it's the seemingly small events in our lives that come to take on more and more meaning. Just as philosophy can help us set better goals, it can also help us get a better sense of the meaning of our lives right now, which pieces are missing, and how new developments might change an unfolding story. Aquinas's point is that as the story comes into fuller philosophical view, we are inevitably going to get interested in these spiritual and existential questions.

Toward the end of his own life, Aquinas reportedly started to have mystical experiences while celebrating Mass. As often happens around such eccentric and singular figures, stories started circulating within the monasteries he visited of his supernatural gifts, and of reported visions and visitations. At the time, he was trying to finish the third massive part of his *Summa*, which was a philosophical account of how we come to have a relationship with God. Thomas had started to write about grace and the sacraments, the way we can know God only partially here on earth, "as through a glass, darkly," to quote Saint Paul. As he began to write about the more personal aspects of this relationship, Aquinas stopped working. Reason had allowed him to sketch what only his faith could allow him to embrace. For the most formidable philosopher in the Christian tradition—the one who literally spent his life wedding doctrine to the theories of Aristotle—arguments were just his jumping-off point.

His spiritual director claims to have heard him say that he could not continue to write because he'd experienced a taste of union with God, and, compared to that, "Everything that I have written seems like straw. . . ."

Soulcraft: Arguing about God

Religion is, infamously, one of those topics that we're taught to steer clear of in polite company. For this exercise, we want you to channel Socrates and subvert this conventional wisdom.

To start, find someone who is willing to go into that philosophical cave with you. Maybe also remind yourself of the big goal of the dialogue—getting closer to understanding together.

Next, find a religious claim you disagree about. There should also be some personal stakes for each of you, so make sure it's something that, if true, would somehow change the way you live. The big ones are "God exists" or "life ends at death." There are more specific ones as well: "We are better off not joining churches" or "There must be an answer for why <insert specific tragic event> occurred."

Instead of disagreeing about the claim directly, take five minutes each to sketch out some of the reasons you have for believing it. These might be philosophical arguments like the ones we considered in this chapter, but they don't have to be. You might believe that God exists because of the way you experience the world, or because you think you can feel his presence in quiet moments. You might think organized religions developed on false claims because of the various ways in which you've seen corrupt organizations exploit their members.

Now, try out a Socratic dialogue. Have one person serve as interviewer, asking about the reasons you have for thinking the way that you do about the particular issue. You're looking for a deeper claim than the initial one you disagreed about that helps explain the crux of your disagreement. This should be a claim that serves as a hinge for the broader belief; if you could be persuaded that it was false, you'd change your mind.

When you've identified the "crux" belief, go back and forth, sharing reasons why you think this claim is true or false. Help each other identify information that might assist you in settling whether or not it's true. You may find your mind is changed by this method, but that's not the point. The point is to make sure you're understanding—as best you can—the deeper disagreement underlying the disagreement at the surface level. Then you might take the next step of considering what it would take to change the underlying structure of your own beliefs or the beliefs of those who disagree.

Here's an example of an exchange that brings out the rhythm of this kind of dialogue:

PAUL: Being in a religion requires having certain *beliefs.* For example, being a Christian means going to church, praying, and such but also being willing to say you believe that God exists. That Jesus rose from the dead.

MEGHAN: Why do you think that religion has to come with belief requirements, especially on such hard and strange questions?

PAUL: Because religions are supposed to tell the truth about the most important good life questions, and religions can't do that if members are divided about the most basic claims of the faith.

MEGHAN: But what about disagreements that help members seek the truth together? If a religion outlaws dissent, they'd make this goal much harder to achieve.

PAUL: Fair enough. So how about I make a modest claim: Religions have got to have some core, essential beliefs that can't change. These beliefs should be fixed. If you are a believer in the pews, you need to trust they are true.

MEGHAN: If I could show you an example from your own religious tradition in which a belief that was thought to be a "core belief" came to be reinterpreted later, and that we think now more truthfully represents reality, would you change your mind about this?

PAUL: Probably. I don't know what such an example would look like. I tend to think my faith tradition has maintained its core beliefs throughout history without any genuine change or innovation. But if you could show me an example of that, I think I would change my mind.

And there we go—we've reached the crux of the matter!

7.

Take a Leap of Faith

> Believe truth! Shun error!—these, we see, are two materially different laws; and by choosing between them we may end by coloring differently our whole intellectual life.
>
> —William James, "The Will to Believe"

A CRISIS OF BELIEF

William James had just finished medical school when, in the early months of 1870, he returned to his parents' home on the verge of "moral collapse." According to a diary he kept at the time, James's despair—which was deep and paralyzing—was at least partly the result of his medical training. He had been taught to think of the human being as a machine; environmental, genetic, and social inputs all resulted in fairly predictable physical and behavioral outputs. The doctor's role in all this was to keep the human machine fine-tuned and running smoothly.

This mechanistic view left no room for free will. He could not see how anything *he* did could matter—or even how a machine could "do" anything at all. Unsure if he had any capacity to plan and choose, James just couldn't see any path to a good life.

His thoughts ran in tight circles: If his life was determined right down to the exact thoughts he was having, then he was unfree, a victim of his circumstances and a hostage to fate. How could anything he do matter if he had no choice over it?

James struggled with depression for much of his adult life, but this episode was particularly acute and fed by the philosophical worries. He spent hours of each day in this torturous mental cycle. He "about touched bottom" and considered suicide as a way out of the loop. In the language of contemporary psychology, James completely lost his internal locus of control, and he experienced the loss as a mind-numbing moral dread.

But then, one day, the storm broke. James had an epiphany:

I'm either free or I'm not, James thought. *If I'm not and I believe that I am, who cares? I'm deceived, but I'm not miserable. And if I am free, and I believe it, then, and only then, can I act freely in the world.* As his thought process gained momentum, James had another realization. Believing in his freedom could, itself, be a free act. To allow himself faith in his freedom was the only hope he had to be free.

In his diary, he abandoned the topics of suicide and despair, and resolved, "For the remainder of this year, I will . . . voluntarily cultivate the feeling of moral freedom, by reading books favorable to it, as well as by acting. . . . Now I will go a step further with my will, not only act with it, but believe as well; believe in my individual reality and creative power."

Even if James's thought process is a bit abstract, the results for his life were anything but. He threw himself into psychology, in many ways inventing the scientific discipline as we now know it during his thirty-five-year career at Harvard. He cofounded a major philosophical movement—American pragmatism. His work inspired John Dewey to lead a major reform in American education. It shaped the thinking of the Supreme Court. And in his downtime, James spent much of the next few decades developing and expanding his account of how our beliefs connect up to our hopes, our choices, and our freedom.

Perhaps surprisingly for someone who's come to be known as "the father of modern psychology," James was one of the nineteenth century's fiercest defenders of the rationality of religious faith. He knew that we live in an uncertain world, and that we're sometimes short on good evidence for the big philosophical questions. Am I really responsible for anything I do? Is there a God I could know? At the same time, he knew that these are questions many of us find inescapable at certain junctures of our lives. In the urgency of the hospital waiting room or even just in the quiet of our beds at night—we find we need an answer.

You might be tempted to not let your mind wander into these topics without a sense of where you'll end up. Skepticism is the view that you ought to doubt (or at least be indifferent toward) any hypothesis that you don't have decisive evidence for. James viewed skepticism on these major existential questions as a recipe for despair because, in these and a number of more mundane cases, we don't always have the luxury of simply holding back and waiting for more evidence.

OUT OF THE WOODS

When Amanda Eller set off for a hike in Maui's Makawao Forest Reserve on the morning of May 8, 2019, she didn't even take her cell phone or her water bottle. She didn't intend to be gone long enough to need them. On her way back to her car, however, Eller became disoriented and started walking in exactly the wrong direction. Instead of returning to her car in time for lunch, Eller walked all afternoon and into the evening, moving farther and farther into the massive two-thousand-acre Hawaiian forest. Here's where things get nightmarish—she wandered the reserve for days that turned into weeks, desperately trying to find her way out of the wilderness. She fell from a twenty-foot cliff. Then she lost her shoes in a flash flood. She survived on berries, unidentifiable plants, and whatever moths happened to land on her. Finally, against all odds, she was rescued. Seventeen days after she went missing, some volunteers flew a helicopter five and a half miles beyond the central search area on a whim, and came upon Eller, desperate and emaciated.

In interviews she's given since her incredible misadventure, Eller describes her mind-set, one that is familiar from reports of people who have survived such extreme situations: "I was really starting to doubt if I could survive. . . . I wanted to give up. . . . But the only option I had was life or death."

Eller could have taken an objective look at her situation, thought seriously about her likelihood of survival, and realistically calculated that she didn't have much chance. She could have fit her beliefs about survival to her evidence. But that's not what she did. She chose instead to believe, against the odds, that she'd survive if she just kept moving. And, against the odds, she did.

We see how such a belief was crucial for Eller's survival, so clearly important to her good life. And, as William James suggests, this appears to be the sort of case where waiting for more evidence just wasn't an option. But how can we reconcile this with the fact that rationality requires concern for the truth?

Here's how James thinks about predicaments like the one Amanda Eller found herself in: "In such a case (and it belongs to an enormous class), the part of wisdom as well as of courage is to *believe what is in the line of your needs*, for only by such belief is the need fulfilled. . . . You make one or the other of two possible universes true by your trust or mistrust—both universes having been only *maybes*, in this particular, before you contributed your act."

Eller's is an extreme case, but James thought that we face a number of decisions over the course of our lives where we've got to decide whether or not to have courage in what we can't know for sure and take a leap.

Another example he gives, and one that tends to hit pretty close to home for our students, is the confidence-inspiring role such leaps of faith play in nascent romances or friendships. Does she love me? Will people on this campus think I'm cool? It's a weird feedback loop: the confidence inspired by faith in yourself changes you in a way that makes the goal more attainable, and as a result, your belief is more likely to be true.

But we can surely go too far. Believing that you'll one day be president might be delusional, and refusing to acknowledge that she really *doesn't* love you—despite all incoming evidence—can turn romantic confidence to creepiness or worse. One key question we have to ask ourselves before we take a leap of faith is: Where's the line? And what distinguishes cases in which we're being ambitious from those in which we're being just downright irresponsible?

THE DARK SIDE OF "WILLING TO BELIEVE"

Readers of bestselling books on how to succeed in business start to recognize patterns in the advice that's offered as winning strategy: learn to fail, take big risks, disrupt "commonsense" principles, and—above all—believe in yourself and your product. Business gurus advise, "You've got to fake it till you make it." Such catchphrases are often illustrated with inspiring stories of wildly ambitious moon shots that ended up paying off, purportedly meant to illustrate the value of such advice. For example, how Microsoft poured millions of marketing dollars into the Xbox, a brand-new gaming console that no one had ever heard of, and captured a huge portion of the market. Or consider any of the prediction-defying successes catalyzed by Steve Jobs, Apple's innovative late CEO, who once said: "You can't connect the dots looking forward; you can only connect them looking backwards. So you have to trust that the dots will somehow connect in your future."

That's great advice if the iPhone is a hit. But there's a dark side to such a strategy. Consider the examples of Billy McFarland and Elizabeth Holmes.

McFarland was a wealthy kid from the suburbs of New Jersey who founded his own credit card company after dropping out of the college his elite private school had prepared him for. Elizabeth Holmes dropped out of Stanford to found the blood testing company Theranos, which promised to use microfluidic technology to revolutionize the way blood was drawn and tested. In addition to their lofty visions and ambitions, Holmes and McFarland shared something else that every successful entrepreneur since Steve Jobs has worked to cultivate: a seemingly impenetrable confidence in their ideas, their leadership, and their business goals. But their stories are cautionary tales.

McFarland teamed up with the rapper Ja Rule to plan a luxury music event, Fyre Festival, meant to promote his credit card company. Neither McFarland nor Ja Rule had ever planned such a production, but McFarland promised that it would be better than Burning Man, the gold standard for bohemian, culture-defining creative festivals. The advertisements should have been the first warning. They featured models frolicking with wild pigs on what was advertised as "Pablo Escobar's private island." Unfortunately, especially for those who shelled out between one thousand and one hundred thousand dollars for tickets to the event, it was too good to be true.

The months leading up to the festival were—to use a technical term—a total shitshow. McFarland quickly lost access to the private island where he initially (impossibly) planned to hold the festival, and it was eventually decided that the festival would be held on what looks like a construction site or a water treatment plant jutting off what is most definitely *not* a private island. The luxurious accommodations—private cabanas and oceanfront mansions—were reduced, in the end, to a field full of leftover emergency hurricane tents with soggy carpets and wet mattresses. The "private planes" meant to ferry concertgoers to the island ended up being a used 737 the organizers rented, slapping their logo on it at the last minute.

One of the most incredible things about the case is that none of the organizers, almost up until the end, had any idea whether or not McFarland was going to pull the whole thing off. In a documentary that captures the months leading up to the catastrophe, veterans of actual culture-defining music festivals and longtime colleagues describe Billy as having an almost godlike power. They'd seen him perform financial miracles for investors, acquiring millions of dollars in funding at a moment's notice, and saving his company from the brink of ruin time and again. It's easy to see, too, how they could have been so deceived. In the documentary, McFarland is handsome and enigmatic. He's always incredibly relaxed, with a half smile. His furrowed brow suggests that he's always thinking ten times faster than anyone around him.

Elizabeth Holmes's story follows a similar trajectory. After dropping out of Stanford to start her blood-testing company, Holmes started to peddle a machine called "the Edison" that she claimed could perform many major blood tests, and with just a single drop of blood. In a matter of just a few years Theranos had five hundred employees and was worth about nine billion dollars. The company struck a deal to offer blood tests on its devices in forty Walgreens locations, with plans to scale up to more than eight thousand. The only problem was that Holmes's revolutionary technology did not work. Theranos was never able to develop viable machines to perform the new blood tests.

John Carreyrou, a reporter for *The Wall Street Journal*, broke the Theranos story in 2015, and he came to our campus in 2019 to discuss the ethics of the case with Notre Dame students. During his visit, we asked him: Was there a leap-of-faith moment for Holmes? Carreyrou pointed to the days leading up to the September 2013 Walgreens launch. When the head of Holmes's lab stopped into her office then, he found her drained of her usual confidence. Shortly after the meeting, Holmes was back to her confident self, at least publicly. On September 9, the day of the launch, Holmes claimed in *The Wall Street Journal* that her device could "'run any combination of [blood] tests, including sets of follow-on tests' at once, very quickly, all from a single small blood sample." Holmes's leap would ultimately land her on trial for fraud.

How do we distinguish the stories of Theranos and the Fyre Festival from those of Xbox or Apple? In retrospect, of course, the answer seems obvious. We sort the good cases from the bad cases based on their consequences. Did the project get off the ground? Did it make investors rich? Or was all the investment money lost? But we know the dangers of just focusing on the consequences. Success or failure in business is as much a matter of skill as luck. We need to consider how virtue ethicists manage risk.

TAKING RESPONSIBILITY FOR YOUR BELIEFS

In 1896, the Brown and Yale undergraduate philosophy clubs invited William James to give a presentation. The eminent professor not only agreed to take the train down from Cambridge to Providence to address the students, he wrote an original paper for them: a short talk that would go on to become one of the most important papers in the philosophy of religion. He called it "The Will to Believe." James's overarching aim was to argue that, at least for some of us, cultivating religious belief, in all of its complexity, with all of its risk, can be a crucial part of the good life.

James's project faced a serious challenge: distinguishing virtuous leaps from reckless, fraudulent, lucky, or irrational ones. He'd been publicly debating this issue with a prominent British atheist named William Clifford. Clifford was basically the Richard Dawkins of the mid-nineteenth century, a scientist who made important advances in geometric algebra and an outspoken moralist. Today, Clifford is most remembered for arguing that we should be just as careful with our religious beliefs as we would be with any other beliefs. He defended his "anti-leap" stance with an example.

A shipowner is debating whether to send an old ship packed full of emigrants across the ocean. Some advisers suggest that the ship isn't seaworthy; it won't make it. But the shipowner chooses instead to have faith in the old vessel, which had weathered many storms in the past. As the ship set sail, "he watched her departure with a light heart, and benevolent wishes for the success of the exiles in their strange new home that was to be; and he got his insurance-money when she went down in mid-ocean and told no tales."

The shipowner is disastrously wrong to have faith in the vessel rather than to ensure its seaworthiness. His hope certainly does not make the situation better for the men and women aboard. The shipowner is responsible for his confidence in his ship, and that responsibility requires investigating the truth about its safety. Clifford draws a stark moral from the story: "It is wrong always, everywhere, and for anyone, to believe anything upon insufficient evidence."

Responding to Clifford's challenge, William James offers us three criteria we can use to help us distinguish responsible from irresponsible leaps of faith. You can and sometimes should take a leap of faith only when you face a choice in beliefs that is "forced," "momentous," and "live." James's three conditions are meant to help you realize when you are at the edge of a good life cliff. Each of these conditions has implications for how we conduct our religious lives, as well as our business and personal lives. And James thought once we properly understand what a leap of faith is, we'll realize that we are navigating them all the time.

First, in order for a leap of faith to be rational, it must be "forced" upon us by some external circumstances. Suppose someone asks you if you'd like to go on a trip to Hawaii tomorrow or stay home. Refusing to choose either option will, eventually, have the same consequences as selecting the option to "stay home." In either case, you'll never leave the house. A choice is forced if refusing to make a decision results in basically the same scenario as choosing one of the options.

We sometimes face the same forced choices with respect to our beliefs. Suppose you must decide whether to believe that your love interest genuinely loves you back. You could go ahead and believe the love is mutual, or you could hold back and wait for more evidence. Wait long enough to decide what to believe in this case, and it will be a self-fulfilling prophecy—the relationship will go nowhere. Intimate beliefs require trust, and at a certain point in most relationships we face a forced leap. And if your date rejects you? You face the double loss of a mistaken belief and a broken heart. The risks are real.

James also thinks more internal needs can force a leap, and in this he takes a sharp departure from the more skeptical philosophers. René Descartes, for instance, would insist that ultimately the only thing we should consider in forming a belief is our confidence that the belief is true. In contrast, James allows our desires, hopes, and passions to play a role alongside the evidence. For James, the skeptics use belief-forming policies that are no less influenced by emotions than his own. It's just that Clifford and Descartes are emotionally attached to having the evidence and fearful of making mistakes, whereas James is hopeful and optimistic about his ability to find truth through leaps of faith. James thinks the skeptics owe us an argument for why intellectual risk aversion leads to a better life.

Second, for the leap of faith to be justified, James thinks the options you're facing must be "momentous." The relevant choice over what to believe should have important consequences for your life. It might have tremendous consequences whether you live the rest of your life in a religious tradition or whether you put your heart out there for a potential romantic partner. It isn't particularly momentous whether you decide to believe that there are an even number of stars in the Milky Way galaxy. Your answer to this question does not connect back to any life you might live. For James, the question of whether God exists is momentous. To require someone to withhold belief in God could entail vast revisions to how they approach every aspect of their life. To force someone to adopt a religious outlook that they don't identify with would, likewise, he thinks, be deadening.

To illustrate James's third condition—the importance of options being "live"—we'll take a brief detour into another one of the most famous thought experiments in the philosophy of religion.

YOU BET YOUR LIFE

To see what is at stake in considering whether we should take a "leap of faith" into religious belief, it helps to consider a famous argument put forward by Blaise Pascal.

Pascal was a French Enlightenment mathematician and philosopher who took religious belief very seriously and frequently found himself involved with intense Catholic subcommunities in seventeenth-century France. In a notebook in which he detailed his thoughts and musings, Pascal sketched out an argument that it's in everyone's best interest to believe in God, even if the evidence for God's existence isn't overwhelmingly strong. He reasoned about it in cost-benefit terms.

If God exists, then there are two possibilities:

1. You believe in God and are eternally rewarded.
2. You don't believe in God and are eternally damned.

If God doesn't exist, then the only cost to believing in God is that you maybe lose your Sunday mornings going to church when you could otherwise have been pursuing some hobby or sleeping in. And if God doesn't exist and you don't believe in him, you don't gain all that much either—you can't even enjoy the smug satisfaction of knowing you were right, since there won't be an afterlife. Because the stakes are so high, Pascal urges his reader to bet on God: "If you gain, you gain all; if you lose, you lose nothing. Wager, then, without hesitation, that He is."

For Pascal, religious belief is *forced* and *momentous*: refusing to believe has the same consequences as actively disbelieving, and the entry ticket to the afterlife is what's on the line. Unlike Pascal, James isn't aiming to be pragmatic in the face of eternal damnation; he thinks the momentousness of religious belief is realized in this life. Hold back and you will miss out on a potentially supportive and meaningful religious community, you'll forfeit your access to a moral code that's guided and inspired millions throughout history, and you'll forgo the chance to cultivate any understanding of the divine.

James didn't think we could follow Pascal's cold arithmetic into religious life. Imagine someone does Pascal's calculation and realizes that it is in their self-interest to start worshipping God. Imagine them showing up at a Catholic church, asking to join, not really having a clue about the teachings of the religion or any particular connection with the divine. James thinks such a person would be a long way from having anything we'd recognize as "faith." Faith requires an authentic emotional connection. Against Pascal, he writes: "A faith in masses and holy water adopted willfully after such a mechanical calculation would lack the inner soul of faith's reality. . . . The option offered to the will by Pascal is not a living option." So James distinguishes his approach from Pascal's by adding the third condition that he thinks Pascal's argument fails to recognize: a virtue ethics condition.

For James, a belief we might leap to must be a "live" option for the person considering it. It must be authentic: something they could envision living out in their everyday life. A claim might be dead because there is just no reason to believe it—converting to flat earthism is a dead option for Paul because he just has no justification for the view. Other claims might be live for some people and might even have some evidence behind them but fail to be live for you, because there is no way (at least currently) you could find yourself genuinely adopting the belief. For instance, Meghan might be able to see a way forward for her life as a Catholic or a Lutheran or a Methodist philosopher. She might be able to imagine her life continuing as a staunch atheist. But it may not be a live option for her to carry on as a Buddhist—she has no personal connection with Buddhism, no awareness of its traditions, and no self-image where Buddhism could play a key part. Our colleague Ted is in a similar situation, except for Ted, it is Christian philosophy that is not a live option. Meghan or Ted could, with some effort, try to make new options for belief live. But James warns us against leaping into options that aren't sufficiently authentic possibilities for us.

So how do we apply these conditions to figure out whether we ought to take a leap of faith in our own lives? As James would put it, if belief in God's existence is a live option for you—then given the fact that it's seemingly forced and momentous for everyone—you'd be rational in taking the leap into religious faith.

What about more earthly leaps? As the cases of Billy McFarland and Elizabeth Holmes illustrate, we often treat questions as forced and momentous when, in fact, they are not. In business, as in life, we've got to take risks in order to accomplish anything. We set deadlines to generate a little creative pressure, or we make promises—to ourselves, our bosses, our editors, or our investors—that we can achieve something that's still just an idea or a goal. Inevitably, such attempts often end in failure, and we know this. But we also know that if we don't believe in ourselves, or in the project we're undertaking, our chance of success drops to zero. So we take calculated risks: we commit to building a prototype of a blood testing device, and we let our confidence run out ahead of the facts.

Problems arise, however, when we let that confidence run out too far ahead, or when our motivations don't actually include seeking the truth. Holmes's life illustrates an important danger that we open ourselves up to when we aren't willing to face the truth about whether our faith is genuinely forced and momentous. If we're not carefully guided by a desire for the truth and an understanding of our own capacities, we can make such leaps where we really shouldn't. We can convince ourselves that we can jump over canyons, and not just crevasses.

At this point, we've got to consider a complication. James and Pascal treat belief like a verb—believing is something that we do. It is part of our life that we have control over. But sometimes we can't just decide to believe, even if we desperately want to, and even if we think the stakes are momentous and the decision is forced. Consider the husband or wife who fears their marriage to be doomed, but desperately wants it to continue.

They realize that their hope will only be vindicated if they can somehow find a little faith in their partner and the relationship, and yet . . . despite their desires, despite their recognition of what's at stake, belief just will not come. Sometimes faith is impossible to conjure or maintain, and we just feel ourselves floating further and further into the depths of uncertainty without knowing why. Does James, or anyone, have advice for us if this is the position we find ourselves in?

The Seminary
(Paul's Apology)

I spent three years in the seminary, discerning whether or not I should be a Catholic priest. During this time, I went on a lot of retreats, many of them weeklong silent retreats in beautiful locations. One of them was at St. Mary of the Lake Seminary in Mundelein, Illinois. The semi-secluded campus of this seminary was absolutely stunning. We woke up on the first day to a perfect layer of crisp white snow under fierce blue skies.

I'd entered the seminary in 2008, well into the clerical sex abuse crises, and—like everyone else—I'd assumed that things had been pretty much cleared up; that offenders had been dealt with and that the structural changes that the U.S. bishops (among others) were touting would help us avoid the kinds of rampant abuses and cover-ups that have been coming to light since the 1960s. All the priests and bishops I'd come into contact with had assured me that abuse, while tragic, was a problem of the past. And I believed them.

But, during my time in the seminary, this confidence was slowly worn away. I was gradually exposed to a culture of secrecy and strict authority. We were encouraged to obey our "superiors"—which in-

cluded not just pastors and priest formators but also other college-aged men like ourselves who'd been given positions of leadership—even when their instructions and advice were deeply confusing or worse. Questions—about particular directives, programming, or the way things were run—were treated like dissent, and inquisitive seminarians were assumed to be disloyal.

I couldn't bring myself to believe the reasoning behind what we were being taught about human sexuality and the moral life. All sexual indiscretion—like consensual violations of the discipline of celibacy and the sexual abuse of minors—was lumped into a single category and discussed exclusively in spiritualistic terms. We were told that there were particular demons whose job it was to tempt men into sexual sin. It was suggested that priests who abused children just hadn't had the spiritual wherewithal to resist such demonic influences. That it really was as simple as that.

The approach disturbed me deeply. As a Catholic, I obviously believed—and still believe—in spiritual realities. But the overly spiritualized approach to one of the Church's deepest, most difficult systemic problems left me unsure whether the appropriate steps had been taken to address a crisis with clear criminal, organizational, psychological, and sociological dimensions. Worse, I saw the ways in which the hyper-spiritualization of sexuality could lead seminarians and priests down exactly the wrong paths. How overemphasizing a problem's spiritual dimension could mask its more human elements, and how this could give cover to predators and bureaucrats alike.

At Mundelein, I had frank conversations about my concerns with the priests leading the retreat. They heard me out, nodding along, and I felt—for the first time in a long time—that I might be getting through.

But then, to my horror, they offered their diagnosis: Now I *was being tempted by the evil one, by the "spirit against Christ," to feed these doubts, and the answer was to engage in "spiritual warfare"; to ask for God's help in exorcising such thoughts. It was recommended that I pray for the strength to better practice the priestly virtue of obedience.*

My experiences in the seminary shook the very foundation of my faith. I left the seminary soon after I returned from that retreat, and found myself barely motivated to keep attending Mass. Although I knew that my experiences didn't directly have anything to do with the bigger questions of faith—like whether God exists, or whether the sacraments were vehicles of supernatural grace—I found, with a mixture of sadness and apathy, that I started to drift away from the Catholicism that had been my primary source of meaning over the course of my entire life. I've read and heard many stories about people who have lost faith in their churches or similar social institutions. Others who experienced this deep and abiding sadness share a sense that something they wish would remain fixed is dissolving or fading away.

Still, for me, my faith was, and is, more than just the set of beliefs that make up its core, or a collection of abstract principles. For me, faith is alive and embodied—as much a verb as a noun.

If we take James's forced, momentous, and live picture of faith seriously, there are reasons why we might find ourselves in a situation where we want to take a leap of faith but philosophically cannot.

In one case, the hypothesis itself is dying. Perhaps the evidence has just been accumulating, and you've realized that you can't continue to cling to the possibility of its truth. In such cases, clearly, the virtuous thing to do, the thing lovers of the truth will do, is to let it die. Perhaps this will require a period of acceptance, and even mourning, but neither James, nor any philosopher, would ever encourage anyone to put a hypothesis on life support if its implausibility has become clear. Leaps of faith shouldn't conflict with a virtuous love of the truth. That's how you end up crashing . . . or in federal court on fraud charges.

In another case, though—and this is the kind of case Paul found himself in during his crisis of faith—the hypothesis isn't dying due to an accumulation of counterevidence. Instead, there are obstacles to faith that may or may not have anything to do with the plausibility of the hypothesis. In such cases, there's still a great deal we can do to put ourselves in the right position with respect to the truth.

We might focus much harder on our evidence, and ask how we could improve our chances of figuring out the truth. Perhaps, instead of mulling over the same few pieces of evidence again and again, or returning to the same books or arguments we've always looked to, it's time to open up a more active investigation; to seek out inspiration in the experiences of those who may or may not agree with us; to explore what other belief systems are out there that might provide a better position with respect to the truth.

We might also give serious introspection a shot. Try to determine your motivations, and see whether they are truth oriented. Do you want to believe just because that's the more comfortable scenario? Or do you really think there's something to this hypothesis that you think is live, forced, and momentous? In the course of such introspection, of course, you might uncover areas of intellectual growth and identify particular habits you'd like to cultivate. All of this, obviously, is to the good.

Finally, you might allow practice to inform your life as you continue your investigation. Live "as if" your hypothesis is true for a few months. Ask yourself how you'd live differently if it were false. Sometimes, the way we interact with the world is the key to accessing the evidence we need to see the truth. To take two of James's most famous examples: you won't be able to exercise your free will in the world unless you believe you're free; you won't know whether people enjoy your company unless you just assume, for the time being, that they do.

A couple years after leaving the seminary, I found myself in a position to take stock. I'd been attending Mass purely out of habit, but I wanted to make a decision. Was I going to take the leap back into full-fledged religious belief, or was I going to quietly back away?

I thought long and hard. I connected with others who had also navigated crises of faith. I explored, attending any religious services to which I could find a plausible connection and participating to the extent that it was appropriate. I also talked to those with no stake in the matter at all—friends and fellow graduate students with all manner of religious backgrounds whom I respected intellectually a great deal. I asked myself if pride and arrogance could be getting in the way of my thinking on religious questions.

My road back to faith involved many small leaps and a couple of big ones. For one thing, I surrounded myself with wise and honest Catholics who saw corruption in the Church as a cancer to be rooted out. I also realized that my desire to work to fix the problem of priestly abuse was itself a sign that I wanted to remain in the Catholic community. I saw the abuse and its cover-up as a perversion of something good, something that could be, and needed to be, resolved. And I realized that I could more authentically work to address the problem if I remained a part of the Church; if I worked on it from the inside.

One of the bigger leaps involved my decision to come to Notre Dame to study for my PhD. I visited during the week leading up to Easter, which, for Catholics, is the most important liturgical week of the year. There are church services every day of that week, and I attended several of them in Notre Dame's ornate basilica. I saw, in the subjects of each of these services, a reflection of my own faith journey. I knew, during that week of services, that I could live my faith once again by taking a leap that was both geographical and metaphorical—moving to South Bend and continuing my search for the truth there.

William James's approach to faith was novel and important, and it may have literally saved his life. In an essay entitled "Is Life Worth Living?" James quotes at length from his contemporary James Fitzjames Stephen on why faith is so necessary to those who live in an uncertain world like ours:

> In all important transactions of life we have to take a leap in the dark. . . . If we decide to leave the riddles unanswered, that is a choice; if we waver in our answer, that, too, is a choice. . . . We stand on a mountain pass in the midst of whirling snow and blinding mist, through which we get glimpses now and then of paths which may be deceptive. If we stand still we shall be frozen to death. If we take the wrong road we shall be dashed to pieces. We do not certainly know whether there is any right one. What must we do? "Be strong and of a good courage." . . . If death ends all, we cannot meet death better.

Soulcraft: Practice Leaps

Each semester we challenge our students to put William James's views on religion and faith to the test. Along with peer leaders, our students are encouraged to set aside fifty minutes to test out some religious hypothesis that's live for them. In groups of about fifteen, these students design a "Religious Experience," picking a location on campus that has some meaning for a religious tradition and engaging in an appropriate ritual or practice meant to bring that religious tradition to life. The students themselves come from a variety of backgrounds. So the first task is to decide as a group how they might find a shared experiment. We also encourage them to research how the particular religious tradition prefers to engage with explorers.

The form these experiences take varies greatly. There are always a good number of groups who choose to sit in silent meditation in Notre Dame's basilica, pondering the religious art that covers the walls and windows, and perhaps allowing their contemplation to be guided by whatever choir happens to be practicing at the time. But there are others who take a walk around Notre Dame's two lakes and read naturalistic or transcendentalist poems. After these experiences, students discuss what stood out to them and turn in short reflection papers based on the exercise. We're always pleased by how much students value the simple act of dipping their toes into a spiritual tradition, discussing it seriously with others for whom it is a living tradition, and reflecting on the experience.

So here's what we suggest if you want to explore some live options: arrange your own test leap. Find a ritual, practice, way of life, or spiritual tradition that's "live," "forced," and "momentous." The "live" question requires a bit of ambition and curiosity; find one that you could see yourself maybe incorporating into your life. Then put yourself in a position to actively participate in it. Ideally, you'll have some sort of guide, a friend or family member who knows that tradition well, who can walk you through the experience and help you debrief afterward. To complete this exercise like a true Jamesian, turn off your inner skeptic for the duration of the experience, allow yourself to really enter into it, and then reflect on what you found after the fact. At some point, of course, you'll want to turn that skeptic back on and ask what evidence you have—or what evidence you acquired—for thinking that the particular practice or exercise is connected up in the right sort of way with the truth. But to complete this activity in the spirit of William James, it's important not to let the calculating, evidence-processing part of you take over. It's important to realize that this part of your nature belongs to a bigger belief-processing system, and that the other part—the "passional nature"—is a crucial component in making sure that we don't miss the opportunity to acquire big, important truths.

Whatever happens, your time won't be wasted: discovering that a religious option isn't live for you, or that evidence suggests that taking the leap isn't something that's being forced on you, is itself valuable good life data.

8.

Struggle with Suffering

> The weight of this sad time we must obey,
> Speak what we feel, not what we ought to say.
>
> —William Shakespeare, *King Lear*

MADISON'S STORY

The summer after first grade, Madison spent her days like any other kid in her suburban Ohio neighborhood, running free outdoors, scraping her knees and bumping her elbows. She was an active kid, full of energy and enthusiasm, so when she came home one day with a particularly large bump, her mother's first reaction was mild curiosity. Had she tripped while running around with her friends? No. Did she fall off the trampoline? Madison said that she had not. Her mother's curiosity turned to concern. They called the pediatrician. Within the week they were able to get into the Cleveland Clinic, and a short while later the clinic called with the results. It was her parents' greatest fear: a fast-growing cancerous tumor. They consulted with Massachusetts General and Texas Children's Hospitals, both of which confirmed the diagnosis.

Though devastated, her parents put on a brave face. Madison understood that the situation was serious, but her parents never used the words "cancer" or "tumor." All she knew at the time was that she had a "bad bump," and that it needed to be removed before she could get back to running and playing with the neighborhood kids.

Her surgery took four hours longer than anticipated. When her parents were escorted into a special consultation room, her mom braced herself for the impact of bad news.

But the doctor said that everything went perfectly. A few weeks later, he followed up with a call: "We don't know how to tell you this, but the tumor isn't cancerous anymore."

After they removed the tumor, they ran further tests on it. They sent biopsies back to Massachusetts and Texas, both of which confirmed the mysterious development. Somehow, overnight, Madison's tumor had gone from malignant to benign. The doctors were baffled, but Madison's parents had an explanation: they'd been praying—and not just them, but their friends and family and kids from Madison's school. Her whole community had surrounded her and made a divine appeal. Apparently God had heard their cries.

Madison was our student in the fall of 2019. She shared her experience with us in office hours and in her philosophical apology. "We use God to explain things we don't understand or that can't be explained," Madison told us. "My parents were like 'Okay, God spared her,' and they've always been very religious so naturally after that time in my life I grew up to be very religious and close to God."

This was a picture of God that made a lot of sense to Madison. God was good and caring and powerful, and when something went wrong, he would fix it as an answer to fervent prayer. After her recovery, Madison prayed often. She went to Mass at the Catholic school she attended and threw herself into religion classes. She was filled with gratitude and love and a sense that she'd been chosen, blessed, and spared.

But then one day her mom woke up in terrible pain. Her symptoms were mysterious, but her condition deteriorated to the point that her family was making regular trips to the ER. The doctors searched diligently for a diagnosis, but it was all in vain. As far as they could tell, there was nothing medically wrong with Madison's mom. Even after the doctors gave up on finding a diagnosis, Madison prayed. She knew, from her own experience, that God could transform the most desperate circumstances. She felt like she had a special connection to God. So, for years, she prayed and trusted and waited.

And, for years, nothing happened.

THE PROBLEM OF SUFFERING

The world is full of suffering. This is an inescapable fact. Some of it we humans directly cause and bear responsibility for. A president can start a devastating war with a short missive. A negligent city manager can deprive thousands of families of clean drinking water. And even those of us with comparatively less power can be responsible for willfully ignoring opportunities to improve others' lives.

But not all suffering can be traced back to human choices. There was plenty of horrific animal suffering before we came on the evolutionary scene. And there are natural disasters and epidemics that nobody seems to choose and everyone would prefer to avoid.

In 1755, a massive earthquake shook Lisbon in the Kingdom of Portugal, decimating the city. Those who survived the first wave flooded into the streets in a panic, only to be swept up in an enormous tsunami. Survivors of both of these catastrophic events were then subjected to five long days of raging fires, some caused by candles that remained in the crumbling structures. All told, the events leveled the city. The estimated death toll is between ten thousand and fifty thousand people.

The "Great Lisbon earthquake" came at a crucial time in Western history. Enlightenment thinking was taking root, and people in Europe were increasingly looking toward naturalistic explanations to make sense of the world they lived in. A few hundred years prior, such an apocalyptic event would have been taken as clear evidence that Lisbon had somehow displeased God. Like the destruction of the cities of Sodom and Gomorrah in Genesis, the leveling of Lisbon would likely have been interpreted as divine retribution for sins and vice.

Such a response initially makes a certain kind of sense to those who are committed to the existence of a God who is perfect, all-powerful, loving, and just. Assuming that such a God exists, one natural response to extreme suffering is to ask what we've done to deserve it: perhaps the inhabitants of the city offended God, or maybe the destruction of the city was just the result of our shoddy construction. Maybe God allowed the devastation to teach us an important lesson. Such thinkers might encourage skeptics to consider how parents, if they are to be both just and loving, are sometimes required to punish their children, or to sit by and allow them to suffer the painful consequences of their own bad decisions. In such cases parents would surely want to intervene, but would allow the "evil" in order to give their child the space to develop character.

Such explanations were standard for centuries in the West. But for a culture powered by the Enlightenment, events like the Lisbon earthquake became fuel for new thinking about the role of God in the good life. Some philosophers held fast to the traditional arguments. Gottfried Wilhelm Leibniz maintained that even with all of its flaws, the world we live in is the best possible world God could have created. Baruch Spinoza, a prominent Jewish philosopher, challenged the notion that human conceptions of "good" and "evil" can even be applied to our thinking about God. For many, though, the destruction of the earthquake could not be explained away as part of a bigger picture of an ultimately balanced cosmos. The violence and damage seemed to be proof of God's indifference rather than his righteous indignation. Or even—though it often couldn't be articulated in such explicitly atheistic terms—reason to believe that God does not exist.

In one of the most influential treatments of the Lisbon disaster, the Enlightenment philosopher and poet Voltaire skewers the traditional theistic response to such tragedies. In a poem published at the time, Voltaire challenges the theistic philosopher to listen to himself and note the callousness of all of these defenses. He details the tragedy in all its gruesome detail, painting a picture of innocents, including children and infants, massacred. He then poses the challenge starkly:

> Say, when you hear their piteous, half-formed cries,
> Or from their ashes see the smoke arise,
> Say, will you then eternal laws maintain,
> Which God to cruelties like these constrain?
> Whilst you these facts replete with horror view,
> Will you maintain death to their crimes was due?

Is it really plausible that a God-governed universe requires destruction and pain on the scale of the Lisbon earthquake? Or is this just a desperate attempt by the theist to rationalize away what is clearly great and unnecessary suffering? Elsewhere in the poem, Voltaire points out that there are numerous cities that are blatantly more hedonistic, and manifestly less God-fearing, than Lisbon. If God were sending a message, it seems like Paris would have been a better target.

The reasoning here is captured even more economically by David Hume, a skeptic and one of the most important philosophers of religion who lived and wrote at roughly the same time as Voltaire:

> Is [God] willing to prevent evil, but not able? then he is impotent. Is he able, but not willing? then he is malevolent. Is he both able and willing? then where does evil come from?

Philosophers know this argument (expressed here through rhetorical questions) as "the problem of evil," and it is historically one of the most powerful arguments against the existence of God. Part of the power of the argument from evil is the emotional punch it carries—where was

God when those people were screaming in the earthquake? But it's also been an enduring argument because its underlying logic seems elegant and airtight. It just doesn't seem like the following three claims can all be true.

The Evil Trilemma

1. God is all-powerful and morally perfect.
2. Any being that's all-powerful and morally perfect would prevent all unnecessary suffering in the world.
3. There is unnecessary suffering in the world.

For some philosophers, logical consistency demands that one of these beliefs has to go and belief in God is the prime candidate to be nixed. Indeed, for some philosophers this rejection can be a key episode in their attempts to understand their experience of the world. The philosopher James Baldwin reflects on the arbitrary, inhuman, loveless conditions wrought by racism and famously concludes "God is white." In other words, what we call "God" isn't really a force of supernatural power and justice in the universe but rather just another name for secular power and overwhelming injustice. For Baldwin, acknowledging this as a response to the problem of evil was a revelation. Leaving his childhood church and taking responsibility for finding meaning in his own suffering, these are the turning points in his philosophical apology "Letter from a Region in My Mind."

For others of us, questions of suffering and meaning drive us further into religious life. This was Meghan's experience with trying to grasp the tragedy of 9/11. This was Stephen Colbert's experience trying to understand how joy could be possible after the deaths of his father and brothers.

All of this raises a question: What can reason-seeking theists believe when faced with the problem of evil? This challenge calls out for philosophical thinking about both God and whether there is a moral logic to our universe. Religious philosophers tend to divide into camps based on whether they think point 2 or 3 of the evil trilemma is the source of the problem.

GOD ON TRIAL

The point of a philosophical apology is to make a person's intentions understandable, to show the reasons behind them, and to show how they aim at a worthy goal. Up until this point in the book, we've been focusing on developing a personal apology—a picture of your vision of the good life and the reasons that feed it. But we can also try to construct the apologies for other people, especially when we want to try to understand *them*. And many philosophers have thought that the problem of suffering requires such an apology for God. If God exists, we need an explanation for why he permits these earthquakes, tsunamis, and childhood cancers. Not so much because he owes us an explanation (though he might). Rather, understanding God as a person—a core tenet at least of Christian belief—would seem to require also understanding what he is aiming at with all of this chaos.

Many "apologetics" offered in response to the problem of evil try to show—contra Hume and Voltaire—that it is logically possible for God to exist and permit suffering. Accepting the underlying logic of Hume's argument, such philosophers take their job to be proving that it's conceivable for God to have an adequate *reason* to permit all the suffering in the world. These philosophers think that if we can imagine a plausible excuse for God's allowing the suffering we observe in the world, we can get him off the hook.

We can think of these kinds of theist philosophers almost like a team of defense attorneys, offering alternative narratives and alibis, challenging the way in which Hume, Voltaire, and their numerous contemporary counterparts use suffering as an indictment of God's existence or goodness. In his opening remarks, the atheist stands up and points to the sheer amount and degree of suffering in the world. He reminds the jury of particular instances of horrendous suffering, telling us stories so awful that we're tempted to turn away. "Now imagine God witnessing such suffering," he tells us. "If he exists, he's right there. He's perfect. He's all-powerful. He could stop this suffering at any moment. But he doesn't." The courtroom is silent. "The only explanation," the atheist concludes, "is that the God you've been led to believe in does not and cannot exist."

Any serious response by the theist would presumably start with a concession. Of course the world is full of suffering. And surely it must pain God, as it would pain any good parent, to watch as creatures endure it. But we have to recognize that the atheist's argument depends on a stronger claim: that the world is full of *pointless* suffering. A defense, then, can be slowly built up by coming up with a number of possible justifications for the suffering we observe. These don't have to be God's actual reasons for allowing suffering; they just need to sow reasonable doubt that the suffering is pointless.

Here's one attempt at a defense. Consider how good it is for the world to be governed by laws. All things are subject to gravity. And it's predictable. So predictable, in fact, that we're able to calculate its effects on massive objects scientifically. This knowledge allows us to build bridges and skyscrapers, send humans to the moon, and develop technology beyond our distant ancestors' wildest dreams. But, of course, the regularity of gravity has consequences. When people fall from great heights, they are injured or die. It may sound insensitive, but isn't it better for the world to be subject to these laws? To be calculable and comprehensible and subject to our scientific understanding? Some suffering is the price we pay for this predictability and all it affords us. For it to be a scientific law that fire burns and scalds, God can't intervene here and there to save us from it. Surely we can all appreciate how this is worth the price, even while maintaining—as perhaps God himself does—that these consequences are regrettable.

Or consider another great good: free will. Sure, a powerful father could help his son avoid all short-term injuries, physical, emotional, and moral. But, in the long run, these bumps and bruises are what build character, and they are necessary in order for children to grow up with a sufficient amount of responsibility and agency. That's why helicopter parents get such bad press. Now think about the world we live in. If God swooped in to intervene every time someone tried to seriously hurt another person, even when they used their freedom to torture or maim that other person in awful ways, wouldn't our lives resemble those of overparented children? Again, we regret the fact that freedom is put to bad use—as God surely must, too—but isn't it better, overall, that we're free?

With this strategy, the philosophical problem of suffering comes down to this: Do we think that the amount and degree of suffering that we observe in our world can all be justified by reasons like those we are collecting above or others we might suggest? The problem of suffering then becomes a problem of understanding the relative weights of cancer, gravity, freedom, and souls.

But should it all come down to this consequentialist logic? It's true that we do sometimes think about pain and minor sacrifices in this "weighing up" way. Is it worth it to suffer the pain of a shot to avoid the more serious disease? Is there enough of a benefit to sacrificing a vacation this summer for a better retirement down the road? But there's something off, even monstrous, about using such comparisons in more serious cases. In the movie *The Tree of Life*, we cringe when a mother who's just lost a son is told "It'll be all right, you've still got the other two." Profound loss, as anyone who has suffered it will tell you, isn't something to be reframed by comparisons with other goods. It's not something that can or ought to be outweighed by future gains.

There's a different way to look at the fundamental philosophical problem that suffering raises. Perhaps we don't want this "weighing up" defense of God or a method of moral accounting for this universe. We want God's actual apology—some insight into his divine good life. What is he doing? Staring down the problem of suffering, some philosophers have thought a better approach is to fire the legal department and turn instead to the creatives in the office.

FEAR AND TREMBLING

Søren Kierkegaard was a nineteenth-century Danish philosopher known as "the father of existentialism." His intense Lutheran upbringing led him to be deeply worried about suffering. He reimagined the role philosophers might play in helping us to understand it. Like Plato, he frequently wrote in dialogues, with characters representing the various hypotheses he entertained. He is just as hard as Socrates to pin down, because like Socrates, Kierkegaard took the point of philosophy to be primarily in prodding us to ask better questions and consider new details that might transform how we see things. *Fear and Trembling* is his attempt to pose strong questions to God.

Kierkegaard starts by sharing that growing up he was always taught to admire Abraham, who is held up in the Christian tradition as "the Father of Faith." But as he grew older, he increasingly saw the strangeness of Abraham and his relationship to God.

Here is the basic "Sunday school" version of Abraham's story from Genesis that you need to know in order to make sense of Kierkegaard's contribution to the problem of suffering. Abraham and his wife, Sarah, were an older, childless couple, living where they both grew up. God reaches out to Abraham directly and instructs him to move to an unknown land. Abraham and Sarah pack up without question. God then tells Abraham that, with Sarah, he will be made "the father of a great nation." Both Sarah and Abraham find this hilarious—he's nearly one hundred and she's approaching ninety. They laugh and laugh at the thought, and yet, they are open to the possibility. Abraham decides to hedge his bets and has a son, Ishmael, with his servant Hagar. But God makes it clear that Sarah is key to the plan. And miraculously, Sarah does eventually have a child, Isaac, and Abraham understands that God's promise is to be fulfilled through Isaac and his descendants. He's a beloved son, and also the person who God promises will complete Abraham's life's mission.

Then . . . a shocking turn of events. One day God commands Abraham to travel to Mount Moriah and sacrifice Isaac, to murder his son as an offering to God. Once again, trusting in God blindly, Abraham travels up the mountain with Isaac, the naive kid asking along the hike where they are going to get an animal for their sacrifice. When they arrive at the place of sacrifice, Abraham ties Isaac up and raises his knife. According to the story, once God is satisfied with Abraham's demonstration of faith, he sends an angel to stop the murder in progress. God provides a ram instead that Abraham and Isaac can sacrifice together.

Kierkegaard finds himself *obsessed* with the last part of this story. In his essay about it, he explains that this obsession was something that grew as he matured and started to realize how truly bizarre and upsetting the Abraham story is. He admits that many Bible stories we are taught to accept as kids are weird. But here's one in which Abraham—the so-called Father of Faith—is depicted as being willing to carry out God's request that he *kill his own son* seemingly out of nowhere. What does this tell us about Abraham? About what Christianity holds up as the model of faithfulness? More important: What does it tell us about God?

Kierkegaard realizes he could offer us a legal defense of God's command and Abraham's faith—something with premises and a conclusion along the lines of "God has standing to test Abraham's faith through this command because . . ." or "In his particular circumstances, Abraham could be confident God's will was good because . . ."—but he rightly discerns that this isn't what we want. We want to understand what God and Abraham are *doing*. And we start with the assumption that God's got perfect intentions—it's the actions that need an explanation.

Think back to a time when a loved one did something you found to be out of character. Maybe it was something hurtful or offensive, or just something you literally could not make sense of. When we find ourselves asking questions like "How could he have done that?" or "What was she thinking?" we almost never fire up the logical analysis part of our brains. We don't calmly assign probabilities to various possible motives and then calculate the odds that our loved one was acting out of spite. Instead, we grasp at stories that could explain, contextualize, and make intelligible the behavior of our loved one. Usually we seek out a story that is true and that we can live with.

To use Iris Murdoch's phrase, we look at the puzzling behavior, and then we "look again" to see if we can ultimately make sense of it. Sometimes the stories we come up with take the form of simple excuses: "I know she was tired, so it must not have been about me." Sometimes they involve supposing that we lack—and cannot now acquire—the relevant details: "I must have misunderstood what he said." Sometimes, the best we can do is reaffirm our trust in the other person, and humbly remind ourselves of our own fallibility: "This isn't in her character. I know it seems clear that what she did was intentional. But I've been wrong when I jumped to conclusions before."

In these instances, we're offering apologies, but not for our own sake. We're telling morally thick stories to try to make sense of the behavior, beliefs, or actions of someone else. And it's usually someone we love, someone we have a relationship with, and someone with whom we want to remain close. What does this look like for Kierkegaard in the case of Abraham and God? To do Kierkegaard's method justice, you really should read his beautiful, strange attempted apologies for yourself in their entirety (Paul does this, out loud, during the course period devoted to this question). But here, we'll offer our own brief summaries of each of Kierkegaard's retellings.

Kierkegaard decides he will try a few different attempts to fill in the missing details of Abraham's intentions that fateful morning, and along the way he hopes indirectly to come to a better understanding of God's will and Abraham's faith.

> 1. Maybe Abraham awoke early in the morning. He prepared a caravan and set off toward Mount Moriah with his terrible mission still a secret from Isaac, and from the wife who'd so joyfully begotten him in her old age. Abraham is stoical. He knows what God has asked of him. He dismisses the servants; turns away from Isaac. And then? He screams at his son. He tells him that his decision to kill him is his and his alone, wanting to spare his son's faith in the last few minutes he has remaining on earth. Isaac cries out to God, "Be thou my father, for I now have none." And Abraham thanks God in his heart, for his son's faith has been spared.

Is that it? Abraham is "the Father of Faith" because he spares his son's faith rather than his own. He puts that faith above all else. He embraces the absurdity of his task, aligns his action with God's intention, and does whatever it takes to preserve Isaac's trust in God as his father.

Kierkegaard isn't satisfied and looks at the story again.

> 2. Maybe Abraham awoke early, kissed Sarah good-bye, and undertook the entirety of his grim task. Just before he was to slaughter his son, the angel intervenes and they find a ram to sacrifice instead. Abraham lives the remainder of his life a broken, quiet man. Isaac recovers, but Abraham grows old and weary, unable to ever again enjoy the son God had given him.

How about this? Abraham here is destroyed as a man. Miserable. He's lost even the happiness and joy he once took in his family life. Perhaps this sacrifice, the sacrifice of his eudaimonia here on earth, is what God really required. Perhaps this is why he is known as "the Father of Faith," an example of what it means to put the things of heaven even before our own earthly function.

Unsatisfied, Kierkegaard looks for a third time:

> 3. Maybe Abraham awoke early. He kissed Sarah and saddled up the caravan. Before he could kill Isaac the angel intervened. He spent the remainder of his years wondering how God could require him to have abdicated his fatherly duty to protect Isaac. Was it a sin to obey? And how could he be forgiven when the only one capable of forgiving sin is the one who demanded this of him in the first place?

Here's another possibility: Abraham properly sees what the "right thing to do" is, and that it's incompatible with God's command. And then he chooses to put God's command over his own perception of morality. Like a lover who has a choice to save a dozen drowning children or just the life of his wife, Abraham sees the right thing to do and then chooses love of God over even his ethical commitments. Is this it? Is this how he becomes "the Father of Faith," by recognizing an authority and a value even greater than all earthly good?

But Kierkegaard still doesn't see it. He goes in a fourth time:

> 4. Maybe Abraham awoke, traveled to the mountain with Isaac, and the angel intervened. They return home in silence, embarrassed by the horror of it, and never speak of it to each other, or to Sarah, again. Abraham moves on, but Isaac cannot. He is destroyed and has lost his faith.

Notice: these stories are not all the same story; nor do the characters all come out the same in every version. In one of them Abraham all but loses his faith; in another Isaac does. In each case God is doing something to Abraham or Isaac. Kierkegaard's struggle to come up with an accurate, morally thick story does not guarantee that he'll end up in the comfortable territory he might hope for; we must sometimes admit at the end of this process that the behavior or action of our loved one is, indeed, unintelligible—sometimes terribly so. And he is open to the possibility that none of his attempts to tell the true story will work. In fact, the stories lead Kierkegaard to seriously consider that faith in God is absurd.

Absurdity, for Kierkegaard, is a technical concept. To embrace the absurd is to recognize that in some situations we're in a territory beyond reason and rationality. Importantly, this doesn't mean that once you've embraced the absurd "anything goes," but just that there are some areas of life—some decisions or claims or life plans—that are stubbornly resistant to our attempts to reason through them.

Kierkegaard's method of offering apologies for God and religious believers isn't just a way of interpreting biblical stories. It is also a way of dealing with the absurd forms of suffering we encounter in our lives.

The Song of Solomon
(From Paul's Apology)

When my wife and I found out that we were pregnant for the first time, we cried. My wife came running out of the bathroom with the positive test, pointing at it and shouting, "Two lines! Two lines!" We danced around the apartment, shaking and hugging each other. There were great rooms inside our hearts behind doors we'd thought were walls, and our capacity to love expanded.

Then there was the preparation and the waiting. Picking up hand-me-down onesies from friends and family, assembling a crib, and googling the hell out of prenatal development.

But when Shayla was ready to go into labor, something felt terribly off. We'd discussed minimizing medical interventions with our doctor, but at every step we were presented with decisions we didn't anticipate, each of which seemed to lead to another situation that demanded another decision. Somehow, over the course of the delivery, the room had filled up. I didn't notice the additional doctors and nurses, but I felt added urgency as each arrived. In my memory of the event I count fourteen medical professionals in scrubs and masks in a couple of rows surrounding the doctor.

And then he was here. A boy! But the room was so quiet.

He should cry, *I thought. But no cry came. And they were handing him around, and then he disappeared into a circle of nurses who'd gathered around the neonatal incubator. I heard myself ask if he was okay, and a nurse nearby said something reassuring, but I was listening to the nurses who were surrounding him and they were saying something about his mouth and a potential obstruction. When we finally heard him squeak—he was breathing—we all caught our own breath, and they brought him to my wife and then to me, and he was beautiful.*

But they'd put something into his mouth, to force it open, because there was a growth of some sort that was forcing his tongue up into his palate. And with that we were told that we could see him again a bit later, in the NICU.

We spent the next few days in the NICU in South Bend. Solomon Blaschko was baptized there, surrounded by plastic candles and plugged into feeding tubes. (Meghan was there, as his godmother.) We were eventually transferred down to Riley Hospital for Children in Indianapolis. When we arrived, we'd narrowed the diagnosis down a bit. It wasn't a benign cyst, which is what we'd been hoping for, but it also wasn't clearly a tumor, which is what we so desperately feared. We lived, for a few weeks, in the fog of medical terminology that all seemed to boil down to different ways of saying, "We don't know either."

Because I'm a philosopher, and because I'd thought about God's relation to suffering quite a bit over the years, I'd come to have certain expectations about what it would be like to encounter such suffering firsthand. I thought it would feel abstract and theoretical, that it would arrive as a rational challenge to my faith, and that my response would be, primarily, to argue my way out of it.

I also came into the experience expecting God himself to react in a particular way. For lack of a better way of putting it, I expected God to be apologetic—maybe even a little sheepish—about the fact that I'd come up against a flaw in his creation. At the very least, I expected to encounter a patient and loving God in prayer who would give me strength, and maybe explain through prayer how all pain and suffering worked together for the good.

But this was not my experience at all.

The second day of our stay at Riley, we were invited to stay at a shelter for the families of sick children, and we moved in only to discover an infestation of bed bugs that reached an almost biblical proportion. We moved to a hotel a few miles south of Riley, and—on the way back to the hospital on the morning of Solomon's surgery—witnessed a terrible and fiery crash on the freeway. I knew, rationally, that these were unrelated events. But the encounter with pain and uncertainty had opened up something raw and emotional inside of me, and the world around us started to seem more violent and inhospitable and almost apocalyptic. I remember walking the halls of the hospital at night, praying for Solomon, and seeing room after room of babies with devastating medical conditions. Many of them were alone, and I imagine some of these had parents, possibly in different states, who needed to return to work to pay for ongoing care, and to save up, in some cases, for a lifetime of such care.

When I prayed, and I prayed often during these days, God was oddly silent. I'd almost describe him as chilly. Like a friend who'd inexplicably neglected me, and now refused to give me any sort of story or explanation. I didn't feel betrayed; I just sort of expected God to say something comforting or to provide some sort of clarity or reassurance.

After about a week at Riley, going back and forth between the hospital and hotel, I was exhausted and needed a break. I told my wife that I was going to go for a walk around the downtown area to clear my head and get some air.

About a block into the walk, I realized it was way too cold to be outside, and I hadn't brought a winter jacket, so I ducked inside a massive mall. It was almost Thanksgiving, so, of course, the mall was decorated for the holidays, and there were lights and garland and bells everywhere. The whole thing was a bit overwhelming, so I put my headphones in and pulled up an audiobook version of the Bible I'd downloaded earlier in the week. Because I didn't want to pay for it, it was an old translation—I think it was the King James Version—and was read by, of all people, James Earl Jones. I didn't really know where to start, so I picked Ecclesiastes, which is a book I'd never read before, and walked toward the Apple Store. Here's how the walk went:

Vanity of vanities; saith the Preacher,
vanity of vanities; all is vanity.
What profit hath a man of all his labour
which he taketh under the sun?

Through the Apple Store window, I saw that they were running a special on Apple Watches and I wondered for a second if the calendar function could be integrated with my Google calendar because I'm a religious user of Google calendars.

All things are full of labour; man cannot utter it:
the eye is not satisfied with seeing, nor the ear filled
with hearing.

Suddenly, in that moment, I was taken in by the text, and the world of the mall all around me seemed strange and too bright and full of anxious movement.

> *There is no remembrance of former things; neither shall there be any remembrance of things that are to come with those that shall come after.*

I imagined the mall dark and empty, fifty or a hundred years into the future. I imagined the broken and unilluminated dust-covered signs from companies that no longer existed. I realized that we'd all, every last one of us in that mall, be dead or marching toward death, and that—when we did die—we'd join the Apple Watches, and empty cologne bottles, and plastic bags someplace under the earth, and that the glory of creation depended on not one of these things, and not one of my efforts, and refused to be diminished by me or my inability to see the full picture . . . and I was filled with gratitude.

This is what I now think of as my "Job moment." It was the moment when I was challenged to let go of my attempts to control and comprehend my life and experiences, when I saw, for a moment, that I was framing my conversation with God in the wrong way. I was, in a way, demanding something of him—answers, comfort, comprehension—but in response I was reprimanded. God finally decides to answer Job, not with an explanation or even some reassurance, but with indignation:

> *Where wast thou when I laid the foundations of the earth?*
> *declare, if thou hast understanding.*
> *Who hath laid the measures thereof, if thou knowest?*
> *or who hath stretched the line upon it?*

At the end of the Book of Job, God gives back to Job the material things that were taken from him. God also gives him children, as many as he had before, but you've got to think that he looks at all of these things differently.

The growth in Solomon's mouth was successfully removed, and it was not cancerous. But when we brought him home from Riley, we left hundreds of other children behind. Some of them will not leave that hospital, or even that unit, during their lives. I don't believe that God spared my son's life; or—at least—not as a simple transaction in response to my prayers. I've seen other parents pray desperately for their children to no avail.

The grace I was given during this experience—and I do believe this was God's grace—was a perspective on my life and plans that I still struggle to live up to. It was an understanding that things—all things—pass away, and that in this life we can try to obscure the facts of pain and suffering and evil, or we can arrange our lives in response to this fact. We can try to hide and ignore this pain, or we can encounter it. And, in some way that I still don't fully understand, for those who put their faith in the God of Job and Ecclesiastes—for those who can appreciate Kierkegaard's conviction that faith is, in some sense, absurd and difficult and true—pain and suffering need to be reckoned with directly. Not as an embarrassment, or as a minor flaw in the system, or a discrepancy to be written out of the final balance sheet of life, but as one of its fundamental elements.

THE PRICE OF ADMISSION

There are two components to how Christian existentialists like Kierkegaard approach the problem of suffering. The first step, as we have seen, is to reject the consequentialist assumption that judgments about "goodness" in every case boil down to judgments about whether net benefits outweigh the costs. Our good lives are not governed by this consequentialist logic. God's goodness is not either. Fire the lawyers.

But a complete apology also demands, as we have seen, that we tell the right morally thick story about someone's intentions. And suffering—Madison's story, Solomon's story, Isaac's story—poses to us the very difficult, quite possibly absurd, challenge of trying to tell the story of what God means by all of this.

In Dostoevsky's masterpiece, *The Brothers Karamazov*, Ivan Karamazov finds the only story he can possibly tell truly about God is a horror story. He recounts to his brother Alyosha the specific atrocities he knows God has permitted—murdered children, abused animals, horrific and pointless wars. He goes into excruciating detail over pages about what he "knows" God has done. And then he tells his brother that, in light of this, there is no apology for God that could make God worth respecting or loving: "[The apologists] have put too high a price on harmony; we can't afford to pay so much for admission. . . . It's not that I don't accept God, Alyosha, I just most respectfully return him the ticket."

Recall Anscombe's critique of President Truman from the chapter on responsibility. She cannot find any plausible way to tell the story of his decision to bomb Hiroshima and Nagasaki that does not indict Truman as a murderer. Any hope of understanding Truman (and any hope of forgiving him) involves first facing the fact that he is responsible for a grave moral harm. We might wonder, How much the worse for God, who also permitted those bombings and everything on Ivan's terrible list besides? Why are Christians like Anscombe willing to work so hard to find the apology that redeems God but not so hard to find an apology that redeems Truman?

One crucial difference is in the target of who we are attempting to understand with the moral apology. In the case of Truman, there is no reason to believe he is *by nature* incapable of viciousness. There is no reason to believe our good lives will be hurt if we can't reconcile with him over the bombings. Most of us don't even know the guy—we couldn't know him.

But for religious believers, those even entertaining the possibility that they are in a relationship with God, matters are quite different. God would be by nature incapable of viciousness. For Stephen Colbert and Thomas Aquinas, God is who we are directing our joy and gratitude for the good life toward. And our lives are seriously threatened if we can't even try to reconcile with him over the suffering we face. With Truman, it seems at least plausible that the true story is one in which he killed civilians to stop the war. With God, no story that views him as a murderer could be the true one, the one that makes him intelligible to us.

For Christians, the core of God's apology takes the form of the Gospels—the story of the life, death, and resurrection of Jesus. It's a story that the faithful have to retell again and again and again, wrestling with the absurdity, but—in paying attention to the detail—thereby also getting glimpses into the person of God. Christians use the Gospels as the key narrative for framing the rest of the texts of the Bible, trying to understand God's intentions and eventually reading more of our lives into the big story. This is what happened to Paul as the lines from Job and Ecclesiastes came to him in his search for meaning in Solomon's hour of crisis; those lines, Paul's need, and God's intentions come together to partially help Paul grapple with the incomprehensible.

Learning to think philosophically and religiously about the problem of suffering means learning to dwell on these stories. Here is a detail Meghan lingers on when trying to figure out what she thinks about suffering. In the Gospel of Luke, Mary, a teenager and a virgin, discovers she is pregnant with Jesus and that she will be the mother of God. She gives birth in an animal stable while traveling with her betrothed, Joseph. Around the same time, some shepherds are also made aware of the imminent arrival of God. The shepherds are dumbfounded and afraid; Mary should have been as well. But we get an interesting detail in her quite different reaction: "She treasured up these things and pondered them in her heart." Which things? Mary presumably knows what the shepherds know—the world order they are used to is about to be turned upside down. But she also knows something they don't, something she could feel in her body from that day onward. Something she loved.

Meghan "looks again" and again and again at this passage of Luke and starts to see . . . God is known both intellectually and in our bodies. What could that mean for someone in the hospital who is sick from chemotherapy? Look again. Faith—the apologies for God that it provides—gives us the material to look at as we try to comprehend our suffering. And it is an ongoing, complicated, borderline absurd process.

It's also one you can try. Suppose you find a faith tradition that is a "live option" for you, in William James's sense. Ask someone in the tradition, "Where is a good place to start the story?" Maybe it is the opening of the Gospel of Luke for a Christian. Maybe it is the story of Moses for someone whose Jewish faith is live. Read through the text and look and look again. Where is a potential connection? Where is a hypothesis about God? Are there people with more established habits of reading and looking who can nudge you toward more meaningful ways of doing it? And what from your experience can you start to see in that story?

TEACHING MADISON PHILOSOPHY

When he teaches God and the Good Life, Paul uses his story about Solomon to illustrate one way philosophers use apologies to respond to the problem of suffering. The story is also a way for Paul to share part of *his* apology with his students, and one that he's still working through. Paul has told the story often enough that he knows what he's able to safely share, but he usually still becomes visibly emotional when he talks about it in class. Paul feels like it's the most authentic thing he can say on the subject. Every semester, Paul's apology opens the door to a deeper discussion with some of our students about suffering in their own lives.

That's how he came to know Madison.

This happens to both of us every semester with at least some students. We prod them to ask some of these strong questions about their lives, we share our stories and questions, and students inevitably want to share their own. We invite it. We aren't therapists or spiritual directors, and we make sure our students know that. But we can help them ask the philosophical questions that weigh on them, good life questions they've often been grappling with long before they took our class. And these discussions aren't aimed at conversion—far from it. The views students develop are as unique as they are as questioners.

After a few years of her mom's mysterious illness, Madison stopped praying. She still believed in God—and she said this belief continued to be one of the most important aspects of her identity—but she didn't much feel like talking to him. She couldn't forget her experience as a young child and was understanding more and more how much credit her parents gave to God for her recovery. But she couldn't stop wondering why God remained so silent now that her mom needed a similar miracle. She captures the dynamic perfectly in metaphor: "It's like God was an ex and cheated on me or something. But we're in the same friend group so it's awkward."

She explained that one of the reasons why she found the class so powerful is that this was one of the first times she'd started to think about these problems in terms of God's personality rather than which box to tick when asked for her religious affiliation.

When we first discussed the problem of suffering in class, Madison was struck by David Hume's argument. We'd just finished discussing Aquinas's arguments for God's existence, and Madison found herself now more convinced than ever that some creative, all-powerful being existed; that this was the God she'd known her whole life, and that he was indeed capable of miracles like the one she'd experienced as a child. Then Hume's argument pushed her in the opposite direction, and she suddenly started to think that God must not exist. Much philosophy of religion leaves you with this argumentative whiplash.

But by the end of the course, Madison had landed somewhere else entirely. Inspired by Kierkegaard's retelling of the Abraham and Isaac story, she'd started experimenting with stories in which God was a deeper, more complicated figure. "God can be wrathful," she told Paul. "Maybe he can play favorites." For Madison, a picture of a more personal God—a God like Job's whose silence turns to fury, or a God like Abraham's who asks the impossible and requires the absurd—makes more sense than the bland omnibenevolent handyman we've come to expect. Maybe we can't perfectly predict how a perfect being will interact with us.

When Paul talked with Madison, it got him thinking about how Solomon would make sense of all of this as he grew up—his illness, his father's faith, his own relationship with God.

When they were last in touch, Madison told Paul that she's still working it all out, but that something in this story speaks to her. For the first time in a long time, she's found a picture of God that's intelligible to her. And for now, that's enough.

Soulcraft: Food for the Journey

In the Catholic Church, as a person approaches death or is seriously ill, they are given sacramental communion bread (the Eucharist) as viaticum, which comes from an archaic Latin word that initially meant "food for the journey." The idea is that we sometimes know that a particular journey will be difficult, or can sometimes anticipate challenges in passing from one state to the next, and that we want to store up grace for those dark times.

We want to invite you into this tradition in a metaphorical sense, and ask you to think about what sorts of traditions, rituals, practices, or relationships you can cultivate so they are there with you when you must deal with serious suffering (your own or in the lives of those you love). It's certainly possible to appreciate the role such things might play without objectifying or instrumentalizing them. For Paul, in the apology shared in this chapter, his faith took the form of scriptural narratives and the community of support that had been built up over years. Reflecting on this story, you might be able to point to things in your own life that you have stored up—or could—as sustenance for the difficult times.

If you're having a hard time coming up with concrete things, consider the following list. Think about if any of these practices might have "shelf life" for you. What do they offer us when we are suffering? Select one or two items and try them out. Think a bit about how you could store them—as habits, as reminders, as experiences you have already tested out, as conversations you have already initiated.

Potential Food for the Journey

- **AESTHETIC OBJECTS:** poems, literature, stories, music
- **TRADITIONAL RESOURCES:** wisdom stored up in guidebooks, memoirs, or just the minds of elders in your community
- **SELF-REFLECTION:** journaling, gratitude exercises, sustained dialogues with an intimate partner or a close friend
- **RITUALS:** meditation, contemplative practices, mindfulness exercises (more on this in the next chapter)
- **COMMUNAL RESOURCES:** friendships organized around common values, book clubs or Bible studies, more or less formal systems of support (e.g., meal trains, calling trees)
- **RELIGIOUS RESOURCES:** practices of prayer, examinations of conscience, spiritual exercises, sacred texts, sacraments, the witness of exemplars

9.

Contemplate Your Purpose

> It may be that when we no longer know what to do
> we have come to our real work.
>
> —Wendell Berry, "The Real Work"

CANCEL EVERYTHING

On March 10, 2020, *The Atlantic* ran a jarring piece on the front page of its website. The headline: CANCEL EVERYTHING. At that point there were 259 confirmed COVID-19 cases in the United States. Eleven days later, there were over 31,000. It became clear by the second week in March (although this clarity came too late) that the greatest moral imperative for each of us was to pause our lives—at least, every aspect of our lives that involved physical interaction with other people.

On March 12, Notre Dame told all of the students we were moving to remote learning. The dominoes fell rapidly over the next forty-eight hours. March Madness: canceled. Tokyo Olympics: postponed. The suggestion to work from home soon became an order. Schools, day cares, parks, restaurants, gyms, theaters, clubs, job interviews, choir practice, any in-person volunteering: all canceled. If you weren't a health-care professional or a key player in the supply line of food, drugs, utilities, or safety equipment, then you needed to stay home. And even those aspects of work that could carry on over the internet were canceled by kids home from school, family drama, the stress of uncertainty, or furloughs and layoffs. The economic and social aspects of the good life ground to a sudden, shocking halt.

For us, pre-virus life was structured mainly around meetings and deadlines, planning various lengths in the future, setting goals for ongoing projects. That all went out the window. The highlights of the day instead became long walks by the St. Joseph River, cooking elaborate family meals, checking slowly rising bread dough, discovering a forgotten copy of *Walden* on the bookshelf.

In the ancient world, philosophers drew a sharp distinction between the life of action and the life of contemplation. Politicians, military commanders, and the hardworking citizens that kept the wheels of society turning were seen as living "active" lives, while philosophers and poets and those devoted to learning for its own sake lived characteristically "contemplative" lives. While almost every philosopher concedes that a good life will contain some active and some contemplative elements, the debate focused on which life (which mix) was inherently better.

Nowadays, we tend to think of the life of contemplation as something that eccentric or exceptional individuals choose. Contemplatives are people who want to set themselves apart from the "real world." Henry David Thoreau moved out to his cabin at Walden Pond to make a point about the shallow materialism in nineteenth-century Massachusetts. Carmelite nuns enter cloistered life because they feel they have been set apart by God for a life of constant prayer.

And if we think of the life of contemplation as something exceptional, then it also seems open to an important kind of moral objection. The off-grid hippies, the cloistered saints, the bearded ivory tower types . . . their lives can appear selfish. The picture of the good life we have developed in this book so far is a life of action. You are recruiting mentors, earning money to give away, making friends, joining religious movements, trying to "escape your caves" through deep conversations with friends and family. Contemplatives do none of these things. The whole point of the contemplative life is to not *do* anything.

The contemplative life also seems exceptionally lonely. Many famous contemplatives are also famous misanthropes. Here's how Thoreau describes family meals: "We meet at meals three times a day, and give each other a new taste of that old musty cheese that we are." Journalist Kathryn Schulz wrote a blistering retrospective on *Walden* for *The New Yorker*, arguing that Thoreau shouldn't be considered an American philosophical hero: "Few things will thwart your plans to live deliberately faster than those messy, confounding surprises known as other people. . . . And yet we made a classic of [*Walden*], and a moral paragon of its author—a man whose deepest desire and signature act was to turn his back on the rest of us."

But as it became clear in March 2020, this is not the only way to think about the role that contemplation plays in the good life. Exceptional circumstances, like a global pandemic, can completely upend the action-packed goals that typically guide our moral and social lives.

WHEN THE LIFE OF ACTION FAILS US

Remember Aristotle's definition of happiness? Eudaimonia is the state of having fulfilled your function as a human being. It is the overarching goal of our lives in virtue ethics. And the goal is determined first and foremost by what kinds of creatures we are. For Aristotle, our function is that we are reason-seeking, goal-driven, social animals. This would seem to suggest that we should want to be better friends, better parents, better citizens, better <insert career>. It's *action* that leads to habits that turn into virtues. And, as goal-oriented creatures, carefully thought-out rational *action* is how we attain justice in our cities and love in our personal relationships. Aristotle insists that the way that we become better parents, better citizens, or better workers is by performing the right action, with the right feeling, at the right time, in the right way, and for the right reason. Elsewhere he counsels: "Thinking itself moves nothing, but thinking that is for the sake of something and concerned with action does."

But by the end of his own good life course, Aristotle starts to worry that all this emphasis on action is misplaced. If eudaimonia is a matter of living an action-packed life, then three serious threats can derail your ability to achieve it.

First, despite your best efforts, you might fail in the life of action. Your business might be disrupted by economic forces beyond your control. Others may not want to be friends with you. You might just happen to have been born into a morally bankrupt society at a low point in human history. You might be the subject of discrimination or oppression. In these cases, virtue ethics seems to entail that you are doomed to a bad life through no fault of your own. But shouldn't we have some meaningful control over whether we are living good lives?

Second, even if you are successful in all of your pursuits of the good life, eventually these pursuits will end. Your children will grow up and move away. You will retire. Your friends will pass away. Is there any part of our function, any goal we could aim at, that won't eventually run out on us? The emptiness of a pure life of action is captured (painfully) by Robert Sapolsky, a professor at Stanford: "We study hard in high school to get admitted to a top college to get into grad school to get a good job to get into the nursing home of our choice." One question that drives virtue ethics is whether there is any state we could get to that would be complete, that could break the cycle of achievement and disappointment.

Finally, Aristotle starts to worry near the end of the *Nicomachean Ethics* that he hasn't quite nailed down what our goal should be when it comes to our *thinking* lives. His teacher, Plato, thought the most important dimension of the good life was getting ourselves out of the cave—getting beyond mere appearances in the world to a genuine understanding of ourselves, and other people, and everything. The philosopher's job was to find the deep, unchanging insight in the storm of life. In the *Republic*, Plato gives a beautiful analogy of the philosopher as the seemingly useless stargazer on a ship. He appears to be distracted by distant concerns, but in fact he has the knowledge to navigate for everyone else: "Always love the sort of learning that makes clear to them some feature of the being that always is and does not wander around between coming to be and decaying."

At the beginning of this book, we discussed how Aristotle thought that philosophy should be deeply practical: "We are conducting an examination, not so that we may know what virtue is, but so that we may *become good*, since otherwise there would be no benefit from it." He criticized Plato for being too abstract and metaphorical—in other books he goes so far as to call his teacher's main idea useless. But Aristotle also worried that something in Plato's view is indispensable. We care about escaping the cave. What makes humans special is our capacity to solve geometry puzzles, to write literature, to make art. To contemplate the world.

We moderns wrestle with this same question. Our cultural default view tends to be that contemplation, meditation, prayer, and the like are useful insofar as they are performance enhancers. You need a meditation app to remind you to meditate because if you don't meditate, you will be too stressed to work. You should stop during the day to pray or practice gratitude because otherwise you will miss opportunities to be a better friend or better fulfill your moral obligations. Calm, a popular meditation app, even teamed up with LeBron James for an ad campaign to promote "mental fitness." In one commercial, James uses the app on his phone while calm music plays and white text appears on the screen: "Want to train like LeBron James? Train your mind." Meditation is the secret to dominance on the court. None of this takes contemplation seriously as a distinctive part of our human function. It just sucks it back into the life of action. Is there a better way to honor the thinking dimension of our good lives?

TRAINING LIKE A ROMAN

Enter Marcus Aurelius.

Marcus was emperor of Rome in the second century AD (unlike Caesar, he is typically referred to by his first name). He had been trained in all four of the major virtue ethics traditions of his day—Plato's Academic school, Aristotle's Peripatetic school, Epicureanism, and Stoicism. Of the four he was most taken by the Stoics' views about the nature of the universe and the sufficiency of virtue for happiness. Stoicism's big idea is that because virtue is the only thing that ultimately matters, we should be as indifferent as possible to the vicissitudes of fate and the parts of life beyond our own character. Someone might take your money, but they can't take your generosity. A plague might take away the things you enjoy doing, but it cannot make you boring. You may not get into law school, but you don't need law school to become just, honest, and prudent.

Much of Stoic philosophy aims to help its adherents cultivate their "inner lives" and navigate the adversity and obstacles that life tends to throw in our way. Anxious about the success of your projects? Remind yourself that the only thing that ultimately matters is the state of your soul. Fearful of what suffering or evil might come your way? Remember that nothing outside of you can ultimately cause you harm. Jealous of a rival's success or someone's arbitrary fame? Call to mind the fact that everyone before you, commoner and emperor alike, has died, and that you will die, and that someday all will be forgotten.

For Stoicism, the key to weathering any hardship or difficulty is to continually remind ourselves that what matters is not what happens to us but how we respond to it. Can you respond with kindness to those who offend you, or are you stricken with inner rage? Are you able to appreciate the ways in which those who aim to hurt you are themselves hurting, or do you simply seek vengeance? The Stoics believed that once we realize that the only thing that really matters is the state of our soul (or character), we can respond to any external obstacles in life by summoning this truth.

It is tempting to read the Stoics and conclude that this is a fine view until you must actually face down adversity. But Stoicism was not pure philosophical navel-gazing for Marcus Aurelius. He had one of the most demanding jobs imaginable, governing an empire and leading armies. His Rome battled its own serious plague that hit in 165. The Antonine Plague was likely a version of smallpox that traveled with Roman troops returning from Asia to the city. It killed around 10 percent of the Roman population. Death, glory, fate, empire—these were daily life for Marcus.

A few years after that plague, in the midst of another European campaign, Marcus began keeping a truly remarkable journal. It documents almost nothing about his day-to-day life. Instead, he captures his Stoic reflections on nature, death, and the people he loves. He reminds himself to tend carefully to his inner life, and offers himself advice on what is worth caring about and reminders of his deepest philosophical principles. It is a philosophical apology like the kind we've discussed throughout this book, but with a key exception—it is not the story of what Marcus is *doing* but rather the story of how he is *thinking*.

Marcus responds to some of life's biggest anxieties—death, his lack of influence, the potential of losing material wealth and power—by reminding himself of his Stoic principles: "How all things quickly vanish, our bodies themselves lost in the physical world, the memories of them lost in time; the nature of all objects of the senses—especially those which allure us with pleasure, frighten us with pain, or enjoy the applause of vanity—how cheap they are, how contemptible, shoddy, perishable, and dead." Marcus was apt to respond to his own worries about not having achieved enough fame by listing the great emperors who'd come before him and rhetorically asking whether they could transcend the grave.

One of the remarkable things about Marcus Aurelius, and about Stoicism in general, is that it predicted some of the most effective and widely used therapies of our own time. In a way, we can see Marcus's meditations as an exercise in cognitive behavioral therapy, a journal devoted to exposing himself to his deepest anxieties in order to defuse the charged moral and emotional reactions they might otherwise incite. But, and this is a crucial point for the virtue ethicist, we need to resist the temptation to use contemplation as just one more instrument that simply allows us to pursue our goals more efficiently, to better live our most active lives. Even though this is the default view in our busy modern world, Marcus Aurelius, Aristotle, and any serious virtue ethicist would see this way of thinking about contemplation in the good life as a missed opportunity. Rather we need to work to see in our goal-driven function a dimension that defies the logic of achievement.

CONTEMPLATION IS POINTLESS . . . AND THAT *IS* THE POINT

A few years ago, the MIT philosopher Kieran Setiya wrote an apology about the philosophy that helped him navigate a midlife crisis—a book called *Midlife: A Philosophical Guide*. Setiya is a life-of-action guy if ever there was one: Cambridge graduate, tenured faculty member at a top university, rich family life. He's published dozens of articles and several well-received books, and given talks at top universities across the world. But he eventually hit his wall: "Accomplishments matter to me, but each one is bittersweet: longed for, pursued, and ultimately, disappointingly, complete. That's over with. What now?"

It's important to note that such crises—although sometimes precipitated by external events like a pandemic or a tragic accident—are ultimately crises of *meaning*, and that they draw our attention to the fact that no achievement (at least none we've discovered or know of) will ever provide your life with enough meaning or purpose to reach eudaimonia.

In such moments of crisis, the subject can become unable to act—unable to keep up their work, go out with friends, or even to get out of bed.

But under the right conditions, crises can provide us with a unique opportunity to examine our values and reorder our priorities. So long as we can weather the initial disruption, and so long as the crises aren't so serious that we're stuck in perpetual survival mode, there's a way in which they can get us "unstuck" from the everyday habits and routines that had come to structure our lives, and can allow us to examine and contemplate the values underlying those routines. A sudden job loss that induces a crisis of meaning can prod us to realize something about what the common good means in our lives. The unexpected end of a relationship can force us to reckon with the question of whether we're really the person we'd like to be. Approached philosophically, crises can add moral or spiritual thickness to the stories we are telling, exposing layers of meaning we ignore when we are just cruising along.

Setiya diagnoses *his* crisis as one of too much action. He draws a distinction between goal-directed (or telic) activities and activities that are "goalless" (or atelic). Whereas goal-directed activities get their value from culminating in an achievement—crossing the finish line makes the painful marathon worth running—goalless activities have value apart from how they end. Goalless activities are valuable just because you're doing them, and they continue to be valuable as long as you do them and aren't diminished in value because they don't culminate in some big accomplishment. In this category, we can put things like sitting on a quiet dock to watch the waves come in or playing with our kids until we lose track of time.

Contemplation, unlike goal-directed action, is complete on its own terms. Following the ancient philosophers, we can break down this completeness into two more distinct features. Contemplation is continuous—it doesn't have a clear beginning or end. If you are absorbed in a thought or a moment, there is no definite point when you have to turn away. And contemplation is leisurely—there is no set pace you should strive to do it at and no such thing as being an "efficient" contemplative. Contemplative activities don't have bittersweet endings, because they don't really have endings at all. For Setiya, the antidote to the problems caused by excessive attachment to goals and action was to push himself to appreciate goalless activities. In his case, the midlife crisis ended by taking up a serious daily meditation practice (and then, hypocritically perhaps, writing a book about it).

Contemplation can be done by anyone, anywhere, at any phase of life, for any amount of time, and—if we've cultivated the right sort of inner life—contemplative practices will refresh us and provide us with meaning. This is not simply because they tap into reserves of dopamine or give our planning minds a breather. Many goalless activities are ones we tend to find meaningful, refreshing, and full of purpose in themselves. And even if such activities are "goalless" in the sense that they aren't directed at realizing some external aim, they can still have an interior impact by allowing the attention-directing, contemplative part of you to do its thing.

But what the hell are you supposed to contemplate? Aristotle could never quite get a grip on how to answer this. The truth? The Platonic Forms? The best Aristotle says on the question is that when we contemplate, we have the chance to behold "the things we have come to know." So how do we make sure that we're contemplating the right things? And how can we get better at an activity that has no point?

SUCCEEDING AT A TASK WITH NO GOAL

There is a temptation to think you need to go somewhere (a lake house, a meditation center) to get absorbed in contemplation. But one of the most remarkable features of contemplation is its portability—it is a form of the good life you can access absolutely anywhere. This is why we don't know precisely when Marcus Aurelius started his journal—it is a story of his thoughts on retreat, not where he is on any particular day. He writes himself a reminder that even in the most difficult circumstances, he can find happiness in contemplation: "Men seek retreats for themselves—in the country, by the sea, in the hills—and you yourself are particularly prone to this yearning. But all this is quite unphilosophic, when it is open to you, at any time you want, to retreat into yourself. No retreat offers someone more quiet and relaxation than that into his own mind, especially if he can dip into thoughts there which put him at immediate and complete ease." For Marcus, it is a skill to be able to step outside of the demands of a particular situation and to have a set of thoughts at hand that you access instead—your philosophical life is itself the retreat.

So what does Marcus contemplate during these miniature mental retreats? He lingers on three frequent topics.

First, he gives himself advice on virtue and reflects on what he has discovered about the good life in his own adventures. The journal reads most of the time like a strange coaching manual, in which Marcus is having a one-sided pump-up talk with himself. A persistent theme is his desire to try harder to live up to his Stoic ideals. "What sort of soul do I have after all?" So one of the most obvious topics of contemplation for the good life is . . . your life itself. And more specifically, during periods of contemplation, you can offer advice to your active self about your ideals. For example, one day during the coronavirus quarantine, Paul and Meghan finished a long and discerning walk. Meghan came home and wrote on a Post-It: "Don't forget, you care more about having friends than getting credit." The little yellow note is a way of unselfing, of giving herself a nudge about how she should try to see others. If notes are too public, you can keep the same aphorisms in a journal, just as Marcus does.

Second, Marcus reflects on nature, change, death—not just for himself but for everything in the universe. When he has a question about reality, he writes that down as well. Could we all be atoms in a meaningless void? For Stoics like Marcus, the world is a unified material cosmos in a state of constant change and regeneration—"a conflagration." God is the reason governing this cosmos. In the midst of this fiery, chaotic cosmos, Stoics like Marcus thought the good life required focusing your desires on virtue alone and realizing that happiness is just doing your best to live virtuously and avoiding concern for everything else. This latter principle is where we get the image of Stoics as coldhearted and indifferent. (Indeed, they called goods like health, money, and power "indifferents," since none of these goods necessarily increases virtue.)

But just as Marcus tries to scientifically, dispassionately understand the material world, he takes great pleasure in allowing the material world to inspire reflection on his own character. He hones his powers of contemplation by trying to behold the details in ordinary life. Appreciating a meal becomes an occasion for reflecting on imperfection and decay: "Even the incidental effects of the processes of Nature have their own charm and attraction. Take the baking of bread. The loaf splits open here and there, and those very cracks, in one way a failure of the baker's profession, somehow catch the eye and give particular stimulus to the appetite." He uses the concrete, visual (edible!) details of his day to supply him with the bigger "principles" that he returns to again and again. Many contemplative traditions, both religious and secular, ask you to start with the very concrete and mundane aspects of life you can behold (food, nature, your body) and use them as an impetus to reflect on the transcendent (suffering, love, change). Marcus would have been completely unsurprised that our pandemic contemplative practices involved sourdough.

Finally, he reflects on the meaning of others' lives in relation to his own—what he has learned from them and why specifically their lives have been good. In the beautiful opening chapter of his journal, he lists the people he loves by name and reflects on what aspects of his own character they have shaped: "From Apollonius: to always be the same man, unchanged in sudden pain, in the loss of a child, in lingering sickness; to see clearly in his living example that a man can combine intensity and relaxation." One of his principles, to which he constantly returns, is that "men are born for the sake of each other." The contemplative life might be solitary in its execution, but Marcus thought that other people, especially those we love, are a key subject of our thinking.

Later thinkers like Saint Thomas Aquinas would insist that when we contemplate, we're really drawn not just into our own thoughts but into perceptions of God. For Aquinas the contemplation we do in spare moments in this life is just a dress rehearsal for the big understanding we'll achieve in the next one. According to Aquinas, contemplation is what we were made for, but we'll only achieve it perfectly in the next life. Still, on earth, a contemplative life is an ideal to strive for, so that we can start exercising our minds like a muscle, using these meditative or contemplative moments to keep our vision on the things that really matter.

Even the secular virtue ethicists have considered the idea that people are a good source of material for our contemplative lives. We saw this with Plato, Aristotle, and Iris Murdoch in earlier chapters. This is one of the ways we see that the contemplative life does not need to be at odds with the life of love, friendship, and philanthropy. Making time for contemplation develops our capacity for love. For us to have the good life, we have to contemplate the good lives of others.

ADDING CONTEMPLATION TO YOUR GOOD LIFE

Here is a simple activity we do sometimes with our students, to start a philosophical conversation about what it means to contemplate the good life. Close your eyes. Replay in your mind whatever you think, until this point, has been the happiest thirty seconds of your life. We then let anyone who wants to share where their mind took them. Try it yourself. Where did you retreat to?

Sometimes our students' answers are achievements—winning a state track and field race, opening a college admissions envelope—but often they're the opposite. One of our students, Tom, reported that his happiest thirty seconds included a scene just after his rowing team *lost* the biggest qualifying race of the season. Explaining it to a puzzled room, he said that he had never felt as connected to any group of people as he did in that moment. Most often the answers we get involve memories of being with other people. A brawny, six-foot-two student athlete broke down in tears during this exercise one night, remembering the last day of summer camp and the feeling of chasing his brother during a game of capture the flag. Other examples involve reflecting on the state of being with other people: sitting by a lake with a lover, being pushed on a swing, holding a newborn. Some report a poignancy in realizing they would not be able to have those kinds of experiences with those particular people ever again. Others take the reflection and have a realization about virtue, what humans are, or how the world works that they store away as material for more philosophical reflection.

In the spirit of Aristotle, we've tried throughout this book to make the philosophical advice as concrete and practical as possible—to bring the philosophy up against "facts and life." And like Aristotle, we have found that making the life of contemplation concrete and practical is about as easy as nailing Jell-O to a wall. But perhaps the best road into this is that of Marcus Aurelius: to let the life of action you've already lived give you some materials for contemplation. Not telling the story but extracting the meaning.

Rereading the *Meditations* during the pandemic, we were gripped with how much everyday life in the quarantine naturally tended toward Marcus's contemplative ideal. The time at home provided many with an opportunity to contemplate and marvel at the everyday lives and habits of family members, including children. When Paul found himself staring intently at some cherry blossoms on a walk with his kids, he observed a certain sadness in his initial perception. The blossoms had appeared overnight, trees exploding with vibrant colors all around the neighborhood, but he knew they'd just as quickly be gone. As he looked back and forth between his quickly growing kids and the trees, he saw that his sadness was coming from an attachment to a genuinely beautiful thing, and a desire for its permanence. That night, when he got home, he wrote his own Stoic aphorism in his journal: "Appreciate good things while they are present, in front of you. Beauty in *this* moment is something change cannot diminish, but it's something you can fail to appreciate."

We can all reflect on how little control any of us have over our economic futures, our jobs, or our health. In these moments, the contemplative approach would serve us well, helping us remind ourselves that there is still so much—our love for our family, our relationship with God, our cultivation of inner virtues—that remains untouched by external contingencies.

Soulcraft: The Examen

If you're religious, contemplative practices are likely already a part of your tradition. Certain strains of Buddhism encourage more or less structured daily meditations. There's a contemplative element built into daily prayer rituals like those practiced by many Jews, Muslims, and Christians. One of our favorite contemplative practices, coming out of the Catholic tradition, is the Examen of Saint Ignatius, the founder of the Society of Jesus, a religious order commonly known as the Jesuits.

The Examen is one of Ignatius's Spiritual Exercises. Jesuits are famously missionaries, traveling to all ends of the earth to convert and educate. Often Jesuits would be sent out in small groups to embed themselves in foreign cultures, as much to learn from and about the culture as to attempt to transform it. The Spiritual Exercises is a set of contemplative prayers and activities that

Ignatius wrote in the sixteenth century to help the priests in his order sharpen their discernment. It was often important for a Jesuit to try to figure out whether some aspect of culture was a development, something that could be adopted and incorporated into his life and faith, or a distraction that would ultimately lead him away from God. Nowadays it is a useful practice for reflecting on what's constant under our own tumultuous lives.

Here's one simple version of the Examen you might try:

1. Find a quiet place where you can sit and contemplate. Ask for enlightenment. In the Catholic tradition, this means asking the Holy Spirit for guidance to see your life and day as God would.

2. Call to mind all those small things, in their very particularity, that you were blessed with throughout the day. Appreciate these. Say a quick prayer of gratitude.

3. Now walk again through each moment of your day, hour by hour. Try this time to see it through God's eyes. Dwell on any moments that trouble you, or give you comfort, or cause any sort of reaction in your soul. Ask for guidance and discernment to understand what is happening—to tell the story truly. Give thanks for those things that brought you closer to God (or your neighbor, or what is good in life). Make a note of any times when you had bad intentions or made mistakes.

4. Honestly face your shortcomings. Ask for forgiveness and appreciate your fallibility. Resolve to be more mindful in the future and to avoid temptations.

5. Look forward to the day to come. Think through the movements and envision how you can respond to the promptings of the spirit, how you can better love yourself and your neighbor, and how you can cultivate attentiveness

to the best movements of your soul and make continual progress.

There are thousands of versions of the Examen, and entire retreats devoted to helping people progress through the Spiritual Exercises. Even if Catholicism isn't your tradition, there are many elements of this sequence that might still be useful—taking responsibility through story, experiencing gratitude. There's also quite a bit of psychological research to support the practical value of this kind of contemplative religious practice. But, of course, for the believer, some of these findings are quite beside the point. This contemplation is something we do because it's in accord with our nature, and because of its intrinsic value. The fact that it might also help make us calmer, more thoughtful, or more productive is an unintended, if happy, consequence.

10.

Prepare for Death

> The true philosophers practice dying, and death is less terrible to them than to any other men.
>
> —Plato, *Phaedo*

MEMENTO MORI

Take a moment to envision your own death. For the sake of this exercise, imagine it to be a peaceful death at the end of a long life. Suppose that you've accomplished the projects that you now take most seriously, and you've had to make the relevant trade-offs to do so. If you are now set on making it into the C-suite of a Fortune 500 company, imagine that you've done it. But that meant you had to work eighty-hour weeks, which left you less time for family life. Or maybe you set out to create a certain family life, which now means that your impact in the world will likely live on mostly through them. Maybe your project has always been to live with openness to fate and adventure. As a result you now find yourself looking for a through line in all the twists and turns.

Color in the details and mentally locate yourself on your deathbed. What are you feeling? What are you thinking?

If you are anything like the many men and women that Bronnie Ware has interviewed, you might be wrestling with a few regrets. Ware is an Australian hospice caregiver and writer. She spent years collecting the contemplative insights of her dying patients and wrote a book based on them. According to Ware, here are the things people most wish they'd have changed while they still had the chance:

1. I wish I'd had the courage to live a life true to myself, not the life others expected of me.
2. I wish I hadn't worked so hard.
3. I wish I'd had the courage to express my feelings.
4. I wish I had stayed in touch with my friends.
5. I wish that I had let myself be happier.

There is a popular genre of blogs, magazine articles, and memoirs about the insights people have at the end of their lives. Think *Tuesdays with Morrie*, *The Last Lecture*, or *When Breath Becomes Air*. We might call this "beautiful death" literature, because it plays to an assumption that death gives us special and affirming clarity on life.

This kind of writing raises some interesting philosophical questions, too. Should we assume that people at the end of their lives are in the best position to see what's really meaningful? If so, what is it about nearing the end of life that elevates one to this expertise? How do we know that these deathbed memoirs are not biased by nostalgia, anxiety, selective memory, or the well-studied tendency to overemphasize the value at the end of an event—a bias sometimes called the peak-end effect in behavioral economics?

Another set of questions is more practical. What does reflection on deathbed values and regrets have to teach us about how to live the good life now, while we are still in the active phase of it? Should we live our lives in such a way to avoid the regrets of Ware's patients? And how often should a well-functioning person think about the end?

Plato famously hypothesized that all of philosophy was a kind of preparation for death. Indeed, most virtue ethicists in the ancient world thought that habitually thinking about death gives us an appreciation of our function as humans and a better grasp of the goal of our lives (even if we shouldn't want to achieve it quickly). And as with so many of the happiness questions we have considered, when we think about twenty-first-century death, technology gives us new ways to plan around death, while making questions about our ultimate goals even more complex.

PLANNING FOR A "GOOD DEATH"

In 2015, Kim Suozzi was a twenty-three-year-old graduate student studying neurobiology when her doctors discovered she had terminal brain cancer. Faced with such a tragic diagnosis, many of us would be tempted to spend our final years struggling to complete projects and rushing to fill a now-short life with meaning. Suozzi, however, turned to her scientific background to envision a new goal. She learned about a German researcher working on connectome mapping—mapping the neural circuits in the brain that scientists now believe provide the architecture for our consciousness. Suozzi spent the last year of her life leading a successful campaign to raise eighty thousand dollars to have her head preserved at death and her connectome mapped, with the hope that as technology improves, someday she could be "brought back." Her fundraiser started with a social media post soon after she learned her cancer was terminal: "Get ready to feel weird about me!" Suozzi's vision of the "good death" was to wager on another round of conscious life, biologically extending the life she loved at twenty-three, accepting potential memory loss and debilitation, and with a tremendous leap of faith in technology as a live option for her reincarnation.

In Suozzi's vision of the good life, she cares a great deal about her mind, and in particular the part of her that houses her processing abilities. She thinks more of the mental life, even with deficits and differences, is a worthy goal. She cares far less about the particulars of her body. And she is not particularly prescriptive about her vision of the good death—the risk was worth it for her, but she never tried to convince others to preserve *their* mental architecture.

Some people have views of the good death that are more prescriptive and emphasize different assumptions about the good life. A few years ago, the famed bioethicist and Obama health adviser Ezekiel Emanuel published a provocative cover story for *The Atlantic* entitled "Why I Hope to Die at 75." In the article, which was published alongside a picture of the grinning then-fifty-seven-year-old, Emanuel claims, "Living too long is . . . a loss. It renders many of us, if not disabled, then faltering and declining, a state that may not be worse than death but is nonetheless deprived. It robs us of our creativity and ability to contribute to work, society, the world. It transforms how people experience us, relate to us, and, most important, remember us. We are no longer remembered as vibrant and engaged but as feeble, ineffectual, even pathetic." Emanuel says these changes give us all reasons to hope for our lives to end before they take effect.

His central argument draws on his years of medical practice and experience with patients at the end of their lives. Emanuel thinks that our attempts to medically resist death are pathological. Given the amount of suffering involved in hanging on to every last breath, and given the speedy and likely diminishment of your "quality of life" after about seventy-five, you should hope for a quick fade to black before the suffering gets bad, and before you start to become more of a burden than a blessing to your family. Emanuel's vision of a good death is one that is both controlled and accepted. But there are deep philosophical assumptions lurking just below the surface.

First, there's the euphemism "quality of life" that suffuses most of this medically directed good death literature. Quality of life is measurable, and can go up or down based on how you are experiencing your life moment to moment. The "data" shows that at seventy-five (at least according to Emanuel) it will start diminishing. As we've seen, this is the way some consequentialist utilitarians think about the good life. But notice the somewhat grim implications they're forced to accept when it comes to death. If you're suffering from chronic pain with no hope of recovery, or are unable to engage creatively and productively at work—if you're becoming a net drain on global utility—you might just be approaching the threshold below which your life is no longer worth living.

We should also ask about what this good death advice implies about the sources of value in life. Emanuel thinks loss of ability to contribute to society sucks the meaning out of his life. But is it true that someone who never had a high-powered career, or contributed productively to the well-being of society, didn't have a meaningful life in the first place? Surely Emanuel would reject this, but it's hard to see on what grounds he could consistently do so. The kind of consequentialist thinking he's employing here implicitly commits us to some uncomfortable views about the marginalized and disabled. It also assumes, without much argument, that Emanuel's contribution to the common good of his family or society will depend on what he is able to produce rather than who he is for them. As we saw in the chapter on work, this view of what life's work amounts to is narrow and hard to sustain.

Emanuel isn't alone in this calculation-minded approach to the value of life at the end; he is just the most prominent clinical advocate. Peter Singer argues that we can tolerate killing the very young, the elderly, and the profoundly disabled under certain circumstances, for instance "when the life of an infant will be so miserable as not to be worth living. . . . It is better that the child should be helped to die without further suffering." His fellow consequentialist David Benatar takes these arguments even *further* (if that's possible) by arguing that human life is so filled with suffering and pain that nonexistence is morally superior to existence, and so anyone who willingly brings a human into this world (i.e., all parents) are doing a grave injustice to their children.

Of course, you can be a consequentialist and not go so far down these controversial routes. But we would still argue that thinking about life and death just in terms of maximizing would miss much of what else goes into the good life. Here we think virtue ethics can be helpful, especially in giving us hypotheses about the good death that don't depend on consequentialist logic.

The first step is considering, like Kim Suozzi, what options seem live for us when it comes to death and where those hopes spring from.

God and the Good Afterlife
(Paul's Apology)

For much of my life, I've had a mental test to determine what kind of relationship I had with someone. As a child and an adolescent, I'd sometimes think about what life would be like without some particular person—a friend or a family member—and see if I could even imagine myself in that world. For friends from school or church, I'd usually imagine myself sad but resilient. So, yes, I could imagine myself in that world. For close family members—my parents, my sister, and especially my brother, with whom I spent every waking minute—the answer into my midtwenties was always a resounding no. I literally couldn't fathom life apart from them.

But then something changed.

I had a couple of firsthand experiences of death. I'd attended funerals of very old grandmothers or great-aunts as a child, but I'd never experienced death firsthand until one of my father's good friends was dying of cancer in the hospital. His name was Alan, and he was a professor at the local university. He and I would sometimes have conversations at parties he and his family would host. I remember feeling privileged that an adult would take the time, and I was totally fascinated by his view of the world.

Toward the end, we would visit him in the hospital. What was confusing to me was the ordinariness of his death. He treated it like he was packing up and preparing for a really long business trip. Physically, it just seemed like he was slowly suffering from the worst flu imaginable. What struck me in our conversations toward the end of his life was the way he held on to his faith, and the way this informed his thinking until the end. For Alan life was about love, about relationships, and so was death. He would talk in a very normal way about the afterlife. Not as though he knew anything specific about it, but because as a Catholic he believed that he would be in a relationship with God, and with everyone else who'd died and gone to heaven (the "communion of saints"). He imagined it to be much like our human communities here on earth, like a brilliant worship service or a lovely family holiday.

This is how my grandfather thought about death, too, minus most of the explicitly religious stuff. The last time I saw him (and we both knew it was the last time), I read him a letter about all the ways in which he'd had an impact on my life. My grandfather was a notorious joker, a drinker, and a host of over-the-top parties that lasted well into the night. Even as he lay in his hospital bed, he had convened a party. Cousins played cards in the hallway, my grandma bought cookies for anyone who stopped by. He wasn't allowed to drink, but he'd joke with the nurses that he wanted them to put "some of the hard stuff" into his IV drip. Before I left, he and I were able to talk. This was one of the great gifts of my life. And as he smiled at me, he told me he wasn't afraid to die. He believed all the stuff about God and heaven, and he was pretty sure he'd get in. Still, he said, he didn't want to go just yet. He just wasn't ready to leave the party.

All these experiences, in their own way, have shaped how I think about death—my own and the deaths of those I love. They've given me real models of what the end might look like, and of what might still matter to me when I get there.

Over the years, I've become less convinced that I couldn't survive the deaths of my brother, my sister, my parents, or even my wife or children. I see (but don't understand) the difficult possibility of living through such tragedy and have witnessed the incredible resilience of some who have. I now think of death itself in much more relational terms. Not about how it would affect my relationships, but about what relationships might survive.

I maintain a belief in the afterlife, and reflect on what that might look like through literature and philosophy. I'm taken by the traditional Christian view that what matters so deeply to us here on earth will be subsumed and elevated in the life to come. That loving relationships—with God, with one another, and with the communion of saints—will make sense of the virtuous struggle we're all engaged in here below.

A passage in Dante's Paradiso *describes when he's finally brought to a spot on a mountain from which he'll have a view of God, the source and summit of all human striving. He sees circles of intricately detailed angels (with various numbers of wings) swirling around . . . a single perfect dot of light. As he explains it, the illumination is intense, but untranslatable. Once he's finally allowed to see the ultimate vision of God and reality, the poet finds himself unable to speak.*

REASON AS AN ANTIDOTE TO FEAR

Once you have the live options in your sights, you can start to ask the hard questions. Throughout this book, we have argued that philosophical attention can help you come to better understand who you are and how you make decisions. Our hope is that understanding, if it is also aimed at the truth, will help you to love your life fully. How does that understanding accompany us when we realize this life we love is also a life that will end? This is a central question in virtue ethics. And many philosophers in the tradition think that the strong questions that help us direct our lives can also offer us a rational way to shield ourselves from fear of death.

This should surprise you. According to virtue ethics, the underlying point of everything we do in life is to grow more and more into a well-functioning version of ourselves. Death seemingly undoes all of this work. We cease to be rational animals. We are erased from the story. Not only that, our death irrevocably changes the stories of those we love, who live second lives in ours. So how could there be a good death?

Virtue ethicists pursue the question by approaching death itself through appreciation of how it figures in developing the virtues. Here are three intriguing strategies, all drawn from ancient sources, but resonant for us.

One question we might ask is, How does death give us material for our intellectual lives? This approach to the good death emphasizes the virtue of contemplation. In brief: you might think that death gives us something significant to think about in this life, a worthy and fruitful target for our minds. As we saw in the previous chapter, some philosophers like Marcus Aurelius thought the most valuable things in life cannot be disrupted or taken away. Poverty can take our material possessions but not our dignity. An enemy soldier can imprison us but cannot take away our virtue. Marcus goes a step further: not even death can take what matters most. Indeed, Marcus constantly *uses* death as an object of contemplation. Marcus, like all of us, is worried he'll get addicted to fake achievements, so he reflects, "How many who once rose to fame are now consigned to oblivion: and how many who sang their fame are long disappeared?"

We might also wonder, Why do we think our deaths will be bad for us? A second approach to the good death emphasizes the virtue of truth seeking. Socrates asks us to think through every option we might face with death and ask if it would truly be harmful. Facing his own imminent death at the end of the *Apology*, he talks through his options. He entertains two live options for what might come next. Either the dead "have no perception of anything, or it is, as we are told, a change and a relocating for the soul from here to another place." If death is complete nonexistence, Socrates argues, then it's like the deepest, most peaceful sleep you've ever had. If the soul undergoes some sort of transformation, then death is a great adventure in which you get to meet everyone who's gone before you. And what could be a greater blessing than that?

Socrates never considers whether a miserable afterlife is an option. But philosophy can perhaps help here as well. Reasoning can tell us some visions of the afterlife aren't good. (And if God is good, then reason would seem to rule these out.) Hypothesis: hell is a real dimension where people are tortured eternally using medieval farm equipment for arbitrary features of the lives they lived. You can perhaps rule out that kind of hell by asking how such a situation could be compatible with morality or whether such an option is compatible with whatever apology you are working out for God. What about an afterlife where hell is other people? Where hell is the eternal satisfaction of your current desires? Perhaps that's harder to rule out. Importantly, your truth-seeking virtues help you uncover reasonable fears and hopes from ones without any reasons backing them.

There's still another question we might ask: Why is life the sort of thing we want more of? Another approach to the good death challenges consequentialist assumptions that good = more. This approach comes, most famously, from Epicureanism, another ancient philosophical tradition usually remembered for putting a pretty high emphasis on pleasure in the good life. (You might know "epicurean" as a term for someone who loves good food.) The Epicureans thought pleasure was important, but we had to care about it in reasonable ways. And reason does not compel us to pile it on. The most famous Epicurean philosopher, Lucretius, makes the point this way: "Of time the eternal, ere we had a birth. And Nature holds this like a mirror up of time-to-be when we are dead and gone. And what is there so horrible appears? Now what is there so sad about it all?" Lucretius asks us to assume for reductio ad absurdum that death is bad because the length of life is good—we should want longer rather than shorter good lives. He's going to show this is absurd by asking you to apply your "length matters" reasoning to another finite point in life: birth. Consider the (near) infinite amount of time that unfolded before you were born, and notice that, during that time, you did not yet exist. Now consider the fact that—after death—your state of being will exactly mirror this time. None of us wish we had been born earlier just so our lives would be longer. So length itself does not matter. So we ought also to be indifferent about our future nonexistence.

Or so says Lucretius. But this leads to yet another question—the Big One. Length alone is not what we want. What strategy should we use to direct our lives toward a good death?

THE SENSE OF AN ENDING

Asking strong questions about death and then reasoning out the answers can take us some way toward living well in death's shadow. But another key philosophical tool is working to fit inevitable challenges, like death, into the true story we have already developed about our lives. If we imagine ourselves as responsible for the stories we are writing, then even if we cannot change the fact of death we can change the intentions of the person who will undergo it.

The anticipated end of a story can change the meaning of what's come before in powerful ways. To illustrate, consider the following short story: "There were three young men who signed up for war, were shipped off, and never returned." This is a tragedy. But consider what happens if we add a new ending to it: "until one day, when they return, battered and beaten, having had to fight their way back after they'd gotten lost and been forgotten by their platoon." Now the story is epic. Let's give the ending one final twist: "One of the men, after remaining silent for a long time, spoke up: 'We didn't see much fighting along the way. Are you sure we were supposed to be dropped off in Normandy, Ohio?'" Now the story is a comedy.

Any kind of story only makes sense when it transpires against a background. The "up and down" motion a man uses to pump a well counts as "doing something" because wells are machines designed to move water. The same motion performed on a tree branch is unintelligible. Standing in front of city hall with a poster board only counts as "activism" in the context of a certain political system in which authority has been distributed in one particular way.

One reason why we think it's so important to reflect on the philosophical story of your life is because there are a number of twists and turns that you've got to anticipate. To end up addicted to drugs or to join a hateful authoritarian political movement is not just one choice among many (and an expression of your ultimate freedom)—it is a *mistake.* The broader context allows us to judge such life outcomes as bad, partly because they entail that you've failed to live up to your function as a rational, social animal.

Seneca was a Roman philosopher who lived and wrote about one hundred years before Marcus Aurelius. Like Marcus, he was a contemplative caught up in a highly charged political life. Seneca had the dubious honor of being an adviser to Emperor Nero, until Nero in one of his characteristically psychopathic fits ordered Seneca to kill himself.

Like other Stoic virtue ethicists, he thought deeply and systematically about death and counseled many of his friends about how to manage the tragedies and limits within their own lives. Much of his Stoic philosophy comes to us from preserved, deeply moving "letters of consolation." In one, to his friend Paulinus, he discusses the importance of reflecting on the story of the life you have been living: "This is the period of our time which is sacred and dedicated, which has passed beyond all human risks and is removed from Fortune's sway. . . . It is an untroubled, everlasting possession."

Suppose you are climbing toward your future, and the way ahead looks dark, uncertain, and foreboding. According to Seneca, if you have been practicing philosophy, you always have a move available to you. You can turn around and behold the life you have built. That life is securely yours to make meaning out of. Seneca goes further. By educating yourself (i.e., by reading philosophy and history) you can annex other eras to your own. You can make your life extend meaningfully deep into the past: "There is a long period of time through which we can roam. We can argue with Socrates, express doubt with Carneades, cultivate retirement with Epicurus. . . ."

Importantly, when we think of the good life as an achievement or an everlasting possession, that doesn't mean that we will take stock of our lives the way we might take stock of a career or an athletic record. We should resist the impulse to make our virtues into categories with scores—to consequentialize them. When you look back on your life, it will not be particularly fulfilling to say, "I'd give myself a B-plus for honesty and an A for generosity." Eulogies list off the virtues and provide evidence for them. Like a good résumé, a good eulogy downplays the struggles. Eulogies are written by people outside of your life at the end. They are a wonderful, necessary form of bullshit.

Your philosophical apology is different. You are telling that story from the inside. The virtues and vices *are* you. The conversations with Socrates, Anscombe, and the others are meant to get at the truth you will know about your life. For Seneca, the reward for your work living this life is the chance to understand it for what it is, to see what was defensible and what was a mistake. And the hope is that reconciling these parts of your life and taking responsibility will give you more light to guide you into that uncertain future. All of which calls us back to the opening question of how you as a philosopher envision the end of your good life.

Imagining Death from the Inside *(Meghan's Apology)*

I find it much easier to think about my own death than the deaths of people I love. In fact, I find imagining their deaths completely devastating. I am not sure any philosophy will prepare me enough for it. Their deaths feel to me like a dark contemplative box that I can open just the tiniest bit, glimpse inside, and then seal the cover back on. I honestly have no idea how Seneca, Marcus Aurelius, or Cormac McCarthy is able to think about this so often and with such sobriety. Genuine love is an emotional affair, a mixture of awe, joy, grief, jealousy, confusion. Loss of something loved appropriately makes all of these the right feelings at the right time. But they are huge feelings, and for me, there just never seems to be an appropriate space now to let them out.

When I imagine my own good life from the end, looking back to now, here is what it seems to look like. There was a tight-knit, in many ways conventional, family. Friendships, jobs, health scares, and other personal tragedies were lived out against the backdrop of the era in which I lived, which included terrorism, pandemics, extraordinary wealth, extraordinary poverty, historic presidencies and historic protests, incredible technological leaps. I sometimes engaged, but more often was an "extra" in these big events. I spent time on every populated continent. I painstakingly learned and then gradually forgot how to speak Spanish. I wrote books, taught thousands and thousands of students, and was thoroughly, joyfully immersed in the strange customs of university life. These episodes are the plot from the outside, each revealing virtues (curiosity, persistence, friendship) and vices (pride and greed). I hope to look back and see that experience sanded some of the rough edges off my ambition and egotism. But I don't see myself as being ashamed in the least for the things I tried to make with other people.

Money will have turned out to be a mostly effective way for me to develop virtues like trust, forgiveness, prudence, and generosity. I'll have realized by midlife that its moral powers for me were wearing off. I'll trust others to help me with the big problems and trust myself to be able to figure out new ones as they arise. If I'm doing well, I'll realize how small a part it plays in my life. The same cycle of appreciating and letting go will happen with authority, with family, and with other goods that we have to accept should change.

Where are the mistakes being made right now? What might I regret? Maybe waiting so long to decide whether to have children. Maybe not investigating bigger "leaps"—live options that are perhaps even further departures from the relatively conventional academic life. Am I sure I don't have a religious vocation? (Are there nuns who say the f-word as often as I do?) Was I really there enough for my neighbors and friends, the way I like to tell myself I am? I'm curious to figure out the answers. I'm going to have to live with the choices.

But importantly, that's not even the main story. Because there won't be any joy in the end at counting up virtues, even though I hope to figure them out. At the end, I dread dying, not because I have any fear of missing out, but because for many moments of my life, I was shocked and amazed by how great a gift it is to have a conscious life of my own. To be a thinking, feeling, directing, me-shaped part of this universe. I can make myself feel this really profoundly when I think about how incredibly lucky it all seems that I was able to have it to begin with.

And I love all of this. I will be devastated to someday face the prospect that there won't be more of it ahead. So it will matter to me at the end to note that there were many points in my life where I loved it "from the inside," in a way only I can really appreciate. Seneca says that life only feels too short if we have never learned how to use it, to live it well. I'm inclined to think that's right—life commands our joy and awe when we live it well. I just can't imagine ever tiring of wanting to live it well. I think this is the mistake in Stoic reasoning about the length of life. When we're in love with something good, we can't pull our attention away.

Just as I can't put myself at the deathbed of any of my loved ones, I likewise can't seem to gather them around my imagined deathbed. Of course, at the real one, many of them could be there. But I think the movie ending, where hands are held, songs are played, and somebody gently whispers "go into the light" . . . that's not how it will go. They'll be opening that black box, too. My death will be painful and will affect their lives profoundly. That's the heavy mystery of living second lives with others: we have to die with one another.

So who are the people I will do this to? I think about this the way I think about how I love my own life. It came to me, a lucky gift, and I loved discovering its function, developing it, and over time was struck again and again with how beautiful it is. I look upon the lives of my brothers and parents, my friends, and count them the same way. I got a Mary and a Liam, then a Pat, then a Connor . . . and so on, and I beheld them all. I know I will regret the amount of time I spent trying to find good reasons to separate people into categories as worth my love or worth less of it. I'll hope the people in the latter category will forgive me.

What about God? He's the target of much of my gratitude. The Colbert argument from the God chapter speaks to how I think of my relationship with God. I don't think love could let such good lives (mine or yours) end. That reasoning makes me optimistic that the love that has propelled this life all along will keep it going. I'll have a Catholic funeral Mass, with the simple prayers. My favorite hymn comes from the American folk tradition. It's a Baptist hymn, not a Catholic one, and I'd hope my loved ones (Christian and skeptic alike) would sing it anyway. In one version (popularized by the Irish folk singer Enya) the hymn ends "Since love is lord of heaven and earth, how can I keep from singing?"

Soulcraft: Strong Questions about Death

If Plato and the Stoics are right, being willing to ask strong questions about death can help us make meaning out of the life we are currently leading and prepare ourselves for the most significant challenges ahead. Contemplating death requires equal parts courage and imagination—courage to confront the truth about our limitations; imagination to fill in the uncertain hypotheses about what will come next. Here are some prompts that can help you start to contemplate. Imagine you are approaching the end of your good life.

1. **THE SETTING:** Where are you? Who is in the room with you? Is there music or prayer?
2. **YOUR STORY:** What are the memories you return to with pride? With love? What episodes of your life are in the "highlight reel"? What are your regrets?
3. **YOUR GOAL:** What do you hope happens as you die? How do you hope others value your life? What, if anything, would be a satisfying next chapter to your story? And what are the reasons behind these answers? How do your goals connect to the story so far?

4. **YOUR MEANS:** Are there things you could do right now to get closer to your goal, or to get a better goal in your sights? Is there anything you can do to change the meaning of episodes you think you'll likely regret?

Maybe you go a step further and share these thoughts, however tentative, with someone else. One of the ways we include our friends and loved ones in our good life is by letting them in on how we're thinking and feeling about even the heavy mortal questions. This can be very practical—these questions can open up a dialogue about the kind of medical care and end-of-life directives that matter to you. But these life and death discussions, with a bit of practice, also help us better understand how our loved ones are fitting their philosophical views together. You may even realize that they have insights that nudge you closer to the truth about the life you are living and the direction in which it is aimed.

CODA

The Limits of Philosophy

We began this book with a bold pitch for philosophy. We believe, and hope that you now do, too, that philosophical exercises can help you live a better life. But at this journey's end, it's important to debrief what we can expect from philosophy, and what we need to seek elsewhere.

Philosophy is excellent at helping you imagine and test your good life goals.

Plato and Aristotle give us arguments for the value of truth in living a good life. If we don't want to wallow in bullshit, or simply use our minds to deceive, manipulate, or confuse our way into positions of power, we've got to seriously consider the possibility that we're creatures made for contemplation. We've got to take a hard look at ourselves and ask why we sometimes prefer the comfort of dark caves. Contemplation, as we have seen, can be a passive act—looking. But it can also be active—asking dinner party questions. The origin of philosophy is curiosity pursued with friends. Sophistry is our reason-seeking function gone haywire. It tries to dampen both our love for the truth and our love for the people we pursue it with. We've always had to resist its allure.

What should we do with ourselves day to day? In conversation with Karl Marx, John Stuart Mill, Jeremy Bentham, and Peter Singer we've uncovered the deep connections between work, money, charity, and living well. Elizabeth Anscombe's insights—and her surprising friendship with Iris Murdoch—showed us how we might use stories to think deeply about love and responsibility, and about the dire importance of such storytelling for the tough ethical decisions we'll inevitably face in our relationships with other people.

Love is the ur-virtue, one that inevitably pulls us from the quotidian issues of the good life into the existential ones. What is worthy of our love? Saint Thomas Aquinas and Stephen Colbert helped us see the role reason plays in seeking the truth about God, and Kierkegaard and William James showed us its limits. They also showed us ways we might transcend those limits, through leaps of faith based on our trust in ourselves or in religious traditions. Marcus Aurelius, Seneca, and Socrates walked with us through the last few miles, helping us think about anxiety, suffering, and death, and providing us with philosophical practices we can use to redirect the hardest challenges toward a better grasp of eudaimonia.

We hope some of the prescriptions of these philosophical doctors have helped you, especially the questions and exercises they recommend. Maybe you have a sharper appreciation of why you have been earning money or spending time parenting. Maybe the philosophical methods also have started to make your goals bigger (and weirder). You talk about work more expansively. You are less afraid to think about death. Some more of those circles are joined.

Philosophers use reason to give us the structure of the goal, but philosophy cannot color in the details. It cannot tell you what your specific work is going to be, how to love the particular kid you have, how to see God in the twists and turns of your experience. In fact, it can be downright dangerous when a philosophy imposed from the outside eclipses the goals you are discovering for your own good life. If Plato had ever acquired real political power, the city he would have built based on the *Republic* would have been a fascist nightmare with heartless math professors trying to run the military. Many a cult has used philosophical language and frameworks to direct people on pseudo-spiritual journeys of self-discovery. These inevitably end poorly for everyone involved. If a philosopher promises to *give* you the good life, you should become skeptical. At the very core of this enterprise is an assumption that you are a reason-seeking animal, and anyone coaching you on the good life owes you honest reasons.

The best philosophers know this, and are humble about what they can and cannot do using these powers of reason. While we think it's important to contextualize it, we do, in the end, agree with Aquinas that, in a sense, it's all "straw." Aristotle, at the end of the *Nicomachean Ethics*, struggles with the notion that he hasn't been able to completely nail down the good life, or to fill in enough details about how contemplation is supposed to get us there. He gets to the end, tries to grasp how we could ever achieve the contemplative virtues, and then concludes, "But a life of this sort would exceed what is human."

Our view is that this humility and frustration are also, in their way, indicators we are on the right track.

For many philosophers, it's as if reason brings us to the precipice and gives us a taste of what we're all striving for: enough to know certain basic truths about ourselves, our functions, our lives, and the virtues we should strive to embody. But only enough to squint at the most ultimate goal.

So what should you do? We leave you with two final suggestions.

We've worked on four interrelated skills throughout this book:

1. Strong Questioning: posing the kinds of questions that uncover our deeper reasons for believing and doing what we do
2. Agency: developing your intentions and telling the true stories about what you are doing and why

3. Loving Attention: paying the right kind of attention to others' true stories, discovering common goods, and joining your lives
4. Making Meaning: beholding how the episodes of your life fit together, reasoning through major course corrections when you must confront them, and joining up all the circles

Our first piece of advice is to keep working on the practices. Take the skills and context you've acquired from your foray into philosophy, and let them unsettle you. Bring them along with you the next time you get into goal mode. Unpack questions, stories, distinctions, and reflections as they become relevant. You're now part of a living tradition of philosophical dialogue stretching back two thousand years. Socrates is always up for a conversation, no matter the hour. Perhaps you might also try to read some of the original texts and enter more fully into these philosophers' complicated and beautiful lives. We provide some suggestions for your library in the Further Reading section.

Our second piece of advice is to let others in on the life you are building. Having a vision of the good life—a philosophical theory of what you are aiming at—is not crazy, impossible, or impractical. It is one of the most practical exercises we can undertake, since your philosophical views can help you make all of the other very difficult decisions you face. Put the questions or topics that have gripped you together into your own hypothesis about what you are working toward. And then . . . share this vision with others. Invite them in. Ask them for wisdom and insights. Make the philosophical questions part of how you pass the time waiting together, how you structure conversations at dinner or in the car. If it helps, pass this book along.

This drive to find a goal proportionate to life, and to seek to know this goal with others, is, for virtue ethicists, what the good life is all about.

Acknowledgments

In many ways, this book is an expression of the love and gratitude we have for Catholic education. We've had the chance to discover the good life with thousands of students at this point, and every semester they have enlightened us, changed our minds, and brought us more deeply into eudaimonia. Some along the way have become great friends. There are downsides to teaching (grading being the chief one). But creating this philosophical community with them and with our colleagues has been a transformative part of each of our lives.

If we tried to name all of the students and colleagues who've helped us make God and the Good Life, we could, but this acknowledgment section would end up being about fifty pages long. So we'll pick a few who have been invaluable contributors to the research and writing for this manuscript. Blake Ziegler, Lulu Phifer, Chase Miller, and Julia French all served as highly effective undergraduate research assistants in the spring of 2020 and have worked with us on the course. Mia Lecinski and Margaret McGreevy were the book RAs than which none greater can be conceived. They closely read every complete draft of the manuscript, provided excellent editorial advice, tracked down countless research questions, and served as arbiters in internal fights about the problem of evil. You will find their philosophical fingerprints in nearly every chapter. Lauren Spohn, Sam Kennedy, Emma Shimek, Kat Machado, Tom "Murph" Murphy, Elle Dietz, Ryan Cook,

Dane Sherman, Conrad Palor, Madison Wagner, and Jess Reeg provided us with challenges and insights over many wonderful philosophical conversations, read sections, and tracked down passages.

Stephen Grimm, Caleb Cohoe, Steve Angle, Tushar Irani, Steve Horst, and everyone in the Philosophy as a Way of Life community gave us critical intellectual guidance, taught us how to better teach ancient virtue ethicists, and have been our "second teaching selves" for the past five years. We learned about the soulcraft exercise idea from them. We are consistently inspired by their scholarship and their teaching projects.

We also owe a tremendous debt to the rest of our GGL teaching team. On the faculty end, Justin Christy, Laura Callahan, and Brian Cutter have all taught the course with us and been instrumental in developing aspects of the curriculum. We also have the honor of mentoring and teaching with some incredible PhD students, most notably Ross Jensen, Ciara O'Rourke, Will Shankles, Wes Siscoe, Shannon Sandridge, and Haley Dutmer, who have all been creative partners on our team.

Mike Wilsey read multiple drafts and has also played a pivotal role in helping us grow the GGL program. The Andrew W. Mellon Foundation, the National Endowment for the Humanities, the Notre Dame College of Arts and Letters, and Notre Dame Research all provided substantial financial and administrative support to make youth corruption on this scale possible. Some friends of Notre Dame participated in our book clubs as we were trying to finish the manuscript and were incredible interlocutors right when we needed them. We benefited from their patience and insight. Sean Cullinan, Tim and Lynn Murphy, Kevin Mulhall, Mike Stephan, Tim Connors, Joe Sifer, Scott and Loretta Dahnke, Paul Bontatibus, Casey Friedman, Carly Murphy, and Glenn and Suzanne Youngkin all provided great comments that changed parts of chapters. We are also grateful to inspired higher-ed leaders who are willing to make bold investments in philosophy. At Notre Dame, they are Jeff Speaks, Maria Di Pasquale, John McGreevy, Sarah Mustillo, Tom Burish, Marie Lynn Miranda, and Fr. John Jenkins. But we meet so many other deans, provosts, and presidents at our partner schools who realize the urgency with which we teach these questions.

We owe more than we can say to our family and friends who read our drafts closely, who put up with our philosophical questioning and apologizing, who provided feedback, and who always serve as our guides to the good life: Shayla Blaschko, James Blaschko, Katie and Ryan Braulick, Russell Blaschko, Debra Blaschko, the Swartz family, Dena Braun, Annie Tarr, Sarah and Chris O'Brien, and all of the Sullivans (Mary, Liam, Patrick, Ambrosia, Connor). Chris Neubauer, Peter Buttigieg, Fr. Gerry Olinger, and Mike Schur all at various points helped us discover some new magic in our course or this manuscript.

We are also enormously grateful to our editors at Penguin, Ginny Smith and Caroline Sydney, and to our agent, Rafe Sagalyn, for first convincing us that God and the Good Life could be a book and then being excellent coaches to us through the writing process. Ginny and Caroline helped us keep the goal in sight at every stage.

Notes

INTRODUCTION

1 **"Are you not ashamed":** Plato, *Apology* 29d–e, trans. G. M. A. Grube, in *Plato: Complete Works*, ed. John M. Cooper (Indianapolis: Hackett, 1997), 27.

2 **"no benefit from it":** Aristotle, *Nicomachean Ethics* 2.2, in *Aristotle's "Nicomachean Ethics,"* trans. Robert C. Bartlett and Susan D. Collins (Chicago: University of Chicago Press, 2011), 27. (Emphasis ours.)

3 **fundamentally human task:** For an example of the "joining up" language, see Cicero, *On Obligations* 1.11, trans. P. G. Walsh (Oxford: Oxford University Press, 2000). For a discussion of this metaphor in Stoic thought, see Terence Irwin, *The Development of Ethics*, vol. 1 (Oxford: Oxford University Press, 2007), chap. 13.

10 **"scientifically minded Westerners":** Martin E. P. Seligman, *Authentic Happiness: Using the New Positive Psychology to Realize Your Potential for Deep Fulfillment* (London: Nicholas Brealey, 2002), 14.

11 **engineers, managers, and consultants:** Linda Kinstler, "Ethicists Were Hired to Save Tech's Soul. Will Anyone Let Them?," *Protocol,* February 5, 2020, www.protocol.com/ethics-silicon-valley. (Emphasis ours.)

12 **their design-process approach:** Steven Kurutz, "Want to Find Fulfillment at Last? Think Like a Designer," *New York Times,* September 17, 2016.

14 **practical advice needs:** We are grateful to Stephen Grimm and Caleb Cohoe for discussing this framework with us.

15 **"[function] of a serious man":** Aristotle, *Nicomachean Ethics* 1.7, lines 1098a11–15, in *Aristotle's "Nicomachean Ethics,"* trans. Bartlett and Collins, 13.

16 **"You are an Athenian":** Plato, *Apology* 29d–e, in *Plato: Complete Works,* ed. Cooper, 27.

16 **That is the kind of happiness:** Aristotle, *Nicomachean Ethics* 1095a17, in *Aristotle's "Nicomachean Ethics,"* trans. Bartlett and Collins, 4–5.

19 **American College Health:** American College Health Association, *American College Health Association–National College Health Assessment II: Undergraduate Student Reference Group Data Report Spring 2019* (Silver Spring, MD: American College Health Association, 2019), 30–32, www.acha.org/documents/ncha/NCHA-II_SPRING_2019_UNDERGRADUATE_REFERENCE_GROUP_DATA_REPORT.pdf. These are all percentages of students who reported these feelings in the "last 2 weeks," "last 30 days," and "last 12 months." For a deeper look into the social psychological predictors of burnout and suicide, see Sara Konrath, *Culture of Burnout: American Life in an Age of Increased Expectations* (Oxford: Oxford University Press, forthcoming).

19 **psychologists observe plummeting:** Thanks to Sara Konrath for discussion. See Konrath, *Culture of Burnout.*

19 **declines in access:** Anne Case and Angus Deaton, *Deaths of Despair and the Future of Capitalism* (Princeton, NJ: Princeton University Press, 2020), 183.

23 **"It is necessary to examine":** "Happiness and the Structure of Ends," in *A Companion to Aristotle,* trans. Gabriel Richard Lear, ed. Georgios Anagnostopoulos (Malden, MA: Wiley-Blackwell, 2009), 403.

28 **"like patients who listen attentively":** Aristotle, *Nicomachean Ethics* 2.4, trans. W. D. Ross, the Internet Classics Archive, http://classics.mit.edu//Aristotle/nicomachean.html.

1: DESIRE THE TRUTH

31 **"refuting others themselves":** Plato, *Republic* 7.537e and 539b, trans. G. M. A. Grube, rev. C. D. C. Reeve (Indianapolis: Hackett, 1992), 208–10.

35 **find puzzles strangely fun:** We learned this approach from Tushar Irani at Wesleyan University, who taught us how to teach Plato. See Tushar Irani, *Plato on the Value of Philosophy: The Art of Argument in the "Gorgias" and "Phaedrus"* (Cambridge: Cambridge University Press, 2017).

35 **it a shot:** Alex Bellos, "Can You Solve It? Are You Smarter Than a Japanese Schoolchild?," *Guardian*, August 3, 2015.

35 **Maybe you found the answer:** The answer is 37. But you should not be satisfied until you have reasoned it out!

41 **Harry Frankfurt:** Harry G. Frankfurt, *On Bullshit* (Princeton, NJ: Princeton University Press, 2005), 55–56.

42 **jumping into politics:** Plato, *Republic* 8.561d, trans. Grube, 232.

43 **Popper thought Plato:** Karl R. Popper, *The Open Society and Its Enemies* (London: Routledge, 1966), 217.

46 "change your position": Plato, *Republic* 1.345c, trans. Grube, 21.

47 "Such prisoners would": Plato, *Republic* 7.515c, trans. Grube, 1133.

48 he tells Socrates: Plato, *Gorgias* 492a, trans. Donald J. Zeyl (Indianapolis: Hackett, 1997), 64.

48 escape from the grip: Thanks to Chike Jeffers for helping us make this connection between Du Bois's apology and the allegory of the cave.

49 "It is as though one": W. E. B. Du Bois, *Dusk of Dawn,* in *W. E. B. Du Bois: Writings*, ed. Nathan Huggins (New York: Literary Classics of the United States, 1986), 649–50.

50 "sometimes an historical fact": Du Bois, *Dusk of Dawn,* in *Writings*, ed. Huggins, 665.

50 desperately needed figure: Plato, *Apology* 30e–31, trans. G. M. A. Grube, in *Plato: The Complete Works*, ed. John M. Cooper (Indianapolis: Hackett, 1997), 28.

51 role of minority philosophers: Michael A. Peters, "Interview with George Yancy, African-American Philosopher of Critical Philosophy of Race," *Educational Philosophy and Theory* 51, no. 7 (2019): 663–69.

51 "non-violent gadflies": Martin Luther King Jr., "Letter from a Birmingham Jail," in *The Journal of Negro History* 71, no. 1–4 (Winter–Autumn, 1986; ed. Alton Hornsby Jr.), 39.

51 "When they have made it": Plato, *Republic*, 7.519d, trans. Grube, 1137.

53 reaction to the election: We were inspired here by a Walk a Mile activity we learned while doing student dialogue training with Sustained Dialogue International. Sustained Dialogue gave us very helpful guidance on asking strong questions with students while we were preparing the GGL course.

2: LIVE GENEROUSLY

59 "Jesus said to him": New American Bible (NAB) (Washington, D.C.: Confraternity of Christian Doctrine, 2010), https://bible.usccb.org/bible/matthew/19.

59 Notre Dame costs: Marketing Communications, University of Notre Dame, "How Aid Works," Notre Dame Office of Financial Aid, September 2020, https://financialaid.nd.edu/how-aid-works.

60 save the life: "GiveWell's Cost-Effectiveness Analyses," GiveWell, January 2019, www.givewell.org/how-we-work/our-criteria/cost-effectiveness/cost-effectiveness-models.

61 founder of Methodism: Max Weber, *The Protestant Ethic and the Spirit of Capitalism*, trans. Talcott Parsons (New York: Charles Scribner's Sons, 1958), 175–76.

67 murders the king: Plato, *Republic* 2.359a–360b, trans. G. M. A. Grube, rev. C. D. C. Reeve (Indianapolis: Hackett, 1992), 34–36.

68 **he could donate:** Peter Singer, *The Most Good You Can Do: How Effective Altruism Is Changing Ideas about Living Ethically* (New Haven, CT: Yale University Press, 2015), 3.

69 **"pains *must* come":** Jeremy Bentham, "An Introduction to the Principles of Morals and Legislation," in *The Broadview Anthology of Social and Political Thought*, vol. 1 (New York: Broadview Press, 2008), 880.

74 **as much in Philadelphia:** Tina Rosenberg, "H.I.V. Drugs Cost $75 in Africa, $39,000 in the U.S. Does It Matter?," *New York Times*, September 18, 2018.

76 **Singer's take on:** Singer, *The Most Good You Can Do*, 8.

3: TAKE RESPONSIBILITY

85 **"justification of monstrous things":** Elizabeth Anscombe, "War and Murder," in *Nuclear Weapons: A Catholic Response*, ed. Walter Stein (London: Sheed and Ward, 1961), 42–53.

89 **use a remote:** Joshua D. Greene, "Solving the Trolley Problem," in *A Companion to Experimental Philosophy*, ed. Justin Sytsma and Wesley Buckwalter (New York: Wiley, 2016), 173–89.

89 **Paul Bloom, another consequentialist psychologist:** Paul Bloom, *Against Empathy: The Case for Rational Compassion* (New York: Ecco, 2018), 31.

90 **"the right motive":** Aristotle, *Nicomachean Ethics* 2.6, in *The Nicomachean Ethics*, trans. W. D. Ross, ed. Lesley Brown (Oxford: Oxford University Press, 2009), 30.

93 **"know if God":** Lieutenant Colonel Joseph Campo, "From a Distance: The Psychology of Killing with Remotely Piloted Aircraft" (PhD diss., Air University, 2015), 226.

93 **life-threatening danger:** For more on the emotional responses reported by these pilots, see Brett Litz, Nathan Stein, Eileen Delaney, Leslie Lebowitz, William P. Nash, Caroline Silva, and Shira Maguen, "Moral Injury and Moral Repair in War Veterans: A Preliminary Model and Intervention Strategy," *Clinical Psychology Review* 29, no. 8 (2009): 695–706. Also see Wayne Chappelle, Emily Skinner, Tanya Goodman, Julie Swearingen, and Lillian Prince, "Emotional Reactions to Killing in Remotely Piloted Aircraft Crewmembers during and following Weapon Strikes," *Military Behavioral Health* 6, no. 4 (2018): 357–67.

93 **the "lasting psychological, biological, spiritual":** Litz et al., "Moral Injury and Moral Repair in War Veterans," 697.

94 **"in a desperate way":** Marc LiVecche, an instructor at the United States Naval Academy, in discussion with Paul Blaschko, September 2020.

95 **pragmatic, consequentialist approach:** Rachael Wiseman, *Routledge Philosophy GuideBook to Anscombe's "Intention"* (New York: Routledge, 2016), 13.

96 **women of Oxford:** Wiseman, *Routledge Philosophy GuideBook*, 11.

96 **"brash, unreal style":** Mary Midgley, "The Golden Age of Female Philosophy," *Guardian*, November 28, 2013. We first came across this source in Wiseman, *Routledge Philosophy GuideBook*, 12.

97 **two hundred thousand civilian casualties:** "The Atomic Bombings of Hiroshima and Nagasaki," Avalon Project, Yale Law School, 2008, https://avalon.yale.edu/subject_menus/mpmenu.asp.

97 **"The women are up to something":** Wiseman, *Routledge Philosophy GuideBook*, 11.

98 ***Intention* starts with:** G. E. M. Anscombe, *Intention* (Cambridge, MA: Harvard University Press, 2000).

101 **the "Why" question:** Anscombe, *Intention*, 38.

102 **Alasdair MacIntyre . . . "heedlessness":** Alasdair MacIntyre, "Heedlessness," Notre Dame Center for Ethics and Culture Fall Conference 2014, University of Notre Dame, October 31, 2014; available on YouTube, https://youtu.be/ccwTDBMn9Fs.

103 **For Anscombe, the first important:** G. E. M. Anscombe, "Mr. Truman's Degree," pamphlet published by the author (Oxford: Oxonian Press), 1956.

104 **"the intentional killing of innocents":** Anscombe, "Mr. Truman's Degree."

104 **"morally thick":** The idea of "moral thickness" comes from Bernard Williams, who thinks that the need for such language is an important feature of everyday life, and something moral philosophers need to pay close attention to. Bernard Williams, *Ethics and the Limits of Philosophy* (Cambridge, MA: Harvard University Press, 1985).

4: WORK WITH INTEGRITY

109 **"half my days":** John Milton, "Sonnet 19: When I consider how my light is spent," Poetry Foundation, accessed November 9, 2020, www.poetryfoundation.org/poems/44750/sonnet-19-when-i-consider-how-my-light-is-spent.

109 **The statistics we monitor:** John I. Jenkins, CSC, "President's Annual Address to the Faculty," September 17, 2019, https://president.nd.edu/homilies-writings-addresses/features/2019-faculty-address/.

110 **Airbnb's leadership team:** Erin Griffith, "Airbnb Was Like a Family, Until the Layoffs Started," *New York Times*, July 17, 2020.

113 **following thought experiment:** This is our modernized take on a thought experiment from Bernard Williams. We've changed and added details, and, in Williams's case the main character is named George not Jim. Bernard Williams, "A Critique of Utilitarianism," in *Utilitarianism: For and Against*, with J. J. C. Smart (Cambridge: Cambridge University Press, 1973), 97*ff.*

115 indispensable tools for: Sophie-Grace Chappell and Nicholas Smyth, "Bernard Williams," *Stanford Encyclopedia of Philosophy*, August 31, 2018, https://plato.stanford.edu/entries/williams-bernard/.

115 monks have lived: *New Melleray Abbey: One Thing*, produced by Chuck Neff, New Melleray Abbey, 2013.

117 When a pandemic ravaged central Iowa: Yonat Shimron, "As Coronavirus Death Rates Multiply, These Monks Are Giving Caskets Away," *National Catholic Register*, April 6, 2020, https://www.ncronline.org/news/people/coronavirus-death-rates-multiply-these-monks-are-giving-away-caskets.

118 feel meaningful regardless: Nellie Bowles, "God Is Dead. So Is the Office. These People Want to Save Both," *New York Times*, August 28, 2020.

118 Karl Marx . . . "alienation": Karl Marx, "Economic and Philosophic Manuscripts of 1844," in *The Marx-Engels Reader*, ed. Robert C. Tucker (New York: W. W. Norton & Company, 1978), 47.

119 For Aristotle, some of the goods: Aristotle, *Politics*, 2nd ed., trans. Carnes Lord (Chicago: University of Chicago Press, 2013), especially Book 1.2.

120 "getting goods": Aristotle, *Politics*, trans. Lord, Book 1.9.

123 true leisure is: Josef Pieper, *Leisure, the Basis of Culture*, trans. Alexander Dru (San Francisco: Ignatius Press, 2009), 46.

5: LOVE ATTENTIVELY

129 "any way to think": Cormac McCarthy, *The Road* (New York: Alfred A. Knopf, 2006), 109.

130 Aristotle thought there were: Aristotle, *Nicomachean Ethics* 8.3, in *Aristotle's "Nicomachean Ethics,"* trans. Robert C. Bartlett and Susan D. Collins (Chicago: University of Chicago Press, 2011).

131 virtues rather than: Troy A. Jollimore, *Love's Vision* (Princeton, NJ: Princeton University Press, 2011), chap. 1.

133 cognitive and social: "Mattel's Nabi Brand Introduces First-Ever Connected Kids Room Platform in Tandem with Microsoft and Qualcomm—Aristotle," Mattel, January 4, 2017, https://www.prnewswire.com/news-releases/mattels-nabi-brand-introduces-first-ever-connected-kids-room-platform-in-tandem-with-microsoft-and-qualcomm---aristotle-300385221.html.

133 "Mattel's New Baby": Lauren Evans, "Mattel's New Baby Monitoring Device Is Creepy as Hell," *Jezebel*, October 2, 2017, https://jezebel.com/mattels-new-baby-device-is-creepy-as-hell-1819086146.

133 "some emotional ties": Kate Cox, "Privacy Advocates Raise Concerns about Mattel's Always-On 'Aristotle' Baby Monitor," Consumerist, May 10, 2017, https://consumerist.com/2017/05/10/privacy-advocates-raise-concerns-about-mattels-always-on-aristotle-baby-monitor/.

133 **"By nature, friendship":** Aristotle, *Nicomachean Ethics* 8.1, line 1155a16, trans. Bartlett and Collins, 163.

133 **"Friendship is not spoken of":** Aristotle, *Nicomachean Ethics* 8.2, line 1155b27, trans. Bartlett and Collins, 166.

134 **gray matter between:** Andy Clark and David J. Chalmers, "The Extended Mind," in *The Extended Mind*, ed. Richard Menary (Cambridge, MA: MIT Press, 2010), 29.

134 **brains are connected:** Julian Kiverstein, Mirko Farina, and Andy Clark, "The Extended Mind Thesis," *Oxford Bibliographies*, May 30, 2019, https://www.oxfordbibliographies.com/view/document/obo-9780195396577/obo-9780195396577-0099.xml.

134 **Chief Justice Roberts:** *Riley v. California*, 573 U.S. 373 (2014). Thanks to Erin Egan.

135 **her magnum opus:** Thanks to Margaret McGreevy for biographical research here and in the next section. She relied on Peter J. Conradi's detailed biography, *Iris Murdoch: A Life* (London: HarperCollins, 2001).

136 **"in inner space?":** Iris Murdoch, "The Idea of Perfection," in *The Sovereignty of Good* (Abingdon, Oxon, UK: Routledge, 1970), 13.

137 **learning to look:** Murdoch, "Idea of Perfection," 17. Murdoch is indebted to the work of another virtue ethicist, Simone Weil, in developing these ideas about the connection between love and attention.

137 **psychologists at SUNY . . . "sustained, escalating, reciprocal":** Arthur Aron, Edward Melinat, Elaine N. Aron, Robert Darrin Vallone, and Renee J. Bator, "The Experimental Generation of Interpersonal Closeness: A Procedure and Some Preliminary Findings," *Personality and Social Psychology Bulletin* 23, no. 4 (April 1997): 363–77.

139 **"merely feeding in":** Aristotle, *Nicomachean Ethics* 9.9, trans. Bartlett and Collins, 205.

142 **her final days:** Thanks to Margaret McGreevy for biographical research. See Conradi, *Iris Murdoch*.

142 **"There was a sense that she was":** Conradi, *Iris Murdoch*, 592.

142 **For Aristotle and Murdoch:** Iris Murdoch, "The Sovereignty of Good over Other Concepts," in *The Sovereignty of Good* (Abingdon, Oxon, UK: Routledge, 1970), 82.

143 **"his friend's strength":** Marcus Tullius Cicero, *Letters of Marcus Tullius Cicero with His Treatises on Friendship and Old Age*, trans. E. S. Shuckburgh (New York: P. F. Collier & Son, 1909), 16.

147 "Well should he": McCarthy, *The Road*, 162.

147 horror novel as: Michael Chabon, "After the Apocalypse," *New York Review of Books*, February 15, 2007, https://www.nybooks.com/articles/2007/02/15/after-the-apocalypse/.

148 "grasps Mary's action": Giacomo Rizzolatti, Leonardo Fogassi, and Vittorio Gallese, "Mirrors in the Mind," *Scientific American* 295, no. 5 (November 2006): 54–61. See also Eleonore Stump, *Wandering in Darkness* (Oxford: Oxford University Press, 2012).

148 Lovecraft: Strong Questions: This exercise is inspired by the "36 Questions That Lead to Love" exercise described earlier in the chapter.

6: WONDER ABOUT GOD

153 "For I do not seek to understand": Saint Anselm, *Proslogium; Monologium: An Appendix in Behalf of the Fool by Gaunilo; and Cur Deus Homo*, trans. Sidney Norton Deane (Chicago: The Open Court Publishing Company, 1903; rep. 1926), https://sourcebooks.fordham.edu/basis/anselm-proslogium.asp.

153 "Joy is the most infallible sign": Joel Lovell, "The Late, Great Stephen Colbert," *GQ*, August 17, 2015, https://www.gq.com/story/stephen-colbert-gq-cover-story.

154 "What punishments of God": Scholars and Tolkien enthusiasts online think that Colbert is referring here to a letter written to Rhona Beare, which reads in part: "A divine 'punishment' is also a divine 'gift,' if accepted, since its object is ultimate blessing, and the supreme inventiveness of the Creator will make 'punishments' (that is changes of design) produce a good not otherwise to be attained." J. R. R. Tolkien, TolkienEstate.com, The Official Website of the J. R. R. Tolkien Estate, Letter 212 to Rhona Beare (1958), published 2015, https://www.tolkienestate.com/en/writing/letters/letter-rhona-beare.html.

155 "With existence comes suffering": Stephen Colbert, interview with Anderson Cooper, *Anderson Cooper 360°*, CNN, August 15, 2019.

155 "Our hearts are restless": Saint Augustine, "Confessions," trans. J. G. Pilkington, from *Nicene and Post-Nicene Fathers, First Series*, vol. 1, ed. Philip Schaff (Buffalo, NY: Christian Literature Publishing Co., 1887; revised and edited for New Advent by Kevin Knight, https://www.newadvent.org/fathers/110101.htm.

155 "God is that": Saint Anselm, *Proslogium; Monologium; Cur Deus Homo*, trans. Deane, chap. 4, https://sourcebooks.fordham.edu/basis/anselm-proslogium.asp.

155 "prime mover": Saint Thomas Aquinas, *The Summa Theologiae of St. Thomas Aquinas*, 2nd and rev. ed., 1920. Literally translated by Fathers of the English Dominican Province, online edition copyright © 2017 by Kevin Knight, First

Part, Question 2, Article 3, "Does God Exist," https://www.newadvent.org/summa/1002.htm.

158 **liturgy, history, community:** Samuel G. Freedman, "Secular, but Feeling a Call to Divinity School," *New York Times*, October 16, 2015.

158 **count as religions:** Mark Oppenheimer. "When Some Turn to Church, Others Go to CrossFit," *New York Times*, November 27, 2015.

160 **religious traditions demand:** For example, in advising persecuted Christian groups in how to live in society, 1 Peter 3:15 counsels, "Always be prepared to give an answer to everyone who asks you to give the reason for the hope that you have. But do this with gentleness and respect."

161 **family's youngest boy:** Stephen Brock, *The Philosophy of Saint Thomas Aquinas: A Sketch* (Eugene, OR: Wipf and Stock, 2015), 1–2.

162 ***Summa Theologica*:** Saint Thomas Aquinas, *The Summa Theologiae of St. Thomas Aquinas*, https://www.newadvent.org/summa/.

164 **"The Five Ways":** Saint Thomas Aquinas, *The Summa Theologiae of St. Thomas Aquinas*, First Part, Question 2, Article 3, "Whether God Exists."

164 **continue to disagree:** An anecdote shared by Peter van Inwagen in *The Problem of Evil* (Oxford: Oxford University Press, 2007), 38.

164 **"Argument from Causation" . . . "Argument from Necessity":** Saint Thomas Aquinas, *The Summa Theologiae of St. Thomas Aquinas*, https://www.newadvent.org/summa/1002.

168 **God in 9/11:** Meghan Sullivan, "Uneasy Grace," *First Things*, April 1, 2014, https://www.firstthings.com/article/2014/04/uneasy-grace.

171 **professional philosophers are:** David Bourget and David J. Chalmers, "What Do Philosophers Believe?," *Philosophical Studies* 170, no. 3 (2014): 465–500.

172 **"as through a glass, darkly":** See 1 Corinthians 13:12, the King James Version translation.

173 **"Everything that I have written":** This anecdote is reported by many biographers and commentators on Aquinas's life. The version we're relying on comes from Brock, *The Philosophy of Saint Thomas Aquinas*, 15.

173 **Soulcraft: Arguing about God:** Duncan Sabien, *Center for Applied Rationality Handbook* (Berkeley, CA: Center for Applied Rationality, 2019). This is based on CFAR's "Double Crux" activity.

7: TAKE A LEAP OF FAITH

177 **"by coloring differently":** William James, *The Will to Believe and Other Essays in Popular Philosophy* (London: Longmans, Green, and Co., 1907), 18.

178 **experienced the loss:** Robert D. Richardson, *William James: In the Maelstrom of American Modernism* (Boston: Houghton Mifflin, 2006), 117–18.

178 "For the remainder of this year": This journal entry is reproduced with commentary in Richardson, *William James,* 121–22.

180 came upon Eller . . . "I was really starting to doubt": Breena Kerr, "Amanda Eller, Hiker Lost in Hawaii Forest, Is Found Alive after 17 Days," *New York Times,* May 25, 2019.

180 "been only *maybes*": James, *The Will to Believe and Other Essays in Popular Philosophy,* 59.

181 gaming console that: Gabe Gurwin, "The History of the Xbox," Digital Trends, October 1, 2020, www.digitaltrends.com/gaming/the-history-of-the-xbox/.

181 "You can't connect the dots": Jobs is quoted as saying this in his 2005 commencement address to graduates of Stanford University: "'You've Got to Find What You Love,' Jobs Says," *Stanford News,* Stanford University, June 2005, https://news.stanford.edu/2005/06/14/jobs-061505/.

182 between one thousand: Michael Baggs, "Fyre Festival: Inside the World's Biggest Festival Flop," BBC News, January 18, 2019, www.bbc.com/news/newsbeat-46904445.

182 a total shitshow: Some of the details below were taken from *Fyre: The Greatest Party That Never Happened,* directed by Chris Smith, Netflix, 2019.

182 jutting off what: Wikipedia, s.v. "Fyre Festival," accessed October 22, 2020, https://en.wikipedia.org/wiki/Fyre_Festival.

183 Theranos had five hundred: Roger Parloff, "This CEO Is Out for Blood," *Fortune,* June 12, 2014.

183 drained of her: John Carreyrou, personal interview, October 19, 2019. See also John Carreyrou, *Bad Blood: Secrets and Lies in a Silicon Valley Startup* (New York: Vintage Books, 2020), 171.

183 her device could: See *The United States of America v. Elizabeth A. Holmes & Ramesh "Sunny" Balwani,* indictment, United States District Court, Northern District of California, San Jose Division, filed June 14, 2018.

184 Brown and Yale: Robert C. Fuller, "'The Will to Believe': A Centennial Reflection," *Journal of the American Academy of Religion* 64, no. 3 (Autumn 1996): 633–50.

185 "he watched her departure": William K. Clifford, "The Ethics of Belief," in *The Ethics of Belief and Other Essays,* ed. Timothy J. Madigan (Amherst, MA: Prometheus, 1999).

187 "leap of faith": Blaise Pascal, *Pensées,* trans. W. F. Trotter (London: Dent, 1910), section 233.

187 "If you gain": Pascal, *Pensées,* trans. Trotter, section 233. As quoted in Alan Hájek, "Pascal's Wager," *The Stanford Encyclopedia of Philosophy* (Summer 2018), ed. Edward N. Zalta, https://plato.stanford.edu/archives/sum2018/entries/pascal-wager/.

188 "A faith in masses": James, *The Will to Believe and Other Essays in Popular Philosophy*, 6.

195 "death ends all": James Fitzjames Stephen, *Liberty, Equality, Fraternity*, 2nd ed. (London: Smith, Elder and Co., 1874). As quoted in James, *The Will to Believe*, 31.

8: STRUGGLE WITH SUFFERING

197 "not what we ought": William Shakespeare, *King Lear*, ed. Stephen Orgel (New York: Penguin Books, 1999), 142.

199 estimated death toll: Mark Molesky, "*This Gulf of Fire* Examines the Lisbon, Portugal, Earthquake in 1755," interview by Robert Siegel, *All Things Considered*, NPR, November 2, 2015, https://www.npr.org/2015/11/02/454051690/this-gulf-of-fire-examines-the-lisbon-portugal-earthquake-in-1755.

201 "Say, when you hear their piteous": Voltaire, "Poem on the Lisbon Disaster," in *Candide: Or Optimism*, trans. and ed. Theo Cuffe (New York: Penguin Books, 2005), app. 2.

201 "Is [God] willing": The triad originally comes from the Greek thinker Epicurus, who is talking about the indifference of the Greek gods. It is even more powerful when directed toward a morally perfect, unitary God. David Hume, "Dialogues Concerning Natural Religion 9–12," *Early Modern Texts*, ed. Jonathan Bennett, 2007, https://www.earlymoderntexts.com/assets/pdfs/hume1779_3.pdf.

202 inhuman, loveless conditions: "And if one despairs—as who has not?—of human love, God's love alone is left. But God—and I felt this even then, so long ago, on that tremendous floor, unwillingly—is white. And if His love was so great, and if He loved all His children, why were we, the blacks, cast down so far? Why?" James Baldwin, "Letter from a Region in My Mind" (1963), in *The Fire Next Time* (New York: Vintage International, 1993).

206 strangeness of Abraham: Søren Kierkegaard, *Fear and Trembling*, trans. Alastair Hannay (New York: Penguin Books, 2005), 8.

208 each of Kierkegaard's: Kierkegaard, *Fear and Trembling*, 9–13.

214 "What profit hath a man": Ecclesiastes 1:1–11, New American Bible (NAB) (Washington, D.C.: Confraternity of Christian Doctrine, 2010), https://bible.usccb.org/bible/ecclesiastes/1.

215 "Where wast thou when I laid the foundations of the earth?": Job 38: 4–5, New American Bible (NAB) (Washington, D.C.: Confraternity of Christian Doctrine, 2010), https://bible.usccb.org/bible/job/38.

217 "[The apologists] have put": Fyodor Dostoevsky, *The Brothers Karamazov*, trans. Richard Pevear and Larissa Volokhonsky (New York: Farrar, Straus and Giroux, 1990), 245.

218 Mary, a teenager and a virgin: Luke 2:1-20, New International Version (NIV) translation.

9: CONTEMPLATE YOUR PURPOSE

223 "no longer know what": Wendell Berry, "The Real Work," in *Standing by Words* (San Francisco: North Point Press, 1983), 205.

223 a jarring piece: Yascha Mounk, "Cancel Everything: Social Distancing Is the Only Way to Stop the Coronavirus. We Must Start Immediately," *Atlantic*, March 10, 2020, https://www.theatlantic.com/ideas/archive/2020/03/coronavirus-cancel-everything/607675.

225 "We meet at meals": Henry David Thoreau, *Walden and Civil Disobedience* (New York: Penguin Classics, 1983), 181.

225 "moral paragon of": Kathryn Schulz, "The Moral Judgments of Henry David Thoreau," *New Yorker*, October 12, 2015, www.newyorker.com/magazine/2015/10/19/pond-scum.

226 "concerned with action": Aristotle, *Nicomachean Ethics* 2.6 (right-action argument) and 6.2 (quotation), in *Aristotle's "Nicomachean Ethics,"* trans. Robert C. Bartlett and Susan D. Collins (Chicago: University of Chicago Press, 2011), 117.

226 "into the nursing": If we want to follow this thought to its logical, naturally stoic end, we might add: "in order to secure a top-quality burial plot." Robert Sapolsky, "This Is Your Brain on Metaphors," *New York Times Opinionator Blog*, November 14, 2010.

227 "wander around between": Plato, *Republic* 6.485b, trans. G. M. A. Grube, rev. C. D. C. Reeve (Indianapolis: Hackett, 1992), 158.

227 "no benefit from it": Aristotle, *Nicomachean Ethics* 2.2, trans. Bartlett and Collins, 27. (Emphasis ours.)

227 teacher's main idea: For example, see Aristotle, *Metaphysics* 1.991a, trans. W. D. Ross in *The Basic Works of Aristotle*, ed. Richard McKeon (New York: Random House, 1941), 707.

229 around 10 percent of: Edward Watts, "What Rome Learned from the Deadly Antonine Plague of 165 A.D.," *Smithsonian Magazine*, April 28, 2020.

229 "How all things quickly vanish": Marcus Aurelius, *Meditations*, trans. Martin Hammond (London: Penguin Classics, 2006).

230 "and ultimately, disappointingly": Kieran Setiya, *Midlife: A Philosophical Guide* (Princeton, NJ: Princeton University Press, 2017), 128.

231 He draws a distinction: Setiya first distinguishes between these on pages 12–13 of his book, but he uses the philosopher's terms "telic" and "atelic" to do so. Setiya, *Midlife*, 12–13.

232 **behold "the things":** See, for example, Aristotle's *Nicomachean Ethics* 10.7 or *De Anima* 2.5. We benefited from reading Matthew D. Walker, *Aristotle on the Uses of Contemplation* (Cambridge: Cambridge University Press, 2018).

233 **"immediate and complete":** Marcus Aurelius, *Meditations* 4.3, trans. Hammond, 23.

233 **"sort of soul":** Marcus Aurelius, *Meditations* 5.11, trans. Hammond, 55.

234 **reason governing this:** Dirk Baltzly, "Stoicism," *Stanford Encyclopedia of Philosophy*, April 10, 2018, https://plato.stanford.edu/entries/stoicism/.

234 **"Even the incidental effects":** Marcus Aurelius, *Meditations* 3, trans. Hammond, 22–23.

234 **"From Apollonius":** Marcus Aurelius, *Meditations*, 1.8, trans. Hammond, 4–5.

235 **"men are born":** Marcus Aurelius, *Meditations*, 8.58, trans. Hammond, 115.

235 **contemplation is what we were made for:** Saint Thomas Aquinas, *The Summa Theologiae of St. Thomas Aquinas*, First Part, Question 2, Article 3, "Whether God Exists."

10: PREPARE FOR DEATH

241 **"death is less":** Plato, *Phaedo* 67e, in *Plato in Twelve Volumes*, vol. 1, trans. Harold North Fowler; Introduction by W. R. M. Lamb (Cambridge, MA: Harvard University Press, 1966), https://www.perseus.tufts.edu/hopper/text?doc=Perseus%3Atext%3A1999.01.0170%3Atext%3DPhaedo%3Asection%3D67e.

242 **"let myself be":** Susie Steiner, "Top Five Regrets of the Dying," *Guardian*, February 1, 2012.

243 **doctors discovered she:** Amy Harmon, "A Dying Young Woman's Hope in Cryonics and a Future," *New York Times*, September 12, 2015.

244 **"feeble, ineffectual, even":** Ezekiel Emanuel, "Why I Hope to Die at 75," *Atlantic*, October 2014, https://www.theatlantic.com/magazine/archive/2014/10/why-i-hope-to-die-at-75/379329/.

245 **"die without further":** Peter Singer, "Taking Life: Humans," in *Practical Ethics*, 2nd ed. (Cambridge: Cambridge University Press, 1993), 175–217.

245 **David Benatar takes these arguments even *further*:** David Benatar, *Better Never to Have Been: The Harm of Coming into Existence* (Oxford: Oxford University Press, 2006).

248 ***A passage in Dante's* Paradiso:** Dante Alighieri and Henry Wadsworth Longfellow, *The Divine Comedy of Dante Alighieri* (Boston, New York: Houghton Mifflin, 1904). See Canto 33, especially lines 82–145.

249 **"How many who once rose":** Marcus Aurelius, *Meditations*, Book 7.6, trans. Martin Hammond (London: Penguin Classics, 2006), 83.

250 **"soul from here":** Plato, *Apology* 40c–41a, trans. G. M. A. Grube, in *Plato: Complete Works*, ed. John M. Cooper (Indianapolis: Hackett, 1997), 35.

251 **Nature holds this:** Lucretius, *De Rerum Natura* 3.972–3.975, trans. William Ellery Leonard (New York: E. P. Dutton, 1916), http://data.perseus.org/citations/urn:cts:latinLit:phi0550.phi001.perseus-eng1:3.931-3.977.

253 **"all human risks":** Seneca, *On the Shortness of Life*, trans. Charles Desmond Nuttall Costa (London: Penguin Books, 2005), 15.

253 **"There is a long period":** Seneca, *On the Shortness of Life*, trans. Costa, 23.

CODA: THE LIMITS OF PHILOSOPHY

261 **"But a life of this sort":** Aristotle, *Nicomachean Ethics* 10.7, in *Aristotle's "Nicomachean Ethics,"* trans. Robert C. Bartlett and Susan D. Collins (Chicago: University of Chicago Press, 2011).

Further Reading

Want to read a bit more by the philosophers we introduced in this book? Here are some of our recommendations for reader-friendly places to start. We have listed them in historical order of when they were (likely) written.

Plato, *Apology of Socrates* (399 BC)

Plato. *The Trial and Death of Socrates.* Translated by G. M. A. Grube. Revised by John M. Cooper. Indianapolis: Hackett, 2000.

Plato, *Republic* (375 BC)

Plato. *Republic.* Translated by G. M. A. Grube. Revised by C. D. C. Reeve. Indianapolis: Hackett, 1997.

Aristotle, *Nicomachean Ethics* (340 BC)

Bartlett, Robert C., and Susan D. Collins, trans. *Aristotle's "Nicomachean Ethics."* Chicago: University of Chicago Press, 2011.

Seneca, *On the Shortness of Life* (AD 49)

Seneca, Lucius Annaeus. *On the Shortness of Life: Life Is Long If You Know How to Use It.* Translated by Charles Desmond Nuttall Costa. London: Penguin Books, 2005.

Marcus Aurelius, *Meditations* (AD 161–180)

Aurelius, Marcus. *Meditations.* Translated by Martin Hammond. London: Penguin Classics, 2006.

Saint Thomas Aquinas, *Summa Theologica* (1265–1273)

Aquinas, Thomas. *Thomas Aquinas: Selected Writings.* Edited by Ralph McInerny. London: Penguin Classics, 1999.

Søren Kierkegaard, *Fear and Trembling* (1843)

Kierkegaard, Søren [Johannes de silentio, pseud.]. *Fear and Trembling.* Translated by Alastair Hannay. London: Penguin Classics, 1986.

Karl Marx and Friedrich Engels, *The Communist Manifesto* (1847)

Marx, Karl, and Friedrich Engels. *The Marx-Engels Reader.* Edited by Robert C. Tucker. New York: W. W. Norton & Company, 1978.

John Stuart Mill, *Utilitarianism* (1861)

Mill, John Stuart. *"Utilitarianism" and the 1868 Speech on Capital Punishment.* Edited by George Sher. Indianapolis: Hackett, 2001.

William James, "The Will to Believe" (1896)

James, William. *Pragmatism and Other Writings.* Edited by Giles Gunn. New York: Penguin Books, 2000.

W. E. B. Du Bois, *Dusk of Dawn* (1940)

Du Bois, W. E. B. *W. E. B. Du Bois: Writings.* Edited by Nathan Huggins. New York: Literary Classics of the United States, 1986.

Elizabeth Anscombe, *Intention* (1957)

Anscombe, G. E. M. *Intention.* Cambridge, MA: Harvard University Press, 2000.

James Baldwin, "Letter from a Region in My Mind" (1963)

Baldwin, James. *The Fire Next Time.* New York: Vintage International, 1993.

Iris Murdoch, *The Sovereignty of Good* (1970)

Murdoch, Iris. *The Sovereignty of Good.* Abingdon, Oxon, UK: Routledge, 1970.

Index